D0984660

St. John of the Cross

of the Cross
(San Juan de la Cruz)

St. John of the Cross

(San Juan de la Cruz)

Alchemist of the Soul

His Life
His Poetry (*Bilingual*)
His Prose

TEXT, NEW EDITED TRANSLATIONS BY
Antonio T. de Nicolás

FOREWORD BY
Seyyed Hossein Nasr

Paragon House
New York

First edition, 1989

Published in the United States by
Paragon House
90 Fifth Avenue
New York, NY 10011

Copyright © 1989 by Paragon House

Library of Congress Cataloging-in-Publication Data
John of the Cross, Saint, 1542–1591.
[Selections. English & Spanish. 1989]
St. John of the Cross (San Juan de la Cruz) : alchemist of the soul :
his life, his poetry (bilingual), his prose / edited and translated
by Antonio T. de Nicolás.—1st ed.
p.   cm.
Bibliography: p.
ISBN 1-55778-027-7.—ISBN 1-55778-089-7 (pbk.)
1. Mysticism—Early works to 1800. 2. Catholic Church—Doctrines.
I. De Nicolás, Antonio T., 1932–   . II. Title. III. Title: Saint
John of the Cross (San Juan de la Cruz).
BV5080.J64213   1989   89-30265
248.2'2–dc19   CIP

Manufactured in the United States of America
The paper used in this publication meets the minimum requirements of
American National Standard for Information Sciences—Permanence of paper
for printed Library Materials, ANSI Z39.48-1984.

CONTENTS

THE MAJESTIC FLIGHT

of the eagle
Harnessing wings to soar
From the side of the mountain
To the rocks at the crest of the horizon
And avoid a life in reverse
Down a spiral of descent

If only we keep memory free
And hold the flight of a wave of air
And train the eyes to separate
Skin from feathers
And descend as lightning

To steal from every cave
The nectar of the gods
With the same accuracy
The same exact measure
As two eagles mating in midair

Controlled free-fall
Through walls of air
Two bodies joined
In the celebration of life
Coming apart
Before they hit
The secure spots
Of the lamb and the ox,

There is no other flight
For the soul!

and
To the brave men and women
Writing poetry in America:
Theirs is the dark night.

FOREWORD

The cacophony of the machine has drowned the voice of the poet in most of the industrialized regions of the Western world. No longer is the poet seen as the seer who is the channel through which truth is expressed. Nor is poetry any longer regarded as a vehicle for anything other than, at best, individualistic sentiments or social criticism if not subhuman inclinations and tendencies. Gone is the role of poetry as the mover of souls toward their celestial origin with a cosmic dimension which reminds the soul itself of the aspects of its reality beyond the ordinarily human. Divorced from principal knowledge and the power of alchemical transmutation, poetry has become debased in the modern world as never before. This holds true especially in America despite the remarkable poetic possibilities of the English language and the fact that this language has been blessed by the appearance of a Shakespeare and has been witness to a poet of the quality of John Keats as recently as the last century.

This eclipse of the sapiental and mystical role of poetry in America has made most modern readers forget the significance of the poetry of a Dante, that supreme Western poet in whose work the reality of the Christian universe became depicted through unparalleled poetic genius into a literary masterpiece of perennial beauty and significance. Likewise, modern American readers remain unaware for the most part of the role of poetry in the Spanish language which alone among major European languages has preserved to this day something of the traditional role and significance of poetry thanks most of all to the figure to whom this volume is devoted, namely, St. John of the Cross, at once one of Spain's greatest saints as well as her greatest poet. One can, therefore, hardly expect the modern reader to cast his eyes beyond the borders of the Western world to the West's historic neighbor, the world of Islam, where poetry continues to enjoy to this day an exalted station such as that of Dante's Italy or St. John of the Cross's Spain and where the very word for poetry (*shi'r*) is related etymologically to (*shu'ur*) or consciousness.

The significance of this translation of St. John of the Cross becomes clear if one realizes his role as at once poet and seer or mystic addressing a world in which poetry and spirituality have parted ways. St. John of the Cross was a Carmelite mystic who was later canonized as a saint and considered as spiritual guide by generations of Christians drawn to the spiritual life. He was also the supreme poet of the Spanish language whose poetry represents the deepest yearning of the Spanish soul for God and in which is to be found the very technique of spiritual realization associated with the way and method of St. John.

The world of St. John reminds one of that of the *fedeli d'amore*, those medieval troubadors of the spirit who sang in beautiful poems about the deepest mysteries of the spiritual path and who saw in all love a reflection of the love of God which is rooted in the very substance of the human soul. In reading him, one is carried to the world of Ruzbihan Baqli Shirazi, Jalal al-Din Rumi, and Fakh al-Din 'Iraqi, the great Persian poets and sages who revealed in the language of love the mysteries of Divine Union. One is also made to recall, nearer to St. John's homeland, the great Arab Sufi poets like 'Umar ibn al-Farid as well as St. John's countryman, Muhyi al-Din ibn 'Arabi, who was at once the supreme expositor of Sufi gnostic doctrines and a Sufi poet of exceptional power equaled and perhaps surpassed in the annals of Arabic Sufi poetry only by Ibn al-Farid.

For one who has walked through the streets of Shiraz and visited Konya, or paid homage at the tomb of Ibn al-Farid in the necropolis of Cairo and the mausoleum of Ibn 'Arabi north of Damascus, there is an almost existential awareness that the poetic world of St. John of the Cross is not totally other than that of the Persian and Arabic *fedeli d'amore* despite the fact that one breathed in a Christian universe and the others in a Muslim. In strolling in the streets of Granada, still witness to the silent presence of Islamic spirituality through the dazzling Islamic artistic heritage of the city, one can hardly forget that the great Spanish mystic and poet lived for some time in this city where he frequented certain Moriscos and that in traveling to that region he gazed upon the same mountains and valleys, the same rivers and fields as the Andalusian Sufi poets and sages such as Ibn 'Arabi.

While the writings of St. John are, of course, Christian and represent one of the heights of poetic expression of Christian mysticism, there are a number of symbols of Sufi origin which can be seen in his work and which bear testament to the presence of certain elements of Islamic literary culture—both Arabic and Persian—in the Spain in which St. John of the Cross flourished. One thinks immediately of the symbol of the "dark night," so prominent in St. John's poetry, which is used by so many Sufi authors, including the Persian poet Shabistari and the Sufi saint of Ronda, Ibn 'Abbad, who established the Shadhiliyyah Order in the Maghrib some two centuries before St. John.

Or when one reads the poem "Love's Living Flame"("*Oh Llama de amor viva*"):

> O Love's living flame,
> Tenderly you wound
> My soul's deepest center!
> Since you no longer evade me,
> Will you, please, at last conclude:
> Rend the veil of this sweet encounter!

How can one not be reminded of the ever recurring theme of the moth and the flame in Persian poetry, where the burning of the moth in the flame, into which it casts itself like an iron filing drawn to a magnet, symbolizes the attraction of the sanctified soul to the flame of Divine Love by which it is finally consumed.

The poetry of St. John of the Cross is not only poetry expressing the mysteries of Divine Union, it is also a vehicle for the methods which in conjunction with Divine Grace make possible that union. The spiritual life has been for too long envisaged in the post–medieval West as an individual quest. For centuries spiritual techniques of Christian origin have become ever more inaccessible. It is only during the past few decades that contact with the living spiritual paths of other traditions has caused many Christian aspirants in the West to seek to rediscover the significance of spiritual techniques, or what the translator of this work calls "technologies," following the original Greek meaning of the term.

St. John's poetry and prose as translated here, and separated from the passages which St. John was forced to add to defend himself before the Inquisition, are themselves carriers of the spiritual techniques associated with the mysticism of the school of St. John. When the poems are recited with this truth in mind, they remind the hearer of the Sufi poems or *anashid* chanted in Sufi gatherings, poems which perform a technical, spiritual function in preparing the soul for the invocation of the Divine Name.

St. John of the Cross has been translated several times into English, but none of the previous renderings made St. John appear with such vividness and significance to the contemporary American reader as the translation of Antonio de Nicolás. A Spaniard who was born and nurtured in the cultural universe of St. John of the Cross, de Nicolás journeyed beyond the Catholic world of his upbringing and even beyond the boundaries of the Western world to delve deeply into the metaphysical teachings of Hinduism. He mastered Sanskrit and became first known in America for his translations and commentaries of Hindu sacred texts. He himself is a poet as well as a philosopher in the traditional and normal sense of the term.

His turning to the works of St. John of the Cross was, therefore, not to add simply to the collection of Spanish literature in translation, but to enable American and English readers to view St. John of the Cross as San Juan de la Cruz, as seen in the Spanish speaking world in which the traditional role of poetry is still alive. He has placed before himself an immense challenge. He has sought to transform the role and function of poetry in contemporary American society by presenting one of the foremost poet-mystics of the Christian tradition as a poet of contemporary literary and spiritual significance.

His critical introduction, which in his own particular language he decries the loss of the "poetic voice," asserts the necessity of reclaiming St. John of the Cross as the poet of the Spirit, whose poetry must be approached not with the analytical eye but with that sanctified imagination of which St. John himself speaks, echoing the vast elaboration of the "imaginal world" (*mundus imaginalis*) of his Murcian compatriot, Ibn 'Arabi. De Nicolás seeks to create a place for St. John of the Cross in the literary and spiritual landscape of contemporary America, a place which would be similar to what San Juan de la Cruz occupied for the translator since he was only ten years old and as the saint has done for countless other Spanish speakers.

De Nicolás has succeeded in rendering the verses of St. John in a poetry that is at once moving and simple; the prose gains much greater significance by having the passages of spiritual importance separated from those containing theological debates which St. John had to carry out with certain Church authorities of his day. Whether de Nicolás has fully succeeded in re-Christening St. John of the Cross as San Juan de la Cruz of the English language, only time will tell, but there is no doubt that the significance of his effort goes far beyond the simple rendition of a masterpiece of Spanish literature into English. De Nicolás has added an important poetic opus to the English language, one which can help to resuscitate the role and function of poetry and the poet in the chaotic conditions of modern society. De Nicolás has in fact dedicated this book to American poets, to "the brave men and women writing poetry in America: Theirs is the dark night."

In reading this translation one cannot but remember, as mentioned by the author in his introduction, the fact that the remarkable poetry of St. John of the Cross was composed in Toledo while he was in prison. It was in this most Arab of all Spanish cities, where the works of Ibn Sina and Ibn Rushd were rendered into Latin and where the Islamic intellectual heritage became accessible to the West, that St. John wrote of the journey of the soul to God in poems of such enduring beauty. The present volume reminds the reader of that remarkable world where Jews, Christians, and Muslims lived in harmony for so many centuries for the poems of St. John, like the city in which they were composed, transcend the confines of a single culture or religious ambience. It is a profoundly Christian work; yet it resonates in the soul of all who are attracted to the world of the Spirit, whether they be Christian or non-Christian.

Antonio de Nicolás is to be congratulated for making available the work of St. John of the Cross in such a lucid and spiritually transparent form in English. Let us hope that his translation will help to revive the role of the poet as the tongue of the spiritual world and expositor of that principal truth which because of its very nature cannot be expressed in a prosaic manner. May the English reader be able to see in these pages an English San Juan de la Cruz with whom he or she can live through various periods of life and to whom he or she can turn in all those crucial moments which punctuate the terrestrial journey of all of us toward that flame of Love, the flame that finally enflames and consumes us, reducing us to that "nothingness" which is none other than eternal felicity and beatitude.

Seyyed Hossein Nasr

CHRONOLOGY

SAN JUAN DE LA CRUZ	CULTURAL EVENTS	HISTORICAL EVENTS
	1515. Birth of Teresa de Avila.	
	1535. Mancebo de Arévalo gathers the doctrines of the *alumbrados* under the title *Breves Compendios* and spreads them through Castile.	
1542. Birth of Juan de la Cruz (Juan de Yepes y Alvarez).		
	1543. The works of Boscán and some of Garcilaso de la Vega are published in Barcelona.	
		1545. The Council of Trent begins in December.
		1546. Luther dies.
	1547. Cervantes is born.	
		1547. Death of Henry VIII and Hernán Cortés.
1547. Juan and family move to Arévalo.		

SAN JUAN DE LA CRUZ	CULTURAL EVENTS	HISTORICAL EVENTS
1551. The family moves to Medina del Campo.		
	1553. Miguel Servet is burned as a heretic.	
		1553. Mary Tudor becomes Queen of England.
	1554. *El Lazarillo de Tormes* (Cervantes) is published.	
		1556. Charles V abdicates. Phillip II is King of Spain. Ignatius de Loyola dies.
	1559–63. Students are forbidden to travel abroad to study. Index of forbidden books appears, one book being *Audi Filia,* by San Juan de Avila, which deals with inner meditation.	
	1560. Arias Montano's *Poliglote Bible* is published.	
	1561. Birth of Luis de Góngora.	
	1562. Fray Luis de León translates *El Cantar de los Cantares* into Spanish, with commentary. Lope de Vega is born.	
1563. Juan joins the Carmelites at Medina, takes the name Juan de Santo Matía.		
		1563. Council of Trent ends.
1564–68. Juan studies philosophy and theology at Salamanca.		

SAN JUAN DE LA CRUZ	CULTURAL EVENTS	HISTORICAL EVENTS
	1564. Miguel Angel dies. Shakespeare and Galileo are born.	
		1564. Calvin dies.
1567. Juan is ordained. He meets Teresa de Avila.		
1568. Juan ends his studies and returns to Medina. He goes with Teresa in August to found the convent at Valladolid, and in October to Duruelo.		
		1568. The Moors are defeated and relocated through Castile. (This became known as the insurrection at Granada.)
1569. Foundation of the Pastrana convent.		
1571. Juan, with Teresa, founds the convent of Alba de Tormes. He becomes the Rector of the Discalced Carmelites College at Alcalá de Henares.		
	1571. Fray Luis goes to jail.	
		1571. The Battle at Lepanto is fought on October 7.
1574. Juan travels with Teresa in order to found the convent at Segovia.		
	1575. Fray Luis de León leaves jail vindicated.	
1576. Founding of the first Chapter of the Discalced Carmelites. Juan is present at Almodóvar, Ciudad Real.		

SAN JUAN DE LA CRUZ	CULTURAL EVENTS	HISTORICAL EVENTS

1577. Juan's brothers in religion take him prisoner to Toledo. There he remains until mid-August 1578.

1578. In October he is named prior of the convent of El Calvario (Jaen). He writes "*Las Cautelas.*" Between 1578 and 1580 he writes "The Ascent" and "Dark Night." He continues writing the "Spiritual Canticle."

1579. Juan goes to Baeza where he founds a discalced convent and becomes rector.

1580. Juan's mother dies in Medina.

1580. Francisco de Quevedo is born. Fernando de Herrera publishes *Anotaciones a Garcilaso*.

1581. In March Juan attends the Chapter of the Separation at Alcalá. Gracián is elected provincial. Juan becomes third definitor and prior of Los Mártires at Granada, while remaining for a while at Baeza.

1582. The founding at Granada of a convent for nuns. Between now and 1586 Juan writes "*Llama de amor viva.*"

1582. On October 4 (using the old calendar) Teresa de Avila dies.

SAN JUAN DE LA CRUZ	CULTURAL EVENTS	HISTORICAL EVENTS

1583. Chapter of
Almodóvar. Juan is
reelected prior of the
convent of Granada.

Fray Luis de León writes
La perfecta Casada and
Los nombres de Cristo.

1584. Between now and
1586 Juan completes the
"Spiritual Canticle."

1585. Juan founds a
convent for nuns at
Málaga. In May he
attends the chapter of
Lisbon, at which Nicolás
Doria succeeds Gracián
as provincial. Juan is
appointed second
definitor while still prior
of Los Mártires. In
October the chapter
continues at Pastrana.
Juan is appointed vicar-
provincial of Andalucía.

Teresa's *Camino de
perfección* is published.

1586. Juan founds a
priory at Córdoba in
May; in August he falls
seriously ill with pleurisy
at Guadalcázar. In
September he assists at
the foundation of a
convent at Madrid with
Ana de Jesús as prioress;
in December he founds
the priory at Caravaca.

1587. At the chapter of
Valladolid Juan ceases to
be definitor and vicar-
provincial, but he is
reappointed prior of
Los Mártires.

1587. The Invincible
Armada is defeated.

SAN JUAN DE LA CRUZ	CULTURAL EVENTS	HISTORICAL EVENTS

1588. In June he attends the first chapter-general of the reform at Madrid. Doria is elected vicar-general. Juan is appointed first definitor and a consiliario on the consulta. In August he becomes prior of Segovia and deputy to Doria during the latter's absences. He remains at Segovia for nearly three years.

1591. At the chapter-general held at Madrid in June, Juan is deprived of all his offices and sent as a simple friar to La Peñuela, near Baeza. He arrives there on August 10 but soon falls ill.

1591. On August 23 Fray Luis de León dies in Madrigal de las Altas Torres, near Fontiveros.

1591. On September 28 Juan leaves for Ubeda, where he dies on December 14.

1592. On February 14 Gracián is expelled from the Order. Ana de Jesús and María de San José are relieved of their offices and sentenced to close seclusion in convents.

1593. Juan's body is transferred from Ubeda to Segovia. In December the Congregation of the Discalced Carmelites is made a separate order by a bull of Clement VIII. Doria is appointed interim general.

SAN JUAN DE LA CRUZ	CULTURAL EVENTS	HISTORICAL EVENTS
1594. Doria is taken ill and dies in Madrid on May 9. Elías de San Martín is elected general on May 23. Fifteen days later Juan's enemy Fray Diego Evangelista dies suddenly on his way to take up his office as provincial of Upper Andalucía.		
1618. First edition of Juan's writings appears at Alcalá, without the "Spiritual Canticle."		
1622. First appearance of the "Spiritual Canticle," translated into French.		
1627. First Spanish edition of the "Spiritual Canticle" published in Brussels.		
1630. First Spanish edition of the complete works published in Madrid.		
1675. Juan is beatified by Clement I.		
1725. He is canonized by Benedict XIII.		
1926. San Juan de la Cruz is declared a doctor of the universal church by Pius XI.		

PART ONE
The Life

Chapter One

THE PROPHETIC VOICE

Not long ago I visited Toledo with a group of international scholars fleeing a very boring conference on religion. We took the road from Madrid early in the morning. It was sunny, though the cool, sharp air announced a long autumn. But as soon as we left the red roofs of Madrid behind, the road was lost within a heavy, white, magical fog. The landscape disappeared suddenly and we seemed to be traveling inside a frosted wedding cake. White fog hung from trees, power lines, road signs, and the wheels of cars. Stones and bushes were dusted white. We drove slowly through a magical land never traveled before by any of us. None of the others could tell where Toledo was: the signs were all covered with fog. But I practically knew the road with my eyes closed and turned up a mountain to the Parador Nacional outside Toledo to wait for the fog to lift. My friends kept asking if I was sure Toledo was really behind that fog. We sat down to lunch and in a little while the sun began to filter through. Slowly, waves of fog began to move and shift, and a whole town rose up as if from the bottom of the sea; first only the stone head appeared—cathedrals and palaces suspended in midair, as if an artist were at work, stealing images from some gigantic canvas. Finally the fog lifted and Toledo appeared as itself—stone upon stone, from heaven to earth, circled by a ring of water that had to be crossed before goats, saints, or tourists by the busload could climb the battlements that surround the city.

It was a day spent recollecting that in this town Arabs and Jews had worked together translating the world's great texts and had established the first school for translators. Through these translations, the knowledge of the Greeks and the ideas that inspired Western civilization entered Europe. In this town Lope de Vega and Cervantes gathered with other poets to talk about poetry and gossip in the *finca* of Buena Vista. In this town El Greco lived and painted. Here monks and nuns built the most famous row of monasteries in Christendom. The poet Becquer called this town "a cry in the desert," and another poet, Rilke, exclaimed: "My God, how many things I have loved because they tried to look like this." And here also the most famous poet of the Spanish language, San Juan de la Cruz (St. John of the Cross), was held prisoner by his fellow monks for over nine months. From the *meseta* of Toledo one can see the old road that winds over the hills of Avila along which San Juan de la Cruz was brought to jail in Toledo. It was in this jail, during the summer of 1567, that San Juan de la Cruz wrote the poetry which made him famous. He created the purest art out of his deepest sufferings at the hands of the same people and the same church that later canonized him. It is also in Toledo that San Juan de la Cruz's family roots and those of Teresa de Avila find a common link. In one of these churches we have documents of how Teresa's grandfather converted with his children from Judaism to Christianity and back; this secret was closely guarded by Teresa and her family and friends. San Juan de la Cruz was, in all probability, unaware of his own roots, though he felt the burden of poverty. In Toledo Arab, Jew, and Christian lived and flourished together.

Our return trip was filled with long silences and declarative propositions: "We could have missed the town altogether, you know? What with all that fog. . . . We English have missed it since the Reformation, eh!" "Organized religion discriminates against the religious act of the mystics, and those who discriminate against organized religion discriminate twice against the religious act." "We have buried the imaginative capacity to recreate the religious acts of people like San Juan de la Cruz. In the name of freedom from religion we have lobotomized the human brain."

I saw in a flash the difficulty of presenting today the religious act as practiced by the mystics. There and then I decided to write this book. San Juan de la Cruz has been present in my life with his verses since I was ten years old. In times of stress or crisis or infatuation I turned to him for a deeper, wider, higher perspective— above all, for a deeper feeling from the stream of life. And I have noticed how our English-speaking young people have no one they can turn to in the way I turned to San Juan de la Cruz for company in the serious moments of life. Unfortunately the young people who have to reach him through English have to make a deeper effort than I because their language has incorporated all the prejudices of the centuries. How could I present San Juan de la Cruz so that his religious act was not only made visible but also became replicable at a level no inquisition could reach? This, then, was the project I committed myself to, and this book is its fulfillment.

For the sake of clarity, however, I will try to summarize here the religious context within which the act of religion occurs in San Juan de la Cruz, and the opposition to it in the contemporary inquisitions to which our individuals and institutions are subject.

INQUISITIONS AND THE PROPHETIC VOICE

The man and saint known in the English language as St. John of the Cross bears little resemblance to his Spanish counterpart, San Juan de la Cruz. To use Plato's language, I can candidly affirm that San Juan de la Cruz is neither the *same* nor *like* St. John of the Cross. Why the English felt the need to translate his name when the translations of his work are so obscure and so foreign to them might already serve as a hint to the colonizing powers of one language over another. It is a disservice to a man like San Juan de la Cruz, and an even greater disservice to the rest of us, to translate his language without translating the experience that drove him to become public through language.

There are three main areas I will address in this book which have all contributed to obscure the real St. John and have substituted instead a shadow deserving of praise but still insubstantial.

First there are the writings about San Juan de la Cruz which take his work as a confirmation of his theological competence. In these writings San Juan de la Cruz is presented as one more theologian who agrees with the party line of the church. These are apologies for the church and supposedly for the man, too. But these writers fail to see that it is San Juan de la Cruz who admits at the start that if the Church willed it differently, he would express himself differently. These writers aim for a reiteration of the beliefs of a small group within the church concerned with orthodoxy of belief. Was not this Church the one that continued to look for a way to condemn Juan de la Cruz and his writings right up to the time of his canonization?

Misunderstandings have also arisen because of those who have acknowledged the fact that San Juan de la Cruz was a great poet, and therefore decided to publish his translated poetry simply as poetry, on an equal footing with other poetry, without further comments or hermeneutics and avoiding the religious experience from which the poetry emerges. But Juan's poetry in translation is not very illuminating by itself; isolated from its context it is neither inspiring, nor great poetry.

The third area of misunderstanding is more subtle. Both those who claim the poetry as religious utterance and equate it with the narratives of the churches, and those who claim it for the secular domain feel that this poetry may be understood using the same cognitive faculties they employ in their narratives or critical theories. But San Juan de la Cruz composed his poetry out of the development of a faculty unknown to them: he used pure imaginings, so that by creating images out of nothing, rather than borrowing them from anything existing around him, a new world of sensation, feeling, memory, and will was created and it is this which is responsible for the power of his poetry. Unless this world is recovered, contemporary readings of San Juan de la Cruz will miss his essence.

This volume will try to recover this lost faculty of imagining so that Juan's poetry can again be linked authentically to its origins. It will, therefore, present his poetry in its entirety, along with those portions of his prose which reveal the workings of his soul from the inside out, and leave aside those portions of theology he was writing just to please the inquisitors. (One must not forget that if he had not conformed to the wishes of the inquisitors, his writing would never have become public, and that even when trying to please them he and the nuns and friends who had some of his manuscripts kept destroying them for fear of condemnation. San Juan de la Cruz wrote with an eye on his soul, but also with an ear to the sounds at the door.

It might help to bear in mind even at this early stage that the project embarked upon by San Juan de la Cruz was to remove from his body any taste for the sensation coming to him from the out-side—to be sensitized exclusively *from the inside out*. His poetry and prose are the narrative of this journey.

In order, however, to be as explicit as possible in defining the context within which San Juan de la Cruz works out his spiritual journey, we need to define in general terms the several meanings of *religion*. In general, religion is a comprehensive image which has organizing power for the whole of life, private and public. In its historical development (that is, examining the role religion has played in history) we may separate religion into two different sys-tems: the first a set of *discontinuous systems* of religions, and the second a set of *continuous systems* of religion.[1]

In the first group we find the monotheistic religions: Judaism, Islam, and Christianity. They claim (1) that there is a Creator above and transcendent to creation, and (2) that their beliefs and moralities are exclusively true because they are legitimized by a unique, sover-eign, divine, and revealing authority. In the second group we find religions that are classified as pantheistic, mystical, or incarnational. These all presuppose an original experience, capable of being re-peated, in which God, cosmos, and human soul are unified in an initial affirmation of the system.

This general division compounds the problem, for in history both systems function at times together, or one through the other, as we see in the case of the mystics within the various monotheistic traditions. Though the practices of mystics are different in kind from the accepted orthodoxy, they are also considered to be part of the group of discontinuous systems because they have expressed themselves in practice within the accepted language of orthodoxy. This happened with the Sufis in Islam, as well as the Christian and Hebrew mystics.

The discontinuous systems of religion claim authority from a transcendent God. They also claim from their followers belief in an axiomatic system of truths derived from theological propositions, and a system of conduct regulated by ethical norms generally attributed to the same authority as the revealer of beliefs. The believer, within these discontinuous systems, is graded in relation to his or her cognitive subservience to the system. In other words, the acts believers perform are identical to acts of surrender of the mind to a set of beliefs. The mystic, on the other hand, might also surrender his mind to church authorities, but this does not stop him or her from practicing religion in a different way, by the use of faculties other than the cognitive, as was the case with Ignatius de Loyola,[2] Teresa de Avila,[3] Juan de la Cruz, and the other mystics, both in and out of the churches.

The continuous system of religious practice brings to the practice of religion something besides cognitive surrender. This is a dedicated discipline of will, memory, imagining, a discipline that is absent in the discontinuous systems of religion, even when the designations of memory, imagining, and will are retained.

Augustine and Thomas Aquinas offer two differing examples of this reductionism. In Augustine the image of God coincides with human actions and faculties as a mirror coincides with its image; life is closed, agonic, passionate, but this image is only human. The images supporting this model are borrowed from the external world, not from the inner world of imagining and free will. Revelation is thus closed and the only hope left is a large dose of "grace" in the face of a hopeless situation. For the Thomists, on the other hand, humans and nature form *analogies* of God, a model-at-a-distance from which, again, participation in revelation has been subtracted. In this model cognition is dependent on the external world, and the best styles of life (that is, Christian life) are equated with individual perfections, individual superheroes, celibate isolation, avoidance of the world, and theoretical contemplation. The impact of these models on Christianity itself will not escape the reader. We have a form of reflection joined with prayer, of thinking and salvation unified in a common project of transformation, a clear yet hybrid mixture of reason and will, thought and tears, intellection and occultism, at the service of a particular way of reading the text of Christianity in the limited context of rational acts and mortal faculties and experiences. Transcendence appears only as a hope of immortality for the believer, although it remains fixed dogmatically in the structure of belief. Incarnation is also treated dogmatically, part of a structure in which revelation is no longer a possibility, but remains a theoretical incarnation subsumed by transcendence.[4]

In examining the general historical confrontation between these two separate systems of religious practice, the discontinuous and the continuous, we may distinguish two ways of identifying them from the beginning of history to the present. When a particular system of religious practice is in power, that is, when a discontinuous system predominates, then other discontinuous and continuous systems are marginalized, expelled, or forced to convert, and their individual representatives are persecuted, suppressed, or executed. Inquisitions appear within the discontinuous systems in order to control other discontinuous and continuous systems of religious practice. Catholics have persecuted Protestants, Jews, Muslims, and mystics. Protestants have done the same, and so have Jews and Muslims, unless the nonconforming individual was willing to convert and express him- or herself using accepted and therefore acceptable propositions. For this reason it is very doubtful that the prose writings of San Juan de la Cruz have any truth value when they deal with theological propositions, for they could easily have been different if the discontinuous system in which he was placed had been other than the Catholic Church. But his writings in prose also offer a description of the kind of spiritual practice he was involved with, and from this point of view his prose writings are indeed important.

The discontinuous systems exert their power with the aid of universal narratives, set down in books and implemented through laws both divine and human. The continuous systems accommodate to any narrative but practice a continuous discipline that is imprinted in the body of the practitioner and leads not only to truths but to decisions in the world (that is, establishing communities) and sets of signs for the reading of those decisions. These signs are not the same signs the discontinuous systems claim for obedience and guidance of the soul. A mystic may practice religion with his or her back to the regulating inquisition of the times, through spiritual procedures so deep that no inquisitor may be able to penetrate or modify them. His or her only guidance is provided by other, earlier recognized mystics. It is only when the mystic speaks or writes that he or she must conform, must confront the established narratives and inquisitors. In this perspective we may observe that texts from the discontinuous systems are in a sense different and thus divisive, while those of continuity are silent as to narrative but detailed as regards the kind of practices they carry out, for in the end the body of the mystic is his or her last evidence of interior practice.

It is by now commonplace to state that the systems of discontinuity have produced divisiveness and war among themselves and among their followers. It is also evident that this fact has been used in modern societies to debunk religion and remove it from the public domain. What is not so evident, however, is that behind the debunking of religion there is a religious attitude borrowed from religion by the debunkers themselves.

The actual human struggle between the discontinuous systems of religion and the continuous ones originates in the fact that the first group claims transcendence in order to destroy immanence, while the second claims immanence in order to build transcendence. The first attitude is as old as the prophets, and we may identify it as "the prophetic voice." The second attitude is the "poetic voice." The prophetic voice claims language as the primary fact, while the poetic voice claims experience to be the origin of language. These two voices present two different versions of the religious act, and their historical struggle is a religious fight, or a fight for or against the religious act.

The prophetic voice, both in the Bible and in philosophy, is dangerous, both for the prophet and for his or her listeners. The prophetic voice acts alone, employing and acting upon the language of another transcendent being, away from human communities and worldly desires. It is unable to separate itself from the speaker's own projects and desires. It is a symbol of disembodied contemplation, of a profound disharmony between the will of another social order and the will of the existing social order. It is a voice that exhibits an extraordinary capacity for self-criticism. Listening to the prophetic voice in the Bible, one has to wonder which is more dangerous to the soul: what scholars do to the Bible with their different interpretations, or what the Bible does to us, and those who read it, with its prophetic voices. Given the prophetic voice, we have inherited such a critical attitude that we are unable to be satisfied with any given state of culture or individual accomplishment. In this vision cities are evil (Matt. 11:21–23,23:37); cultures, like that of Egypt, are evil: "What is the crime of Jacob? Is it not Samaria? What is the sin of the House of Judah? Is it not Jerusalem?" (Mic. 1:5); wealth is treacherous: "Wealth is indeed a treacherous thing" (Hab. 2:4); and any "way of life" is apt to give rise to pride and error—even a man's righteousness is suspect: "Though I count myself innocent, it may declare me a hypocrite" (Job 9:20).

The role of the prophets is to denounce the presently existing culture and probe it to its foundations until it is reduced to dust. Instead of investing the various cultures with sacredness, they deconstruct their claims, undress their monuments and institutions, and obliterate any preferences. In front of their vision of Yahweh, all men and their petty distinctions are as the undifferentiated dust of the desert. The prophetic seers make alienation their home. They are the nomads of discontent. They make those who listen to them feel at home in this alienation by making them share in the seer's vision, and they sit back and contemplate in perfect stoicism the prospect of social and individual collapse. The prophets were the first to discover the sound, often mocking, of the skeptical voice, a sound that for a long time since has pervaded the intellectual life and university corridors of Western culture. In that voice, no matter what happens in history, even if prophecy itself is destroyed, the content—the avid need for change—never changes.

This prophetic voice is nowhere more evident than in the heirs of the biblical prophets who teach at our universities in any department that will have them. Under their critical attitude all the idols of the past must fall: God has no being, being is not analogous, the word is not a mystical experience, faith is not an experience, God cannot be thought of as a substance, God's works cannot be conceived as causally connected to the world, sacred history cannot be conceived as a process, things have no being, no nature, no essence, no appearance, there are no models to be copied, no ideals, no basis for values, no guide (except for some loose messages from the prophets themselves) for morals, no sacred institutions, no sacredness in human acting. The only thing that is permanent is the continuity of the prophetic vision, as much of the prophets of old as of the modern prophets in the academic communities.[5]

The prophetic voice does not have to base itself on any experience, but proceeds by borrowing the language of others and submitting it to a deconstruction of all its claims, demanding that it be changed because it is not good enough; thus it interiorizes an attitude that is critical in the sense that nothing can measure up to the wholly transcendent prophetic vision. But because the prophetic voice does not create anything, it is also impotent when it tries to destroy. Instead of a total destruction, the prophetic voice settles for a transformation. While it pushes the transcendent farther and farther into more distant recesses of abstraction, it also appropriates for itself the attributes of the transcendent. It institutionalizes its own structures, its states, its visionaries. Its modern tale is the conquest of nature through intellectual means: theory replaces nature, the gods, institutions, social and cultural life, individual life; and through theory, faith is replaced by service to humans. God is dead, but His attributes are nevertheless visible in the prophetic visionaries. The simulacrum has become God.

San Juan de la Cruz's life and writings become exemplary if they are allowed to stand against the inquisitions of both his time and ours as they really are: a life without the compromise of surrender of faith to beliefs, of charity to service, of language to experience, of theory over experience. In revealing him as he was and is through our reading him anew, we wish to resurrect the power of the poetic voice over the prophetic. And this is not itself a theoretical war. The reader will discover that the prophetic voice inhabits our own way of reading by inhabiting the language through which Juan reaches us. Our best friend in this enterprise is our memory as members of a species, for the same acts the mystic performs lie hidden there also. We have "biological memory" as a species and as individuals. The mystic's acts—the mystic's language—may be listened to, focused upon, and organized in a way that enables us to set those habits in motion again.

Religious discrimination is not the type of discrimination one discontinuous system exerts over other continuous and discontinuous systems. Rather, religious discrimination is at its worst when, in the name of religious discrimination of the above type, it suppresses the fundamental faculties through which the religious act may be performed, as in the case of the religious practice of San Juan de la Cruz. Religious discrimination in this sense, then, is a discrimination against the capacities of our own body and mind, which the prophetic voice refuses to transmit to the young and the poetic voice recreates in its own body for us to repeat. By listening to the poetic voice we may be able to renew the active imagining that created life, gods, and experience in the first place and out of which our languages were born. We need to recover the imaginative faculty which the poetic voice cultivates and the prophetic voice buried in the course of their struggle through the centuries.

Chapter Two
THE LIFE

The life of any person is necessarily limited when set down in the form of a narrative. This limitation is even more problematic when the life a person lives takes place in one language and the narrative in another, and when the distance of mental habits is as pronounced as that between a sixteenth-century pre-Reformation Catholic with Jewish and Islamic roots, and a modern reader ambivalent about religion, theoretically inclined, tolerant of other people's views, but utterly convinced that his or her theoretical grasp of the man is in itself sufficient to guarantee comprehension. And yet, between San Juan de la Cruz and the modern reader the Reformation intervened, which among other developments introduced within the English language a new understanding of what constituted interiority and exteriority in man. Not only did it establish a different line separating the two, but it buried the acts of imagining through which the mystics of an earlier Christianity and of other cultures practiced their interior life.

Modernity took over the universities, and the theoretical replaced the experiential as the new habit of thought. Language repeated the project of theorizing and adapting empirical objects to fit the theory. It even ordered the objects of the world in a chain of necessity and dialectics, as in Hegel and Marx. As a result, theory appropriated meanings and changed them to fit the continuous need for new theories and the need to theorize as the primary activity of the brain or mind. It became useless in this context to look for history, soul, or experience. Language is all there is: experience comes later.

It would be a trivial exercise to try to read San Juan de la Cruz's life using the criteria described above and ignore the criteria through which he himself made his life. He was pre-modern, pre-Reformation, pre-dialectical, pre-deconstructionist, pre-postmodern. We must, therefore, readjust our reading habits to make them coincide with those he used. It is essential for us to focus on those internal acts and faculties he set in motion to make his life, to write his poetry and his prose. The act of reading is itself different in different periods. No sixteenth-century person could use reading skills the way we use them today. For them, reading was an exercise in memory, and memory served to set the imagination in motion so that in imagination the world they lived in could stay together. For us, reading means reading for information, the gathering of facts. It is an act we perform in solitude. A sixteenth-century person would read aloud, pronouncing every syllable even when reading alone, and would make images as he or she went along, articulating those memories in a language of images. These images provided reaffirmation of a world familiar to them but almost unknown to us. A person's life consists not so much in what happens to him or her, but of the means he or she uses to gather that life, and the particular inner faculties to which those memories, images, and facts are surrendered so that they not only make their lives through those acts but make them knowingly.

This simple fact—a foreground of actions against a known background kept alive through memory and acts of imagination—separates more than anything else a sixteenth-century person from a contemporary reader. We have no cosmos, no cosmology against which to read our actions. Facts, discrete facts, gathered from our environment, and theoretical habits, determine our actions. We have situations, but no background. How, then, are we to understand a sixteenth-century man who directs most of his efforts to building and rebuilding a background through acts of imagining in order that his acts may have a measure of quality? Can we separate a sixteenth-century man into a plurality of personalities (mystic, poet, saint, founder) and not read him as a unified act—the same acts—appearing in several manifestations? Is San Juan de la Cruz really two people, one a mystic and the other a poet? Against which background are we measuring his actions? Which are the acts through which he builds the background? Which are the acts through which he makes this background public? It is necessary to see that one man holds together background and foreground. If either of those is missing, the man is also missing.

This is the narrative I am trying to develop. It is obvious, therefore, that neither contemporary literary theory nor theology is capable of performing such a task. This cannot be construed as a rejection of these disciplines. They are simply irrelevant to the problem at hand.[1]

The decisions a person makes, either out of design or habit, are dependent on a certain background, which becomes manifest through the decisions taken. Since this background and these decisions are mutually illuminating, it is trivial to isolate partial backgrounds or particular acts disconnected from the larger picture. The habits of a person within a limited background are also the habits of that same person within the larger one. In the case of San Juan de la Cruz, it would not be legitimate to separate his mysticism from his poetry, or to presuppose that the acts through which he reaches mystical experience are different from the acts he uses to create poetry. No mystic is so by chance, and no poet is so by chance; the mystic and the poet are not two separate entities when the acts they perform coincide in the same person, revealing the same background and foreground. There is not much difference, methodologically, if we describe San Juan de la Cruz as a mystic or as a poet. Somewhere in him both acts coincide.

We must, therefore, pose the following questions: What did San Juan de la Cruz do internally in order to empty himself of external sensations and become sensitized bodily from the interior only? How does a person become a mystic? And how does a mystic become a poet?

THE HABIT OF POVERTY

Poverty has no pleasant taste in modern literatures. And there is even less taste for it in English literary culture, since the English

Reformation identified possession of riches as a sign of divine favor.
Furthermore, poverty has become a political tool, something to
thrust aggressively in the face of the enemy. Yet, the founders of the
great religions lived in poverty and praised it. But in the modern
mind poverty means only exclusion, discrimination, lack of *things*.
But poverty is more. Those who have things (money and power)
have left poverty behind. And we have carried on this political push
against poverty by subsidizing the poor. It is a sign of the times that
the students doing menial work at the university where I teach are
mostly middle class, while those from lower-income families are
subsidized with grants. It is not therefore surprising that in modern
narratives there is an eloquent silence about the virtue of poverty, a
virtue once cultivated by some for the benefit of the soul. In the case
of San Juan de la Cruz, his poverty is usually hurried over. It is a fact
that we lack good narratives about poverty. Nor do contemporary
saints preach poverty.

San Juan de la Cruz was born Juan de Yepes y Alvarez in
Fontiveros, a town of about five thousand people, northeast of
Avila, the birthplace of Saint Teresa de Avila. The year of his birth is
given as 1542 (by subtracting his age of forty-nine years from the
date of his death, 1591).[2] He was the third son of Gonzalo de Yepes
and Catalina Alvarez. Gonzalo, his father, belonged to a wealthy
family of silk merchants from Toledo. On one of his business trips
Gonzalo met the orphaned and poor Catalina in a small weaving
factory at Fontiveros. Gonzalo must have fallen so deeply in love
that he did not listen to anyone, for he married the girl in 1529.
Gonzalo was at once dismissed and disowned by his family. He
joined his wife and took up her occupation as a weaver of silk.
Gonzalo's family reacted in a strange manner, for in Spain in those
days the wife took the status of the husband and not the other way
around, unless it was felt that he had broken the code of honor and
stained the family. Though there are no documents which verify
this conclusion, it appears that Catalina must have been either of
Muslim descent, or the daughter of a publicly executed felon.
Whatever the reason, Gonzalo left Toledo and settled with his wife
in Fontiveros. The family was from then on condemned to find
housing in the *barrios* where Islamic converts or their descendants
lived—the poorest and most disadvantaged neighborhoods. The

probability of anyone rising up from this milieu to achieve world renown was remote indeed.

Three sons were born of this marriage of love: Luis, Francisco, and Juan. Shortly after Juan's birth his father died. Reduced to extreme poverty, the young widow Catalina tried to place her children in the homes of her husband's family. She traveled to Toledo, Torrijos, Gálvez, and Arévalo with hopes of finding some help at their hands, but she was cruelly repulsed. She finally settled in Medina del Campo, then a large mercantile town, where she returned to her work of weaving. Poverty in this family was so great that Luis, the second son, died while still a young child due to malnutrition; Francisco, the eldest son, never learned how to read or write and could not find employment, though he always gave the impression of having an excellent heart and a simple mind; and Juan de Yepes, the youngest, carried on his body the marks of hunger: the very short height of five feet, due to rickets. Much later on, when Juan de Yepes was already Juan de la Cruz and Teresa de Avila had entrusted his mother Catalina to the care of the nuns of Medina del Campo, the nuns bought her a pair of shoes and wrote down in their accounts "pa *la* Catalina," a sure sign that Catalina was still considered a woman of the lowest social rank and that this condition was not lost on any of Juan de la Cruz's fellow monks, despite the fact that he twice changed his name: Juan de Yepes became Juan de Santo Matía, and finally Juan de la Cruz.

What we know for certain about Juan de Yepes's childhood is that he always lived in Islamic neighborhoods, in Fontiveros, Arévalo, and Medina del Campo, a fact that, while not explicit in Juan de la Cruz's poetry, is obvious in its music.

In 1546 Catalina traveled to Rodilla and Gálvez asking her brothers-in-law, a canon and a doctor, to adopt the children. The first refused to give any help, but the second did take in Francisco. But the doctor's wife became pregnant in 1547 and Francisco was returned home. That same year Catalina went to try her fortune in Arévalo, and in 1551 she moved to Medina del Campo with the same hope. By then Francisco had married Ana Izquierdo in Arévalo, who joined them in the weaving at home. She brought seven children into the world, all of whom died, with the exception of a girl who eventually became a nun.

The children of poor families in Spain had a way out of poverty since the sixteenth century, and that was the church. They could also join the army, but Catalina's children obviously did not. Juan was placed by his mother in a catechism school, an institution resembling an orphanage where the children were given food and clothing along with their training and served as acolytes at monasteries, churches, and the private chapels of the rich. In this semi-orphanage Juan received his elementary education and tried his hand at a series of jobs (carpentry, tailoring, sculpturing, and painting) through apprenticeships to local craftsmen. One after another, however, dismissed the young man as totally incompetent. At the age of seventeen he found a job at the Plague Hospital de la Concepción, and the founder of this hospital, Don Alonso Alvarez, aware of the young man's desire to learn, encouraged him to become a priest. He arranged for Juan to attend the newly established Jesuit College at Medina del Campo. This was the end of Juan's childhood.

Three stories from this early period have come down to us. Playing as a child in Fontiveros with other children, he fell into a little lake near his home. A beautiful woman (the Virgin Mary?) saved him. When the family moved to Medina del Campo a sea monster jumped out of the Zapardiel river (the same river of his childhood in Fontiveros) and tried to devour the child. And also in Medina del Campo, Juan fell into a well. In each case, Juan was saved by the same beautiful woman.

Regardless of how the reader wants to take these stories, the fact is that the child saw them in his way and thus formed the reality of his soul. The child experienced his early years as both a spiritual and physical sinking, a journey down into the pit. How could he rise? It is also true that this type of story was popular then and continues to be popular even in this century in those areas of Spain where Islamic descendants are concentrated. One still hears of wells, lakes, sea monsters, and enchanted princesses in their depths. It was at this very time that Spain tried to Christianize those places that had Jewish or Islamic traditions. Where sea or water monsters were spoken of, where enchanted princesses saved children from death, little by little Christian images made their appearance; and while the sense of enchantment remained, the names changed. What images were buried in the depths of Juan's soul? Whose faces did he see when love or heaven came to his mind? What images were reflected to him out of the depths of wells and rivers? What images did Juan de la Cruz see, feel, touch, and smell when in imagination he created out of nothing his own human origins?

In closing my account of the early period of Juan's life, I am reminded of another persecuted giant of this sixteenth century Fray Luis de León, who summarized in a metaphor his own escape from persecution. As he is engaged in writing *The Names of Christ* in a garden by a river, he sees on the opposite shore a little bird, singing, perched in a tree. The song is so sweet and clear that he is forced to pay attention to it. Suddenly two huge, black crows appear from nowhere and attack the little bird. The bird is caught by them, suspended in midair, and then dropped into the flowing waters of the river. The little bird struggles with the current and the crows continue to attack it viciously. At last the bird disappears within the waters and the crows fly away. His heart sinks with the plight of the little bird while the whole countryside seems to be covered by absolute silence. Suddenly the little beak and then the head appear above the waters. Slowly the bird shakes its wings and stumbles onto the shore, all wet and tired. Slowly other birds join it, flying around in circles, and the little bird takes flight in a burst of exuberance toward the open sky. The silence of the countryside gives way to sounds of joy.

Juan de la Cruz—Juan de Yepes—learned to survive early in his young age and fly high above the appetites of his own compatriots. Who owned the wings, the water, the air was not his concern. Juan de Yepes learned soon that his mission in life, his project, was to fly, and this required his body and soul to carry little baggage.

FORMAL TRAINING

Between 1559 and 1563 Juan de Yepes attended the Jesuit College of Medina, where he studied the humanities: Nebrija the grammarian, translations and originals from the Latin—Virgil, Horace, Cicero, Seneca, Caesar, Ovid, Suetonius, and Pliny. He studied Latin and Greek and, of course, religion. In the writings of San Juan de la Cruz this period of his training does not appear anywhere. He is not given to quoting from the classics, and his writing style does not have the classical elegance of someone like Fray Luis de León. It seems obvious that Juan's soul did not vibrate in harmony with the Jesuits. This may explain why Juan de Yepes did not even try to become a Jesuit. Instead he looked among the solitary places, the orders of contemplation, like the Franciscans and the Carmelites. He was not even tempted to become a secular priest with a pension that would have taken care of his financial problems at home. One night in 1563 he knocked at the door of the Carmelite convent of Medina, and there he became a friar the same year, at age twenty. On February 24 he received the habit of Our Lady of Mount Carmel, changing his name to Juan de Santo Matía.

The Carmelite Order was not primarily dedicated to study, but tried nevertheless to give their members a solid philosophical and theological background. Since 1500 the Carmelites had sent their best students to study at the University of Salamanca while giving them classes in theology at the home college of San Andrés in Salamanca. In the year 1564–65 there were eight Carmelites registered at the University of Salamanca besides Juan de Santo Matía. His name continues to appear there for the next three years. In 1567–68 he registered for a course in theology. This seems to prove that he did most of his studies at San Andrés and took only some courses at Salamanca. But this does not disqualify him as an interested spectator in the battles which took place between professors and the Inquisition at that institution. Several of them, the most prominent being Fray Luis de León, went to jail on account of their teachings. One point of contention was the interpretation of the *Song of Songs,* which constituted the basis of Juan's own poem, "Spiritual Canticle." He thus learned very early that if one dared to speak in public, to make public one's thoughts, one ran the risk of being sent to jail, removed from the mainstream for the rest of one's life. Yet, it is around these controversial writings and teachings that Juan de la Cruz focused his own internal spiritual flight. And it is here, in this spiritual flight, that he finds the source of quotes in the Old and New Testament, and it is this spiritual flight that makes him feel strong in his own beliefs and public exposition. He quotes 684 times from the Old Testament and 376 times from the New Testament, while his spiritual trajectory follows a marked line of

Hebrew interests with his Islamic themes, music, and human love forming the background. This quantity of quotations from the Old Testament was remarkable in a mystic. A few years before, another mystic also wrote abundantly but only quoted twice from the Old Testament, with most of his quotations taken from the New Testament and the Fathers of the Church. This was Ignatius de Loyola, founder of the Jesuits.

What really is a formal education? It is obvious that the formal education of the sixteenth century consisted of learning certain skills: languages, public speaking, writing, and the ability to express oneself in public to the satisfaction of the Inquisition. The fact is that formal education in Spain, England, and Germany differed not so much in the skills taught as in the public propositions that were regarded in each country as correct. This was also the time when the vernacular made its appearance in printed discourse, and translations had to be evaluated and approved by the inquisitors. It was a time when Erasmus on the one hand, Luther on the other, and the practices of the "*iluminados*" and mystics everywhere kept the Inquisition on its toes day and night. And we must accept the fact that education is mostly a social and political decision about which truths become public and how this is accomplished. It is part and parcel of the public domain, a public domain which is always in the hands of one inquisition or another. Those of us who have lived, time and again, under inquisitions or dictatorships operating in the open know the sad truth that none of us believes in public statements and in public rhetoric, since we know they are the product of the visible inquisition at work. And we immediately proceed to discover and promote those internal acts no inquisition can reach, just as was true of the sixteenth century. This experience is missing, however, in contemporary "free" societies that believe they are free because inquisitions are simply not as visible as in other periods of history. But a sixteenth-century monk, a mystic of those days, or even a Spaniard of the Franco era, would be able to detect immediately the inquisitions operating in and through our free systems of education and public communication. What we miss in our free societies is the development of needed acts which occur as a matter of course in a prison where people know they are prisoners, but are absent when the prisoners believe themselves to be free. I do not refer, of course, to specific freedoms, but to the freedom to perform acts we do not think we are missing, in order to be truly free.

The role of formal education becomes clearer when we observe a century like the sixteenth. The different nations of Europe shared the same facts and based their education on the same books and yet local inquisitions made sure the results of that education were not uniform across Europe. Interpretations varied, cultures were built on these differences, and even those within the culture had to learn how to accommodate to the public expressions demanded by the inquisitions. These facts establish certain principles we should bear in mind. First, students arrive at the universities with their lives already formed, their values established, and with a clear idea of who they are and where they are going. In order to do this they already possess certain technologies (images and languages) through which they are able to make their lives. But because cultures are hybrid mixtures of all sorts of familial, clan, and tribal elements, cultures try to homogenize the expression of these elements through new languages and images taught and made authoritative through the universities. All these elements or *technologies* put together, as practiced within an individual, form what we call an educated person. The demand of one technology to become the exclusive practice of a culture is obviously more than an inquisition can achieve, unless the members of the culture agree to that reductionism or are misled as to their many other possibilities. If for a moment we suspend the belief in a unifying ground like "nature," or "common values," we can easily see that what we are as human beings is simply the possibility of being able to practice certain technologies the species has learned and coded into the human neurophysiology. We are never the finished product of a "nature," a "god," a "system." In the name of nature, god, and system, we may suppress or overdevelop one technology at the expense of others, or we may develop our own technologies against those of the public domain while mastering them, or we may propagate local, familial, or foreign technologies from our past or from other cultures now present among us, until they are embodied in the legitimate practice of the public domain. This last alternative is what we observe occurring throughout the sixteenth century with its mystics, and this is the alternative our educational system should develop in

America where most of the cultures of the world are present. We must avoid inquisitions in our midst. Democracies contradict themselves when they operate under any kind of inquisition, no matter how subtle, and democratic societies in order to be democratic need to include the multiple technologies of their constituents, if they are not to be discriminatory.

There is a large difference between the inquisitions of the sixteenth century and those of the present day. In those days the inquisitions would indeed make room for saints, mystics, and other marginal individuals if they could prove—and the proof was entirely up to them—that what they knew or were preaching came from God. If they could not prove this then they were condemned insofar as they did not express themselves as the inquisition demanded. But the inquisitors were open to this slender possibility, and for this reason saints, mystics, and innovators tried to find a place for themselves, forming societies, hospitals, orders, congregations; and writing mystical poetry. Contemporary democracies have no common ground of values, no common language, no common beliefs. They operate simply by imposing one technology over all others. There is no room for the voice of God in the public domain. As long as no other technologies are developed within the individual, even if God spoke no one would be listening.

EXERCISING THE SOUL

Juan de Santo Matía was ordained as a priest in 1567 and returned to Medina del Campo to celebrate his first mass. Teresa de Avila happened to be there at that time after she had opened her second convent of reformed nuns. Already she was thinking of reforming the men. The two met for the first time and Teresa convinced Juan that his call to the solitary and rigorous life would best be served in reforming the men with her, rather than in joining the Carthusian monks. Juan and the Prior of the Medina Carmelites, Father Heredia, became the first two men to join Teresa in her adventure of reform. The two men, or the "one and one-half men," as Teresa affectionately called them, were entrusted with returning the Carmelite order to its original spirituality, austerity, and detachment

from things of this world, its exercise of the soul toward total
nakedness. Their political idea was not to reform the calced Carmelites already living in convents, but to form new communities of
discalced Carmelites in new convents. Juan de Santo Matía saw this
as the beginning of a new life. He again changed his name—to Juan
de la Cruz. From now on his life was a determined effort to make
this reform succeed; it was to be marked with the failures and
successes of this mission. The failures were more visible than the
successes, but seemed also to be directed to the deeper life Juan was
beginning to develop: the flight towards the solitary regions of
mystical experience. He did not direct his efforts toward a political
struggle with the outside world, as did Teresa de Avila. His efforts
aimed at achieving his own internal perfection while serving as a
model for others, making his life an example of the reformed
Carmelite.

Teresa ordered that Juan de la Cruz and his companion Germán
de San Matía live together in a cell built within the walls of the
convent of the Encarnación at Avila. It is a curious irony of history
that the orchard within which the cell was built had, two centuries
earlier, been a Hebrew cemetery for heretical Jews, where the remains of Moshe de León, the celebrated author of the *Zohar* (1250–
1305), had been buried. [3] There is a certain historical irony in the fact
that this is the way mystics from across religions and cultures should
meet: suffering under the incomprehension of their colleagues, persecuted, in solitude, in a totally dark night. For it was here, while
Juan and his companion were sleeping on the night of December 2,
1577, that the calced Carmelites pulled them out of their beds and
took them as prisoners to Toledo. Apparently Juan and his companion managed to destroy or eat some of Juan's own writings so that
they would not fall in the hands of his enemies. What was Juan afraid
of? Which writings was he hiding? Who were his enemies?

The religious practice of the sixteenth century had been crit-
icized by Calvin, Luther, and the Catholic Counter-Reformers as an
empty religiosity, fixated on externalities, the church of a dead God,
of a fantastic Christ, of rituals—sterile because the people practicing
them had made them so. On the other hand, there were those who
believed themselves already saved because they had learned to abandon themselves to God. These were the *"iluminados"* or *"aban-*

donados," conventicles of people who chose as their expression of salvation the erotic language of the Bible and of human love; and the "*beatas*," abandoned to divine love without any practice whatsoever of virtue, who talked to everyone, including the Inquisition, of love ecstasies, erotic visions, and instant salvation. The Inquisition took a radical stand on all these issues. Erasmus, Calvin, and Luther were attacked for their doctrines of salvation through faith and without works, as were all types of interior religiosity. The Inquisition was not fond of a religious experience, such as that of mysticism, which the religious authorities found difficult or impossible to control. Any mystic who flirted with writing for the public was also flirting with the Inquisition. Juan de la Cruz was a victim of this historical equivocation. How would the authorities have read his "Spiritual Canticle"? Its language had already been condemned by the Inquisition.[4]

But Juan de la Cruz was not so much the victim of an external enemy as of an enemy within and close at hand—his own Carmelite brothers. For nine months they held him prisoner in Toledo, in a small room without windows which was used as the lavatory for guests, with one small skylight in the ceiling for ventilation and light.

On his arrival the prior of the convent and other superiors read him the decision taken at Piacenza, Italy, against the discalced reformers. It aimed at getting them to give up their mad project of reform, abandon their habits, and stop recruiting novices. They also informed him that his place was at Medina del Campo, and that in any case he had committed a grave sin of disobedience. However, were he to change his ways and accept their recommendations, they would forget everything and even grant him a post as superior in one of their calced convents. But Juan de la Cruz refused to budge. He felt committed to return to the original inspiration of the order, to austerity and the interior life. And so he was sent back to jail, where he was treated with greater severity than before, since it was learned that his companion Germán de San Matías had managed to escape. He was kept in total isolation. The few friars who visited him went there only to shower him with recriminations and throw his food on the floor. His jailer was not even allowed to talk to him, or remove the chamber pot from his cell, and the stench made Juan sick. His back was full of sores from the scourging he had under-gone at the hands of the friars trying to teach him that it does not pay to disobey. His habit stuck to his flesh, his clothes began to rot, and his body became infested with worms. He lost his appetite, could hardly sleep, and when the hot summer arrived in Toledo he was hardly able to breathe in his cell. In these surroundings he began writing "Spiritual Canticle" and the little poem that begins "Well I know the fountain." In these poems, and others such as "Dark Night," we are able to sense the emptiness he felt within him-self.

After six months spent in these conditions they changed his jailer. He must have been a kinder man, for he gave Juan paper and ink so that he could write "those things that might profit his soul," and he also allowed him to clean up his own excrement and kept the door open to let air in. He gave him needle, thread, and scissors to mend his clothes, and during this slight relaxation of his regimen, Juan began to plan his escape.

Bit by bit he loosened the screws of the lock to his cell and waited patiently. One night he removed the lock, moved quickly over the friars sleeping in the guest room, ran a rope made of blankets and clothes down from a balcony, and descended into the garden. He then climbed over a wall and found he was free. As soon as dawn arrived he went to the Carmelite nuns, who gave him shelter under the pretext that a very sick nun needed confession. Thus they were able to shield him from the Inquisition, which could not enter the cloister. There Juan de la Cruz recited some of his poems for the nuns. They then arranged for a canon of Toledo, Don Pedro González de Mendoza, a friend of the Reformers, to hide Juan in his house. His servants took Juan to Almodovar del Río where the discalced Carmelites were gathering, thus ending his persecu-tion by the non–Reformed Carmelites.

For a few years Juan de la Cruz found a certain peace far away from Castile, as prior of the tiny convent of El Calvario in An-dalucia. Here he wrote "*Noche Oscura*" and finished "Spiritual Can-ticle." His life was that of a hermit, and he was happy. He also lived in Los Mártires, Granada, La Peñuela, and Baeza. His home was in the fields and mountains and not among people. But he was to be subject to persecution nevertheless.

In 1591 there was a gathering of the Carmelite order in Madrid and Juan was sent there as one of its superiors. By this time the reformation of the Order had become widespread and many had joined for reasons other than spiritual advancement. Juan opened the meeting in Madrid by admonishing those gathered there that the Order would be ruined if people were afraid to correct their superiors and if those superiors could turn against them and seek revenge. He proposed, therefore, that all voting be secret. Secret voting had already been an acknowledged success during the Cistercian reform (around A.D. 1112), and it was to influence the political technique of voting in the European parliamentary democracies, the English being the first to adopt it. Juan's proposal was rejected, and he himself was transformed by it into the enemy within. His own reformed friars now wanted to destroy him. There was talk of sending him to Mexico so that he would not become a superior to the nuns; this, however, was averted when a bull arrived from Rome stating the nuns could deal with their own decisions without the aid of a male superior. Juan was then asked to return to Segovia, but he was afraid of becoming more deeply involved with the politics of the Order and refused. Finally he was sent to La Peñuela, in the Sierra Morena, to live peacefully again as a hermit. But this peace would not last long.

Doria, who had taken control of the Order and was the exact opposite of Juan in his vision of the purpose of the Reformation of the Order and how to run it, took it upon himself to destroy Juan de la Cruz. He instructed Father Diego Evangelista, a loyal follower and also someone Juan had reproached for his free ways outside the convent, to open an inquiry against Juan de la Cruz regarding his morality and his behavior with the nuns. Father Diego visited convent after convent, asking the most impertinent questions, arranging the answers as he saw fit, editing the narrative to fit the purpose of his inquiry, putting pressure on priests and nuns to tell all, finally managing to extract from a nun in Málaga that Juan de la Cruz had kissed her through a grating. It was obvious that Doria had started a sexual inquiry against Juan de la Cruz. Nuns and priests protested, but they knew the dangers of the times and while protesting they started to burn whatever correspondence or writings from Juan de la Cruz they had. Doria wanted Juan de la Cruz removed from the Order. He had attempted something similar with Gracián, Teresa de Avila's favorite friar, and succeeded. But Juan de la Cruz was not disturbed, nor did he do anything to defend himself. Much of his work was burned, and this may be the reason why his prose works have come to us in unfinished form, and why we have so little of his poetry.

Be that as it may, no one was in fact convinced or even concerned that Juan de la Cruz might have misbehaved sexually. But as a result of the inquiry he became a marginal man, abandoned by all, and after only six weeks at La Peñuela he came down with a high fever and was ordered to Baeza to recover. But Juan preferred Ubeda, where he was not as well known, and went there instead. The superior treated him with the greatest severity, expressing his vengeance against the man who had reproached him for being too free outside the convent walls. A doctor cut into Juan's foot and removed a great quantity of pus, then cauterized the wound with a burning iron, as was commonly done with people and animals in those days. The superior denied him even the food prescribed by the doctor, alleging extreme poverty in the convent. But Juan told him not to give it a second thought, for he was happy—he predicted that the house would one day have all it needed. The superior finally became remorseful and apologized to the sick man.

On the 14th of December, 1591, just before midnight, as the friars surrounded the sick man chanting the "*De Profundis*" and the "*Miserere,*" Juan arranged his own bedcovers, as if expecting someone to come and visit him, and asked to be read *Song of Songs.* Suddenly he exclaimed: "Oh, what beautiful daisies!" and died.

This is the life of the man called Juan de Yepes, Juan de Santo Matía, and Juan de la Cruz. He received no consolation to carry to his tomb. His only admirers, his only audience, while alive, consisted of women and a few novices. Yet their friendship was offered to him only insofar as they offered themselves to God. Even his greatest and most famous friend, Teresa de Avila, parted with him on unfriendly terms. When they met for the last time in Granada, Teresa had been obsessed with the idea of going to Burgos to found a convent and to see her friend Gracián. Juan de la Cruz tried to persuade Teresa that the voices she heard calling her to Burgos did not come from God. They argued the whole night and then parted, each going a separate way. Juan never hesitated to follow the will of God, and he always chose the hardest way in order to make doubly sure he was not setting his will over God's will. Teresa was different. She felt assured that God's will and hers would ultimately coincide. There is only one hint that Juan retained a tiny attachment to something of this world. As he lay dying he must have remembered his early days at the hospital of Medina del Campo, where he tried to comfort those about to die by bringing them a dish of asparagus, a great delicacy, as their last meal on earth. Juan remembered that he liked asparagus and as he was dying he asked for some for himself. This is the last trace of his humanity given to us. The world around him obviously knew that a saint had just died. The news of his death, and of the smell of flowers his body exhaled as soon as he died, spread quickly. People gathered around the body and soon the ritual of burial, exhumation, and the gathering of relics began. The gruesome custom of dismembering the dead had originated in medieval times. Juan's fingers, legs, and bones were preserved as relics.

In 1675 Juan de la Cruz was beatified, and in 1725 he was made a saint. Even this honor worked against him in some respects. His true background—the stories and places of his birth, his family history—were distorted beyond recognition. Many of his papers were destroyed so that nothing would prevent his human exaltation, for with it his Order, his family, and his country were also being exalted. And so, were it not for his poetry, Juan de la Cruz would have been rendered a marginal figure through the manipulations of theologians.

Juan de la Cruz forces scholarship to face the naked act through which his poetry was able to become the living testimony of his spiritual practice. All the rest is tainted.

Chapter Three
SPIRITUAL PRACTICE

Mystics center their spiritual practice on a maxim that to them is self-evident: desires are images and will their act.[1] If desires are images, then the spiritual practice of the mystic will concentrate on building only those images that will let the will of God enter the human will and thus cancel out all images coming from outside— that is, images that do not bring in the will of God. In short, the project of the mystic is to reverse the normal process in which sensation is fed by external images. He wishes to empty the senses of all sensation coming to them from the *outside,* including the memory of sensation, and sensitize the body only from the *inside.* It is remarkable that the achievement of this goal has been such a well-kept secret. For if one person has been able to accomplish such an impressive turnabout, then all human beings are capable of such a feat. Since this is a human act, it may be reflected upon and articulated so that other humans may repeat it.

The first step along the path of spiritual practice for a mystic will be to discover, promote, and exert through repetition and dedication those faculties capable of building original images that introduce the absolute desire of the origin. This must act as the absolute background which gives light and meaning to the acts of the foreground. The mystics build a background even as they act on the foreground, and all their acts are measured against the background they keep on building. If the mystic is not able to construct that background internally, then he or she will be at the mercy of the enemy: the exteriority of the world, the images which flood in from outside, the sensations of the devil, the flesh, other things. The mystic also knows that images from the outside will not enter within unless he or she so wills. Life is an agonic reading of those signs which come from God or from external agents. But before the mystic even considers these signs, he or she must know with certainty how to distinguish the internal and the external human faculties through which interiority and exteriority are built.[2]

Juan de la Cruz exemplifies ultimate interiority. His spiritual practice demonstrates how the technologies that create interiority are developed; he is a master at revealing the steps necessary to build a background using those technologies to create interiority and give light and meaning to external acts. Since technology is a human device, he makes sure to empty himself, body and soul, of any sensation or attachment which might come to him through these exercises. Thus his spiritual practice constructs as much as it deconstructs along its course.

Juan de la Cruz described his practice as the flight of the solitary bird and wrote down the five conditions of this flight:

> The first, that it flies to the highest point;
> the second, that it does not suffer for company, not even of its
>   own kind;
> the third, that it aims its beak to the skies;
> the fourth, that it does not have a definitive color;
> the fifth, that it sings very softly.

Mystics differ in the way they use the internal signs of the background they create in the conduct of their lives. Ignatius de Loyola used them to bring the will of God to the world; he made use of meditation only as an aid in making decisions. Teresa de Avila delighted in the sensations of the inner signs and used them to found communities for women and also for the sheer pleasure of feeling God's company.[3] Juan de la Cruz, however, used them simply to get rid of them. He is a straight arrow. In his flight he created the clearest document of spiritual practice. Though mystics may differ in the way they use the signs they receive from the background they build, they do not differ in their view of how this background is built and on the need to build it; and this applies equally to mystics within Christianity and those within other traditions: Islam, Judaism, Hinduism, Buddhism, Taoism, and the rest of the distant and misunderstood religions of the Far East. The abilities and skills used to build the background will not by themselves bring God to the mystic, but, as Teresa de Avila wrote in her *Life,* "without them God does not come."

THE BIBLICAL TRADITION

It is essential at this point to make the reader aware of the fact that many of the words used in describing mystical practice sound like words we use to describe religious practice in general and the biblical tradition in particular. Faith, belief, reason, imagination, reformation, transformation, body, soul, language, signs, revelation, charisma, prophecy, voice, preaching, hearing, etc., mean different things according to different traditions or practices. All of them and many others form the pattern of the actual practice of any tradition, but none extends uniformly across traditions. Our mainstream spiritual practice in America is the result of the actual spiritual practice of the early Protestant preachers in America. Their practice, we may say, is the only uniform understanding the English language repeats wherever and whenever we speak of spiritual practice. And the practice of those early Protestants was in essence the biblical tradition. What we are presenting here as mystical practice goes against the grain of that tradition, or runs the risk of being misunderstood if the presuppositions and actual spiritual practice of those early Protestants are not exposed as the actual presuppositions ingrained in the language we ourselves use to speak of mystical practice.

John Cotton (1584–1652), Benjamin Colman (1673–1747), William Ellery Channing (1780–1842), and Ralph Waldo Emerson (1803–1882) may serve us as prototypes for our purposes here. All of these preachers emerged from the Puritan tradition and all had a deep concern for shaping the *rational* and *emotional* aspects of religious experience. While they were deeply engaged in their spiritual pursuit they also contributed greatly to a revival of external literary, religious, and social life. More significantly, they show us how their way of preaching is also their way of spiritual practice, and this influenced the shape of the spiritual practice around them. In other words, how they understood religion is the way most people in America understand religion and its practice today. What would be foreign to them is foreign to most.

For the Protestant preachers mentioned above, prophecy was their practice, and this practice was an art. Prophecy for them was the inspired act of speaking forth the Holy Spirit, but since the Spirit arrives through the faculty of hearing, the preacher needs to direct his words in such a manner as to persuade the audience, or a significant part of it. Protestant thought thus established a "true" connection between Spirit and external form, between the inspiration of a sermon and its delivery. In this manner it broke away from other biblical traditions (Catholic, mystical, Hindu, Buddhist, etc.). All the preacher needed to do was touch the individual with the Spirit, for when the Spirit touches the individual the Spirit is *its own interpreter.* This freed the individual from any mediation by other persons or even by churches. Interpretation, as much as experience, is private, for it is not the result of reason but of experience itself. This conclusion could have opened a Pandora's box of anarchism, but Calvin came to the rescue. He proposed that the Bible contained knowledge that was "objective and informational," although to a great degree reserved for the elect. Thus acts of interpretation of the Bible are legitimate, for they have not only an individual but also a social dimension. And in this interpretation even those who do not share the elect status may participate.

It was on the basis of this double-barreled vision of scriptural interpretation that Protestantism developed its own individual and social theories and also its doctrines of how scriptural truths were to be presented to an audience. Thus the model of spiritual practice as embodied in the Protestant preacher addresses the task of bridging the gap between piety—that mysterious and overwhelming sense of ecstatic union with a transcendent whole—and everyday concerns about moral judgment and conduct in the world.[4]

Official Protestantism in Europe and America is thus a rejection of everything mystical. There is no need to build a background, for it is already built into the written text of the Bible. There is no need to construct mystical experience, for no amount of good works can make you part of the elect if God has not so chosen you. And even if you succeed in the mystical endeavor and God pours his gifts over you, that is all that mystical experience is: a private gift of God to an individual, without social features or returns. In other words, there is no room within Protestantism and the biblical tradition we have inherited for the kind of public acceptance of the practice of religion described by San Juan de la Cruz, regardless of how highly we esteem his poetry. Modern efforts within Protestantism to widen the Protestant mind by writers like Tillich are open to suspicion even though well-intentioned. It is obvious that if we call all words and signs *symbolic,* we might then be able to enlarge the discussion of what constitutes religious experience, but in the process we will have destroyed the experience itself. What would a Protestant divine say of San Juan de la Cruz when in verse and in prose he speaks of God as "My Beloved the mountains"? If Juan de la Cruz lived today I wonder if he would have preferred the damnation of the sixteenth-century Inquisition which called his statement heretical or the condescension of a present-day Protestant theologian who calls his statement metaphorical. A sixteenth-century heretic would have been condemned for holding wrong beliefs, but would not also have been insulted by hearing his beloved called a metaphor and a construction of fantasy, by being perceived as the inhabitant of a world of make-believe, a demented person. San Juan de la Cruz did not need to state in prose that the meaning of his poetic verse "my beloved the mountains," was literally "my beloved is the mountains."

The argument hardly needs to be made that American democracy cannot be built on a plurality of *symbols* declared such by those who control the power of interpretation in the public domain. Only true pluralities will create a true democracy, both political and individual.

THE BUILDING OF THE REAL

Mysticism is not a literary style, nor is there a literary genre which can be identified as mystical, as we identify poetry, stories, novels, and plays. Mysticism is built on an interior experience. In mysticism experience comes first and is followed by its expression through literary genres. But if we are going to use literary categories we may say with accuracy that in the mystical experience the *body* of the mystic is the primary text, for it inscribes the primary acts, the signs of which can be articulated and made public. But this raises the question of what is the real? Is it a given or a construction?

All so-called reality is a substitution. What cannot be known is replaced by that which can be known—explanatory systems—and in some cases, as in science, this may also be predictable and controllable. These multiple substitutions and manipulations of systems of explanation produce the multiple facts that we take as given rather than constructed. The skills or technologies through which we reach those facts remain invisible to the users, and thus we speak about "facts" as if they came into existence without human effort. But the fact of the matter is that all reality is construed through human effort. This effort uses the body to reach out and enlarge itself beyond the limits of its possibilities by means of certain instruments, both external and internal; we are acquainted with the external instrumentalities through which we compensate for the deficiencies of our human body, but we are almost ignorant of the internal instrumentalities through which we reach those external constructs as well as other, internal ones. We are almost illiterate when it comes to knowing about the inner function and extent of our human faculties. Our human interiority is multiple and through inner technologies we can not only build bridges to reach the ultimate and most distant objects in the cosmos, but we are also able to build bridges to the divinity and the world of the spirit. The mystic is a human being who knows this simple fact and is determined to construct those instruments within his interiority through which the divine—the not-human—may appear. Since these inner technologies are human, the mystic knows they are only a preparation, dispensable once the manifestation has taken place. The manifestation itself, however, is a constant affair, not just one shot in the dark.

In short: The human body is not a fact but the repository of a multitude of technologies reaching both inward and outward to extend the two worlds—human and divine—as far as they can reach; insofar as they are human constructs they are not causal of the mystical experience, but the experience would not occur without the development of those technologies. Furthermore, without knowledge of those technologies, internal and external, it is not possible to talk about the individuals practicing them. One does not need to be a mystic or a scientist to have their experiences, but unless one knows something about their technologies, discussion of their work is bound to be misleading.

The internal mechanism of the mystic is geared to build a particular kind of experience: a union of two separate wills, the mystic's and God's. The building of this kind of experience requires him to refrain from using any intellectual technologies or fantasies which borrow from the known world, and from the necessities of thought. The mystic is focused exclusively on an imagination which builds images in the perfection of their originality, for they are created whole and not borrowed from other images. In building these original images the mystic listens for signs of affection and movements of the will. In this search the familiar world of the mystic is reduced to insensibility while a new world with different signs emerges. There is darkness of the senses, of the bereaved sensorium, there is doubt about the origin of signs, there is the divestment of beliefs, there is the loss of hope, at times even of love. This is a journey where only faith traveling in the dark succeeds. And the manifestation of success is the experienced union of two wills, after the death of the individual will of the mystic has survived its own dark burial. The mystics express this union in verses and prose concerned with love: the union of love, of two lovers, a sexual language which expresses the reality of two wills uniting, which expresses a reality that only the mystic experiences: that God is no longer only a transcendent being but lives in the human flesh. He becomes the flesh, the immanent God in the flesh, in the dust, in the earth out of which he built himself a wife, built his own substance, and became one of us—just as Solomon expresses this in the *Song of Songs,* San Juan de la Cruz explains it in his poetry and part of his prose.

Jewish biblical commentators, the heirs of the prophetic voice and suspicious of any anthropomorphism attributed to God, did away with the *Song of Songs* by simply stating that it should be interpreted as an allegory. The same thing happened in Christianity as intellectualism gained a privileged status over other technologies with the primacy of the scholastic version of Aristotle during the medieval period. And Christianity was also responsible for identifying its moral doctrine with the models inherited from Augustine and Roman Stoicism, in which human love was exclusively connected to the mechanism of human reproduction, depriving it of other meanings and expressions, and loading it with animality and degradation.

The mystic experiences love as the unity of two wills. His verbal expression of this experience is erotic. But the experience comes totally from the inside out, as opposed to that of the ordinary lover, who experiences love from the outside in. In the mystic the senses are filled with love from the inside, while in the lover they are filled from the outside. The true experience of love, the absolute experience of love, is that of the mystic. The ordinary lover needs the aid of external, ideal images to justify love to himself, he needs to sublimate love for it to have meaning. The mystic experiences love as the deepest experience given to humans: empirical love, positivistic love, love without constructs, naked love. It is an experience the mystic cannot appropriate or own, but which happens *through* the mystic with him or her as witness. The mystic knows that there are human experiences which are not owned by any one subject, even when they pass through particular bodies—experiences that are eternal because they happened to no one, though the witness was there as if present, and his or her body was the substance and field where the experience took place. But because this sort of experience may be generalized to the point of incomprehensibility, we will, at this point, slow down the process of description and analyze the building of the experience which we call mystical into its different steps, so that we may clearly perceive the exercise involved in the practices of these athletes of the soul.

THE SPIRITUAL PRACTICES OF DISMEMBERMENT

The Catholic Church had the good sense to sanctify Juan de la Cruz, along with so many other mystics. In this way, the Church proclaimed the *reality* of their lives. The same Church was not as wise in trying to describe their mystical practice using the theological cate-

gories of "the purgative, the illuminative, and the unitive ways."
These theological categories cover up rather than reveal the actual
spiritual practice of these athletes of the spiritual life. We must
discover their actual practice so that it does not remain hidden and
therefore ineffectual.

The mystics were not squeamish about their goals. Their spiritual practice was an assault on the divinity. It was neither a theoretical nor intuitive assault, but an experiential one, and this experience
involved a transformation of the sensory systems of the mystic.
How is this achieved? What steps do mystics follow to steal the
background and make the background their own flesh?

Mystics share in one common image that guides their imagination backwards: they believe that the experience they are after *has
already happened,* whether it is called the Trinity in Christianity, the
First Sacrifice in Hinduism, Nirvana in Buddhism, etc. The distance between this original experience and the body of the mystic is
what the mystics tried to bridge through spiritual practice. Christianity proclaimed itself different from the mystery religions, moral
reformers, and free-lance worshipers by establishing the will of God
as the center of this original experience. This will (the Father)
created the world out of nothing, became human flesh in the Second
Person of the Trinity (the Son), and performed these deeds out of
love (the Spirit). This is the cornerstone of Christianity and the
model for the experience that has already happened in the spiritual
practice of the Christian mystics. Will, memory, and imagination
are all the mystic needs to bring to meditation in order to recover
this original experience. But the will of the mystic is already busy
with acts of self-indulgence, memory is occupied with things that
give pleasure or pain to the body, and imagination is busy building
future worlds for the proclamation of individual selves. Spiritual
practice in its beginning is dedicated to retraining the will, the
memory, and the imagination to recreate the original act of the
Trinitarian experience. [5]

The mystic's sense of humility is more than a virtue. It is a
needed ingredient in the spiritual practice, a systematic condition
needed to embody certain practices, technologies, languages, habits
of reading, sensing, feeling, and acting. These new technologies are
radical, and yet they are a revolution against nothing. They simply

prepare the fertile ground where the will of God will make itself present, manifest. These technologies, therefore, are primarily concerned with a single goal: to separate the will of the subject from its attachment to his or her own self as center and origin of action and create a new attachment to the will of God as origin and foundation of all action; and in this manner to live one's life.

PREPARATIONS

The beginnings of this path are always the most difficult, and those who succeed often forget their early difficulties. San Juan de la Cruz often says "this is only for beginners," but adds that without these beginnings there would have been no "dark night of the soul," no mystical path. It is a time of trial, of meandering about, of disorientation, of aridity, but also a time of direct assault on the habits of the initiate. It is a time of violence to the bodily habits of the apprentice. He or she is asked to search for a new place in which to perform the exercises of the soul, away from the ordinary place and ordinary habits, away from the familiar. San Juan de la Cruz was an expert at finding a place in the mountains, a lonely room, a solitary place, a monastery in the country, an unaccustomed place where the mystic-to-be is forced to invent new bodily habits and is immune to all outside communications. In place of the accustomed external communications system, a new and willed system is introduced with new habits of lighting, temperature, distribution of hours, of half-hours, of morning, afternoon, and night. An external timetable is forced on the body to sharpen the will and the new habits: a new diet, new sleeping hours, sharp changes in the timetable, constant exercises of the will.

The body itself is forced into the new environment. It is asked to learn and behave in new positions, positions which prepare the body to endure hours of meditation, hours of doing violence to previous habits. The body is taught how to stand, to walk, to sit, to lower one's eyes, to raise them, to screen out sounds, to listen to signs from inside. The body of the initiate is reeducated until it develops the habit of repelling all of the old familiar external communications systems and habits. All gestures, facial expressions, and bodily movements must be painstakingly examined as if in slow motion so that the body becomes impervious to the outside and begins to habituate itself to facing inward. While the new habits of the body are only the means to an end, the end has been partially achieved. The initiate has started to sharpen his or her own will, and this is what is necessary to proceed with meditation.

But before meditation may begin, the initiate must develop the will even further. What began by changing the outside is now turned inward. The will of the initiate is now used as a surgical knife to cut some openings into that interior world. In order to achieve this, the life of the retreatant, the future mystic, is sliced into separate parts for examination—into years, days, half-days, and hours. He or she must do the same with the different moments of any life, of a day, of an act, of a look, of a thought. He or she must follow the trail of these surgical cuts, giving to each of them the new language from inside, the new emotions and feelings: ugliness of sin, pain and tears at evil, self-pity, gratitude, amazement, disgust, consolation, desolation. Without noticing it, a language of the will emerges in relation to the new background that the will of the initiate has been creating. An interior clock begins to chime. The timepiece of the "solitary region" is now running. And this new timetable determines from now on the actual acts of the day: waking up, the time and kind of meditation, the examination of conscience, meditation on meditations, conversations with the guide, changing of diet, keeping the same diet, changing the hours of sleep or keeping them, preparing the coming meditation—in short, covering the inside and the outside of the future mystic with a whole language/technology that immunizes him or her to others to whom he or she had previously been habituated.

Even at this preparatory level the initiate becomes aware of the new language that has emerged and how it has built around him or her a scaffolding of inner habits ready to sustain the new emerging body of meditation. But soon the drama unfolds: the initiate experiences the excitement of the new and also the bereavement of the familiar. The initiate knows that the exercises do not guarantee that the divinity will enter the solitary region, while he or she experiences the unfamiliarity of what used to be familiar. The initiate can never anticipate what is about to happen, or even if it will happen.

Yet he or she needs to give up everything. There is no guarantee that the empty spaces are going to be filled. This journey needs raw human faith. And this is only the beginning, and it will get worse before it becomes better, if it ever becomes better. There are only two things which favor the initiate: the exercises of initiation themselves, which keep opening horizons of language; and one other boon: he or she is chasing after an experience that has already happened, developing the predictability of that memory.

THE PRIMACY OF MEMORY

The Trinity as the origin of Christianity is an experience that has already happened. It originated outside of time and entered time in the Second Person of the Trinity through the manifestation of the incarnation. It is precisely because this experience has already happened and is originally outside of time that for every mystic the assault on the divinity needs to be made through the mediation of its manifestations. This means that for every mystic the first act of meditation is to remember, to turn all things into memory. Remembering is the first step in the path to mystic knowledge. Meditation properly begins with the ability to bring all things into remembrance. The background is conquered by turning all things into memories and then by turning these memories into imaginings.

Memory makes of Christians communities and religion; it is the common ground of shared memories that joins the group of individuals together as a community. Without memories Christianity cannot be articulated. Christ set down this internal law on which the mystics stand: "Do this in remembrance of me" (Luke 22:19). And even when the Father will send, in Christ's name, the comforter, the Spirit, He will do it to "bring all things to your remembrance" (John 14:25). To be a Christian is primarily to live on memory, but only the mystics put this dictum into spiritual practice, turning memory around, storing memories, turning every sign, whatever its origin, into a memory point. Only the mystics were able to articulate those memories so that memory would remain active. Those memories are the remembrance of the will of God in operation, the return trip to the original act of creation. They are the mediators in any form of meditation: creation, fall, redemption, providence, restoration, angels, Adam and Eve, the life of Christ, the death, the resurrection, the images of the desires of the world, the memories of the acts of God. These are memories of a past actively present and, therefore, being God's will, memories with a future. It is this predictability of memory that carried the mystics through the dark nights of the soul, and it is this predictability that allows the mystic to organize the present in view of the future. Memory, by turning back on itself, vivifies the mystic and guarantees the future. Memory mediates all human action: it is human language, and it is also divine manifestation. Images in memory become the starting point of meditation proper.

THE ACT OF IMAGINING: DISMEMBERMENT

Contrary to modern-day practices in psychology where imagining is guided so that individuals and groups share in the same image, or in which archetypal images are the goal of the act of imagining,[6] the mystics, astonishingly enough, leave the initiate and the curious almost completely in the dark as to how images are created in the mystical imagination, the proper activity of spiritual practice. The reason is simple. Imagining for those mystics of the sixteenth century was as much a part of their inner habits as, say, thinking is to us today. Reading itself was an act through which whatever was read was turned into memories and those memories became the playthings of the mind. For this cultural reason the mystics took it almost for granted that everyone knew how to imagine. Today, however, the situation is different. Imagining today is closer to fantasy, where the act of imagining is directed for the sake of the subject. In the imagining of the mystics it was left completely up to them to exercise their imaginations. The guide was content with providing memory points for meditation and then helping the initiate in reading the signs after the meditation. But the actual act of imagining was unguided, left entirely to the powers of the initiate. For this is true imagining, the ability to make images out of memory, out of original memories. There is no subjective or objective reservoir of images with which to fill the mind of the retreatant or the initiate. Making images is his or her religious exercise. The initiate is supposed to be able to stand by himself on an imageless field with his store of memories, where the absence of images will force him into the exercise of imagining. Thus the actual act of imagining rests mostly on technology rather than on images—concentration, guided and directed will, the closing of external and other internal worlds, followed by the search for the perfect, the uncontaminated, the original, the divine image. This image cannot be borrowed; it must be created. For it is only to the degree that it resembles the original that by its creation signs will appear. It is only through the creation of this pure image in meditation that sensation flows into the retreatant or initiate, and that he abandons his old habits of sensation. Unless this pure image and its signs penetrate the individual and material body of the mystic, they will not, in turn, penetrate the public domain.

The process of imagining, for the mystics, also has particular features that are absent in other forms of using the imagination. There is an element of *dismemberment* which takes place only in mystical practice.[7]

As the body of the mystic in meditation faces the frame of the memory on which he or she is going to imagine—hell, angels, the first sin, a scene of the life of Christ—the body of the mystic undergoes a radical dismemberment. For he or she is not so much *present* in the frame of the memory he develops, but rather lends to the frame, in order to create the image, a dismembered sensorium. The actual birth of signs does not take place in meditation unless this dismemberment is properly executed. The initiate lends the frame his eye, his ear, his sense of touch, of smell, of motion, of taste, and the frame becomes alive as each sense lends sensation to the image being built. The perfect image, the solitary image, is set into motion through the senses of the initiate as he or she runs them, one at a time, through the image as it is being made. It takes the sensitizing of the image by each sense of the mystic to effect a mediation between the initiate and the signs of the will of God. The efficacy of the image depends on the subject being kept elusively absent in the act of imagining. What the initiates do instead is to lend sight, sound, smell, touch, and movement to the image out of their own sensation. They vitalize the image as they dismember their own unified sensorium. Each sense reads the image and sensitizes it separately. And what is done through visualization must be read and repeated through hearing, smelling, touching, moving, and tasting. Images of themselves do nothing; they have no sensation and are not yet desires. The mystic imagines by sensitizing the image in a dismembered fashion, and the image so sensitized returns sensation to the mystic, but his successive unities differ from the original one with which he started the exercises of imagining. The mystic does not destroy anything. He or she simply enlarges the capacity of the body to contain larger doses of sensation, larger unities.

What takes so long here to describe, and what takes so much longer to practice, suddenly becomes a habit. The initial moments are almost forgotten, and steps at first considered essential are skipped over in favor of more delicate exercises. This is simply the technology itself. Having become a habit, it accelerates the process in order to challenge the next horizon. The horizon in the path of the mystic is always a receding one, and it is always a present experience that leads him or her to go on.

All imagining is a mediation. The unity and size of the image is identical with the new identities the mystic keeps receiving and shedding. This fluid mobility eventually desensitizes the mystic to previous images of self except the actual one emerging from the meditation.

As the exercises of meditation progress, the structure of meditation remains uniform. There are always the two frames, that of the retreatant or initiate, and that of God, but the sensations increase. The habit and taste of imagining anticipates the results, making the meditation fly. Imagining becomes second nature and is accomplished with greater ease. The initiate begins, out of experience, to read the different signs and discern among them. He also becomes adept at articulating them to the guide.

There is a moment, however, on the path of mystical progress when all striving—the careful, agonic dedication to concentrate, to sharpen the will, to imagine—accumulate in the initiate with such force that all the habits of the past, all the expectations of the familiar, seem near total collapse. Fear and death seem to invade every corner of the initiate. This is the time of the total death of the old being, the total darkness of the soul, the time to live only on the power of faith. And sadly enough it is at this juncture that most initiates stop and only the truly great mystics continue. This is the most brutal episode that can take place in the life of any human being. One becomes careful not to burn all bridges. At its most successful, it is a complete death for all normal habits of ordinary human life. Naturally this is a painful bereavement for the body and soul of even the strongest person. For there is no guarantee that the sensations of meditation are going to remain. In the dawn of this newly possible life there is not enough light to know if life as we once knew it will begin again, and it is even less clear that what happened during meditation will ever recur. This is the dark night of the soul, the most horrible and desolate tunnel through which all spiritual life must pass. One needs to be very humble to be original. One always wishes one had imitated others and beaten them at their own game. But the light of dawn recognizes that in this fight within the soul that wants both the old and the new, two loves have at last recognized their common origin. Lucky are those like San Juan de la Cruz who crossed the threshold of the light into a spiritual practice that is experience, and can retrace the footsteps of the Beloved through the signs of the woods, the forest, and the fields, for at last memory has stopped being memory and has become life—"My Beloved the mountains." Memory and imagination, matter and spirit, earth and light, creature and Creator, transcendence and immanence have at last found in the mystic a middle ground, a mediation, through which the divine and the human share the same project of transformation.

SAN JUAN DE LA CRUZ

I felt it was essential to place San Juan de la Cruz's writing in this context of spiritual practice. This is what he did; these are the technologies through which he reached the experiences of which his prose and poetry are the expression. For San Juan de la Cruz was first and foremost a mystic, and secondly a guide of souls. His actual human profession was to guide a few souls around him, a few nuns and novices who were under his charge. His writing also is intended mostly as a guide. It is simple, not formally poetic or theological.

From beginning to end it is a reflection of the mystical practice we have just sketched. It is unfortunate for the contemporary reader that San Juan de la Cruz did not feel the need to describe this practice from the first steps on, as we have just done, since the people of the sixteenth century were closer to those meditative skills than we are. It is also unfortunate that several of his writings are missing. But even what we have would be meaningless—or would have been to him—if it is not placed in the mystical context of his religious practice. San Juan de la Cruz starts his best poetry almost at the end of his journey: with the dark night of the soul. But if one follows the sequence of his teaching, one arrives at those poems on the Gospel where he builds, in poetry, the memories that serve as guide for imagining, the basic memories of meditation. The sequence of "Dark Night," "Spiritual Canticle," and "Love's Living Flame," is none other than an acknowledgment of his own experience: the man crossing the threshold of old habits into the new life of the soul; then singing of the world of the Beloved in the "Spiritual Canticle," where presence and absence play in him as the experience of the achieved spiritual life; and finally revealing in the last poem "Love's Living Flame" the whole transformation of his body which has taken place, his sensitization from the inside out and not vice versa. [8] The poetry of San Juan de la Cruz is both an expression of some part of this mystical transformation and the result of this transformation. Luckily he left some traces of this journey in his prose, too, and for this reason it has been included in this volume.

San Juan de la Cruz's poetry and spiritual practice are inseparable, and are the result of the same inner technologies. Otherwise how can one understand the memorable lines T. S. Eliot stole from San Juan de la Cruz for "East Coker"?

> Shall I say it again? In order to arrive there,
> to arrive where you are, to get from where you are
>   not,
> You must go by a way wherein there is no ecstasy.
> In order to arrive at what you do not know
> You must go by a way which is the way of ignorance.
> In order to possess what you do not possess
> You must go by the way of dispossession.

In order to arrive at what you are not
You must go through the way in which you are not.
And what you do not know is the only thing you know
And what you own is what you do not own
And where you are is where you are not.

This is Juan de la Cruz's original:

In order to come to taste everything
You must lose your taste in everything;

In order to own everything
Do not try to own something of anything;

To arrive at what you dislike
You must cross through the place you dislike;

To arrive at what you do not know
You must go by a way you do not know;

To arrive at what you do not own
You must go through the way of no possessions;

To arrive at what you are not
You must go through the way in which you are not.

And this list of maxims was not meant to make poetic reading,
but to serve as an easy memory guide for the readers of "The Ascent
of Mount Carmel."

Chapter Four

THE POETIC VOICE

When a thing is hidden away with so much pain, merely to reveal it is to destroy it.

TERTULLIAN

The physical body of Juan de la Cruz, whole or dismembered, never decomposed. The spiritual practice of sensitizing the body from the inside out produced as a result a physical testimony of embodied technologies that transform materiality to form unions ordinary mortals are not able to perform using ordinary means of sensation. Conversely, the physical unions performed in the flesh of the mystics are the testimony that the technologies used in spiritual practice do achieve mortal transformations. This remarkable achievement is even more remarkable when we realize that Juan de la Cruz's body was filled with pus and sores before he died. Yet, the testimony of those present, even allowing for *a posteriori* exaggerations, establishes the fact that even in sickness his wounds and pus "smelled as if handling flowers."[1]

The same remarkable transformation is achieved in San Juan de la Cruz's body of poetry. The materiality of language, his appropriation of the languages around him, his influences, and the affective power of this language bear witness to the transformation that also took place in his poetry, which must be read in the light of this transformation.

In short, San Juan de la Cruz created his poetry using the same technologies as those of his spiritual life; it effects the same inner transformations and habits of reading, and shares the same spiritual—not aesthetic—intentionality. (This statement does not apply to all of his poems, for reasons to be shown later, but it does

apply particularly to the three poems for which he is best known:
"Dark Night," "Spiritual Canticle," and "Love's Living Flame.") If
this poetry is everlasting, it is not because it is poetry in its normally
understood sense of aesthetic feeling, but because it is spiritual
practice expressed in poetic verse. Its aesthetic quality is secondary
and almost accidental in the mind of the author. The poetry of San
Juan de la Cruz is the visible manifestation of an invisible experience, which shares also the technologies of its own creation and the
intention of its own practice.

THE TEXTS

The primary text of a mystic such as San Juan de la Cruz is his
human body. In it are stored the disciplines of his spiritual practice,
arrived at through the violence of the habits he developed to sensitize his body to sensations coming from the inside, as opposed to
those coming from the outside. The technologies used to achieve
this habit of sensation, the particular ways memory and imagination
are employed, lead to an accumulation in the body of not only the
new type of experience, the so-called mystical experience, but also
sets of signs, mostly affective, which guide the mystic in his progress along the spiritual path. Since both the technologies and the
signs are part of a communications system humans have used across
cultures and races, they are identifiable and may be articulated,
either in private to a human, spiritual guide, or in public in the form
of doctrine or poetry. Thus they may become public language and
join the public domain.[2]

Given the fact that this public articulation takes place at particular times and places, it is obvious that as prose or poetry it will share
the common dress of the times. It will be bound to a certain time and
therefore to certain customs, languages, interests, and inquisitorial
fears as well as to the available knowledge of the historical moment.
On the other hand, the deeper and more human the expression, the
larger and more comprehensive will appear to be the linguistic body
of the expression. In short, the better the poet or writer, the more
influences his or her language will reveal. But the better the poet or
writer, the greater will be the transformation of these common

influences. And this is the case of San Juan de la Cruz's poetry. His writings in prose and poetry reveal a degree of distance from the original experience of his spiritual practice, and my task is to point out this distance and dependence, or (as the case may be) independence.

The four main works, or texts, written by San Juan de la Cruz are: "Ascent of Mount Carmel": poetry and commentary in prose (unfinished); "Dark Night": poetry and commentary (unfinished); "Spiritual Canticle": poetry and commentary; "Love's Living Flame": poetry and commentary.

Besides these well-defined texts, twelve other poems by San Juan de la Cruz have reached us. There are also thirty-two letters which have survived out of the many he wrote, and some minor prose works: "Precautions," "Counsels to a Religious on How to Reach Perfection," and the "Maxims and Counsels," or "Sayings of Light and Love."[3]

There is disagreement among commentators as to when each text was written. But avoiding academic squabbles I will attempt to date all the texts and clarify the circumstances in which they were written.

The poem *"Noche Oscura"* ("Dark Night") appears to have been written around 1579, soon after San Juan de la Cruz escaped from the Toledo jail. "Spiritual Canticle" (*"Cántico espiritual"*) was written in part while Juan was in the Toledo jail in 1578, and finished in Granada in 1582 and 1583; though some critics believe that verses 32 and 34 were written in 1578 and 1579.

It remains a mystery as to how these separate compositions became a unified poem, and why two versions of the poem exist. The first version is the favorite of the critics because of its more poetic ordering (the second one has one extra stanza, verses 53–57). The first version is found, among other places, in the Carmelite Convent of San Lúcar de Barrameda, with annotations in the hand of the author; and the second, composed between 1585 and 1586 while he was superior (prior) of the Convent of the Martyrs at Granada, is found, along with other manuscripts, at the Carmelite Convent in Jaen.[4]

"Love's Living Flame" (*"Llama de amor viva"*) was written in 1584. During that same year and the following one, the poem *"Un pastorcico solo está apenado*" ("A Young Shepherd, Alone, Is Pining") was also composed. "*Qué bien se yo la fuente que mana e corre*" ("How Well I Know the Fountain that Runs and Flows") was written while at the prison in Toledo, and the poems gathered under the heading "Romance on the gospel" also date from this time, as well as the poem "*Super Flumina Babilonis.*"

The little poem "*Del verbo divino*" ("The Divine Word") was improvised by the poet on successive Christmas nights, between 1582 and 1585, while he was prior at Granada.

The poems "*Entreme donde no supe*" ("I Entered Where I Did Not Know") and "*Vivo sin vivir en mi*" ("I Live, Yet Do Not Live in Me") seem to have been written earlier than 1574 and therefore predate Juan's imprisonment at Toledo.

The poem "*Para venir a gustarlo todo*" ("In Order to Come to Taste Everything"), with which I concluded chapter 3, appears in chapter 13 of the first book of the "Ascent of Mount Carmel" and is also included at the beginning of the work under a painting entitled "*Mons Dei*" ("God's Mountain").

The text of these poems and the translations are based on the text edited by Crisógono de Jesus, O.C.D., *Vida y Obras de San Juan de la Cruz*, Madrid, B.A.C. 1969.

JUAN'S AUDIENCE AND ITS HABITS OF READING

This whole corpus of poetry and prose was written by San Juan de la Cruz for a very particular audience: those he directed spiritually. The primary and only real job San Juan de la Cruz carried out in his professional life was the guiding of souls. It so happens, however, that these consisted of nuns or young novices under his care who were living in the sixteenth-century cultural environment of Spain. They and the other pious women he came in contact with were not fully literate in the modern sense. They could read, but belonged culturally to an *audile* and *oral* tradition that had different habits of reading than we do today. In their reading they looked for different things than we do. This is an important point, for it clarifies some of the poems of San Juan de la Cruz and the reason why some appear to be, or are, better than others. It also illuminates why some poems can only be understood in comparison with others: the same memories *feel* different for author and reader.[5]

One little-known peculiarity of the Spanish mystics and their culture which is not as evident in their Flemish and German counterparts, is their immersion in and use of oral/audile technologies. For these mystics reading is not pursued privately in silence, and its purpose is not fundamentally the gathering of information. Their reading was done aloud; every word was pronounced. Reading was an act, the goal of which was to store memories. Information was secondary.

Oral cultures have the ability to organize themselves by criteria (epistemologies) derived from sound, and use these criteria to transmit and repeat their own technology of listening and remembering. All signs are interpreted using these same technologies, and so information is also transmitted. But beyond information there is a whole world of organized experience measured in proportion to the rhythms of oral transmission in chant, in verse, in the cadences of the voice. People are instructed in the norms of experience by listening to the rhythms of sentences, poetry, and speech.

When we say "an oral/audile culture" we mean a culture that knowingly follows an internal, epistemological path or map, and in which this is a basic presupposition of its organization. An audile culture takes the *ear* as the primary human organ of sense, and all its texts are ruled by the correspondence between the innate auditory sense of harmony and tone, and certain mathematical properties and ratios as manifested; for example, in the vibrating musical string. Language within such a culture is primarily a language about wholes, frames, memories, images, contexts, systems, and only secondarily about things and information. An oral/audile culture also possesses inner *mandalas,* or protogeometries, homologous with the arithmetical aspects of music, which chart the path of memory and imagining. In fact, imagining is the language the oral/audile culture develops to mark its origins and its continuity through time.[6]

A very peculiar feature of the spiritual practice of the mystics, and of San Juan de la Cruz in particular, is this: since, ideally, meditation requires conditions of silence more easily found in an acoustic laboratory than in a church, we seldom find these mystics

praying in churches. Juan searched for, or was given, ideal conditions of silence for his meditation and his writing, so that the voice
of God could be perceived. Scientific experiments in acoustics have
confirmed that the perception of tone takes time and is only possible
under ideal conditions, which include quiet surroundings, good
volume, repetition, and so on. To organize perception so that it can
receive the signal frequency takes even longer. Thus we find San
Juan de la Cruz always searching for those solitary places, for those
mountains, lonely caves, monasteries in the country. We must not
forget that his most famous poem, "Spiritual Canticle," was written in the bathroom of the jail of a convent. Could one find a more
solitary acoustical laboratory?[7]

Now let us return to Juan's audience of nuns and novices. They
provide us with a clue as to why some poems were written in a
certain form, and why in fact they were written at all. We know that
San Juan de la Cruz wrote "*Super Flumina Babilonis*" and "Romance
on the Gospels" in jail. We also know that these were the first of his
poems to be read to the nuns after his escape. It is in the contrast
between these poems and "Spiritual Canticle" that Juan's poetic
process becomes clear to us. In certain poems he organizes "memory points" for meditation, and this is the case in the two poems first
mentioned. In others the *result* of his meditation comes through. In
the first two poems he points out the memories that need to be
activated in order to meditate effectively, by directing the imagination towards experiences that have already happened outside of time
as well as those within time, up to the birth of Christ. These are
memories that establish the background story of Christians. But
they are not yet the true background, for Christians have not yet
meditated upon those memories and transformed them into living
reality. Thus it is obvious that San Juan de la Cruz, guide of souls, is
writing didactic poems to help memory to meditate, to help the
nuns and novices single out certain memories to be made real
through imaginative acts. They are meant to guide, and though in
his hands they sound musical enough, they are not of the quality of
"Spiritual Canticle," in which memory has been transformed into
the reality of a background which feels as real and can be named
with the same emphasis as the foreground. But more on this later.
Let it suffice for the moment to point out that the majority of the
poems of San Juan de la Cruz aim at guiding the souls under his care

into meditation, by pointing out the memories that will best serve for such a purpose, and setting them to the easy rhythms of rhymed verse. Thus we can use the criterion of meditation, rather than that of poetry, to distinguish among his poems. With this in mind it can easily be seen that some poems, while better than the didactic ones mentioned, are not as good as "Dark Night," "Spiritual Canticle," or "Love's Living Flame." They are poems revealing the progress of the mystic in his internal life, but lack the deep touch of the total transformation revealed in the best poems. Some were written when the poet was not yet proficient as a mystic, though most probably he was, by the time he wrote those poems, as proficient a poet as he would ever be.

THE MAJOR POEMS

San Juan de la Cruz's major poems are all accompanied by a prose commentary. "Dark Night," in fact, has two different commentaries. The prose commentary is not, properly speaking, a commentary on the poetry, but rather adds to it a different sense, a different direction, that the poetry on its own does not have. The prose commentary is a description of the spiritual practice, while the poetry is art, but art achieved through the same method of spiritual practice. It is therefore obvious that no commentary may be substituted for the poetry. Though the poetry may be read after the commentary, and may find its meanings confirmed through the prose, the poetry may be read on its own, autonomously, even if that was not the intention of the author or the expectation of the recipients—or if in truth it does not mean what it says. In short, poetry is either poetry or it is not, and no commentary will create a poem where there is none. For this reason the reader cannot expect here a commentary on the prose, much less the poetry, of San Juan de la Cruz. What I will try to do instead is to establish a link between the methods Juan used in meditation and those he adopted in writing poetry, to illuminate his own particular way of using poetry, thus redeeming it from contemporary theories of literary criticism which presuppose that language is previous to experience and that poetry provides only an aesthetic and subjective feeling.

The purpose of San Juan de la Cruz's spiritual practice is a

resensitization of the body from the inside out, as opposed to the
ordinary path of sensation from the outside in. To achieve this inner
transformation San Juan de la Cruz sheds, like so many snakeskins,
his habits of ordinary sensation through a spiritual discipline that
completely empties him externally and leaves inside a large void, a
huge darkness of sensation, a total an absolute dark night of the
soul. This total darkness is the result of a dedicated spiritual practice. In his case this total darkness is also the beginning of his
flirtation with the Beloved and his inner sensations from the Beloved. Juan gives us this first stage of his spiritual practice in his
memorable poem "Dark Night." As a poem it is the result and
expression, the complete experience, of his spiritual journey and
practice. It is not a fantasy borrowed from others, or to help others
meditate. For this reason the reader cannot help but feel the lines run
through his own veins as if he or she were writing them. There is, in
all of us, an experience similar to this in darkness, in emptiness. It is
not directed, as it is for Juan de la Cruz, and in most cases it is not the
result of spiritual practice but of the absence of it. Nevertheless this
experience as reflected in Juan's poetry is not subjective: it is the
common experience of each and every member of the human species. What we lack in practice is the happy ending, and it is this
happy ending, hard as the path to reach it might be, that Juan de la
Cruz provides.

The next step, and perhaps the most difficult to understand for
literary critics, is the poem "Spiritual Canticle." Is it an allegory, a
metaphor, a symbol? What does the author really say in it?

"Desires are images and will their act." Thus we began the
journey into spiritual practice. If the mystic does not succeed in
creating a total image of the individual's and the world's desire he
plays a cruel trick on himself. He would then be destitute of all
sensation, human and divine. If he plays the mystic game it is
because he knows that he is only substituting smaller images,
smaller desires, for larger images and larger desires, individual will
for the will of God. If through his practice he is able to link his
will to the will of God, the sensitization that results from such a shift
will not be smaller than before but certainly larger. And here in
"Spiritual Canticle" we have the result of such a transformation.
"Where did you hide, my love?" he begins, and the rest of the poem

is a description of love hiding and becoming present everywhere the poet succeeds in transforming image into reality. What started as memory, what became background through imagining, is now reality felt, seen, touched, heard, smelled, moving in the air, surrounding the sensations of the poet/mystic. Between absence and presence of love we are witnesses to the running spring of love flowing through the lines of the poem—not to metaphors, allegories, symbols, but to realities that feel as close at hand as mother, child, lover, joy, orgasm.

What would a literary critic, or a hurried reading of such a poem miss? Shutting up the world within a fog of theory is a devaluation of both poetry and life. If theory cannot account for the fact that the poetry of a mystic literally expresses his *reality,* then all the worse for theory, for life is not a dream, and failure to describe its many forms is like an unnecessary amputation. We will return to this later.

Juan de la Cruz had to deal in his own time with similar inquisitions. In stanza 8, verse 2 of "Spiritual Canticle," the copyist wrote: "*Oh alma, no viviendo donde vives,*" (O soul, not living where you live), but Juan de la Cruz corrected the verse to read less symbolically and more literally: "O life, not living where you live" (*Oh vida, no viviendo donde vives*). The copyist wanted to spiritualize the poem, perhaps considering it dangerous. The same happens again in "Dark Night" when in stanza 7 Juan wrote: "*cuando* yo *sus cabellos esparcía*" and the copyist changed it to: "*cuando* ya *sus cabellos esparcía*"; the copyist substituted "I spread his tresses" for "the fresh wind from the turret/ already spread his tresses." This is a significant correction which the author returned in his own hand to his original version.

There is more. One expects to find certain liberties in poetry, for example the phrase "My Beloved the mountains," from "Spiritual Canticle." However, one would also expect the poet to correct such obvious exaggerations in his prose, especially since such an expression could certainly prove dangerous if read by the inquisitors. Were not the commentators of the *Song of Songs* who used such language imprisoned by the Inquisition? Was not the great Fray Luis de León thrown into jail, a victim of this same interpretation and language? Why did Juan de la Cruz not correct it? Even in prose his statement is the same: "My Beloved is the mountains."

From a literary point of view it is obvious that the poet is describing what for him is literal reality, experience. But this reality is not the common reality. For us a mountain is a mountain. Between the poet and us there is a certain distance, that of the spiritual practice through which mountains become first signs, then images, and lastly the Beloved himself, not in a new distance of metaphor, but in the reality we attribute to those things we call real because they affect our senses. Mountains affect San Juan de la Cruz the same way our lover affects us, they kindle his senses. It is both spiritual practice and poetry at its best when a mountain affects our sensation as readers to the point of becoming eternal in our memory.

The last great, major poem of San Juan de la Cruz is "Love's Living Flame," or simply "*Llama*," as it is known in Spanish. Here the poet presents the end of the journey; the body is sensitized from the inside, it is described as such in poetry and it reads as truly as if it said what we normally expect it to say—that it is sensitized by the best external things and not the bad external things. San Juan de la Cruz says more. His senses are *closed* to the outside, they are opened only if the internal light shines on them, and this is not only the highest point of spiritual practice but also of poetic achievement. What the poet writes is a dictation from the inside out. Menéndez y Pelayo once wrote that one has to be careful with the poetry of San Juan de la Cruz, for "God has walked through it." A literary critic might find this to be an exaggeration. But his presupposition that *no one* has walked through it is even worse. The fact is that both statements are from literary critics and both depreciate the poet, poetry in general, and the capacity of humans to express themselves and achieve something beyond literary theory.

THE WRITING OF POETRY

San Juan de la Cruz has always been considered the straightest of arrows in the passage from earth to sky. His writings and his direction of souls have always emphasized a journey with no baggage. He used to reprimand Teresa de Avila for her attention to and delight in voices, raptures, consolations. His path was the path to "*nada*" (nothing). "Dark Night," "Spiritual Canticle," and "Love's

Living Flame" are all testaments of this dedication to absolute negation: "*nada, nada, nada, y aun en la montaña nada*" (nothing, nothing, nothing, and even on the mountain nothing). And yet, it is this same San Juan de la Cruz who left us a poetry permeated with feeling. In human terms we may say that this poetry is so fully sensuous, so affective, so filled with the desire of the whole world, that one has to wonder if in reality San Juan de la Cruz was as detached from human sensations as he claimed. Perhaps, on the other hand, we have the wrong idea about poetry.

Our contemporary culture, particularly in America, thinks of poetry in terms of entertainment, perhaps even of literature, but always as an activity of certain people on the extreme margins of the culture. Poetry for us does not have the cosmic and religious meanings it has had for other cultures in different periods of human life. The best poets, and the lesser ones, too, will always write poetry regardless of who applauds, but it is very unlikely that poets will recognize themselves if nobody else does. In all likelihood our immediate audience diminishes poetry, if not the poet. But in any case, the fact of the matter is that what we understand as poetry today is not a universal category and does not indicate the way in which poetry should always be appreciated or indeed written. The best we can do for poetry is to search out other models, other versions of the act of writing poetry, regardless of how this resembles or differs from contemporary criteria.

San Juan de la Cruz may indeed have written poetry as part of his spiritual practice, rather than as a secular act of literature. He could easily have carried his spiritual methods over into his poetry, both part of one single activity. If this is true we have a model radically different than that used in the writing of poetry today, and as such it is exemplary and worth examining.

There is no written guide that I know of for the inner world of poetry. It is difficult to determine what poets do *inside* themselves in order to communicate poetically. We have examined poetic language through its *external* tokens of sound, gesture, rhythm, measure, and word, but have done nothing to examine the *internal* tokens of that same language: intentionality, conceptualization, purposive action. Action, conception, communication are distinguishable in poetic expression but not separable. The external tokens of language have changed and continue to change; how can a poem be called such when the external rules change so often, and when the internal tokens of poetic language appear to be so disparate? We recognize poetry coming from ancient Greece, Rome, Turkey, India, China, Russia, Catholic Spain, Protestant England, Germany, Italy, and from all levels of the social scale, all sexes and ages. Is there a common fire that lights the verses of the poets beneath all this external diversity, which makes poetry a bonding act? And if there is such a hidden fire, how do humans proceed to light it? How is poetry written?

The answer, of course, cannot be formulated as a generalization. We can only proceed by examining the poetic process in specific men and women—in the present case, that of one man, San Juan de la Cruz. How did San Juan de la Cruz write poetry?

As we can see from the previous chapter, there are close similarities between the writing of poetry and the spiritual practice of the mystics. The poet, like the mystic, builds out of his own sensations a background and a foreground. At times the background is built on the ashes of the foreground; at other times the foreground is raised only to discover that it does not equal the background, or is contradictory to it, or moves in the opposite direction. Without this contrast of background and foreground there is no poetry. The other requirement for poetry is that both background and foreground be built out of the sensations, the flesh, of the poet. What separates the poet from the mystic is the depth of the background. The mystic will only want to reach and build the ultimate, the original background. The poet may linger in other, not so definitive, backgrounds.

In the spiritual practice of San Juan de la Cruz there is a laborious and dedicated effort to strip the writer away from any background that is not the ultimate, or in his words, the Will of God. The images of the mystic and the poet coincide in this ultimate region, where we find the Trinity, the images of origin, the ultimate marriage of union, the ultimate eroticism of the soul (which happens to be also the original one). These are all images not borrowed from the senses, but built through interior sensitizations that flow from the senses to the image and back, transforming them and yielding the inspired poetry we know.

In that same spiritual practice there are several ways of building images, or accelerating the process of building such images. In the first laborious efforts the process proceeds slowly through a dismemberment of the senses of the mystic to "member" the image of meditation. These "membered" images are remembered by the mystic in posterior meditations by simply running over those points of the meditation where the "consolation" was greatest. It is these "memories" of consolation in particular that mystics narrate to their guides, or use as the ground of their communication, their descriptions, their poetry. Remembering them is bringing them, and the sensations accompanying them, into memory. Here mystics are close to poets in that they write out of a sensed experience. If the poet is a mystic he has an unending source of poetic writing. It was part of the spiritual practice of the mystics to keep a diary about these "visitations" that take place in the exercise of meditation. Some, like San Juan de la Cruz, went further and used them as the source of their poetry. The intention was not to write poetry so much as to communicate the direct experience of spiritual practice. And this, as we shall see, is San Juan de la Cruz's obvious intention. The eloquence of his poetry arises precisely because of the close connection between its composition and the actual act of spiritual practice.

In short, San Juan de la Cruz builds his poetic experience using the same method he uses to build his spiritual life. He desensitizes himself to the external world and builds inner images out of his own dismembered sensorium. The result is a sensitized image that impinges upon him through all the mysterious ways of grace and divine visitation, but which also changes his inner sensations and builds a chain of memories of those moments: "visitations" which when recalled serve as the warm and inspired base of his poetic communication. This method was, in the case of San Juan de la Cruz, linked to his spiritual practice. There is no reason to suppose, however, that it cannot work without it, or to presuppose that these poetic exercises are so closely related to spiritual practice, or are in fact at times identical with spiritual practice. Only the poetry will bear witness.

We shall soon see that this is indeed how the process worked by San Juan de la Cruz, but even then it will answer only part of the secret of his poetic method, the internal part. But how about the actual poetry? How did he come to write poetry of such high quality, and which influenced so much poetry written after him?

Mother Magdalena del Espíritu Santo put this same question to him: "Does God give you the words of your poems?" And Juan de la Cruz answered: "Daughter, sometimes God gives them to me, but others I look for them."

Where did San Juan de la Cruz look? How did others influence him? Or is it rather the case that through San Juan de la Cruz all the poetry he came in contact with—consciously and unconsciously—became not only present in his own poetry but also transformed into a new kind of poetry? Was he influenced by others, or did he simply raise others with him to the heights of a new poetry?

POETIC SOURCES AND INFLUENCES

It is difficult to imagine San Juan de la Cruz, in the tiny bathroom turned into a jail cell at Toledo, writing poetry; difficult to imagine him consulting other poets for inspiration. It is unlikely that the tiny monasteries through which he traveled had such up-to-date libraries that much of the poetry written before him was ready at hand for his consultation. But we do know, as has been mentioned earlier, that while studying humanities at Medina del Campo with the Jesuits Juan was trained in the classics. While it is true that the formal classical style of writing does not appear in his work (as it did, for example, in that of Fray Luis de León) there is no doubt that many echoes of past poetry are present in his writings. The poetry and prose of San Juan de la Cruz are crisscrossed with the presence of those who wrote poetry before him. But none appears unaltered; the references are transformed in intention, feeling, and quality by the author. It is obvious that Juan had been a good student and his soul had absorbed the classic and popular rhythms. Juan's sensibility found the classic as well as the popular ballad close to his own flesh. While in prison, he heard a passerby sing this song at midnight under the window of his cell:

> *Muérome de amores,*
> *carillo, ¿qué haré?*
> *—Que te mueras, alahé!*

(I am dying of love,
My friend, what can I do?
—Die, then, friend, *alahé*!)

The story goes that San Juan de la Cruz fainted on hearing this
song, in ecstasy or simple delight. Music, rhythm, language were
all present in San Juan de la Cruz with the innocence and spontaneity
of water after rain, and as close at hand. What he did with these tools
forms the remarkable story of how a few verses and poems made
eternal the memory of a man who otherwise would have passed
unnoticed. Were it not for his poetry, San Juan de la Cruz would
have disappeared into the murky background of the sixteenth century, as did so many of his contemporaries. But he is still with us.

It speaks very highly of the education of the young man from
very deprived origins that he learned and remembered so well the
lessons of the academy, the street, and the school. The vast literature
on the influences and sources of his poetry and prose demonstrates
that there is hardly an important or even a secondary writer who is
not present in Juan de la Cruz's writings. Thus, Augustine, Gregory
the Great, Bernard, the Rhineland Mystics, the Victorines, Bona-
venture, Aquinas, John Banthorpe, Michael de Bologna, Raymund
Lull, Osuna, Laredo, Luis de León, and even Teresa de Avila herself
all appear, for Teresa carried on an exchange of poems with San Juan
de la Cruz as a challenge of his spiritual and literary proficiency. Juan
quotes or refers in places to many specific authors: Ovid, Boethius,
Dionysius, Gregory, Augustine, Francis, Bernard, Aquinas, and, of
course, Garcilaso and Boscán. And one cannot ignore the influences
of the Bible, the Islamic tradition, and even Virgil.

The fact that both in prose and poetry San Juan de la Cruz
brings others into his writings is in part a sign of the times. To
quote, in those days, was a sign of traveling in the right company,
and thus a sign of orthodoxy, even when some of the sources he
uses, like Augustine, are not authentic,[8] and others, like the Islamic
angelology he at times propounds, are suspect despite being dressed
in the negative garb of mystical union.

But more significantly, the presence of so many writers in the
writings of San Juan de la Cruz clarifies for us his true understanding of the negative way. San Juan de la Cruz does not empty himself

of anything. He only empties himself of the affirmation that they, he, or his own writing, or life for that matter, *belongs* to him. San Juan de la Cruz transforms whatever appears before him, around him, within him, by raising it to a new space, a new region of light, a divine intention previously absent; and then, in this new light, he both affirms it and denies that the new creation visible to the eye or audible to the ear is his: "And even in the mountain nothing." The poet is simply the instrument of a manifestation; the manifestation, however, is neither God nor author. It is a middle ground of light where both meet. God is not the light seen—if anything, He is the light with which the poet sees.

We should separate poets and Fathers of the Church, since the two groups perform different functions in San Juan de la Cruz's writings. Prose and poetry form two different texts, or two different subtexts of his primary text of meditation. Thus, returning to his poetry, we find that San Juan de la Cruz is not as poetically innocent as it might appear from our previous description of his poetic process. Though it is true he uses language reminiscent of others, he does alter it. In his use of the Bible we find that in "Spiritual Canticle" San Juan de la Cruz changes, adds, and omits verses from the *Song of Songs* in such a way that both dependence and originality are established. San Juan de la Cruz omits in part or whole, or changes the meaning of, the following verses: I—5, 6, 9, 12, 13, 14, 17; II—1, 2, 5, 9, 13, 17; III—3, 4, 6–11; IV—1–8, 11–15, etc. He keeps only those verses that agree with the sensibilities of tradition or the Renaissance,9 those verses that express the encounter of the human and the divine in an experience created in the interiority of the mystic. In this interiority another "reality" appears as the union of the human and the divine, on condition that what is sensed through external means, and even the memory of this sensing, be renounced or canceled. Only then that other "reality" appears and the poetic voice of the mystic expresses it in the only language available to him, that of erotic love with a divine intention. There is no sublimation here. On the contrary, there is an experience that appears in the interior of the mystic and is felt and expressed exactly as it is apprehended, as an overflow of love. Its expression in the poetic voice of the mystic as eroticism is as real to him or her as tables and chair are to ordinary people.

The poetic voice of the mystic focuses on a revelation from the inside, and this revelation appears in the form of a union that feels, in human terms, like the ultimate union of lovers; only these lovers are not two human beings: one is human, the other divine. The language in which this union is expressed is the only one available to the mystic, the language of the union of lovers, for this is the only language in which such a communication is possible. For this reason the mystics are quick to negate as much as they affirm, and are never satisfied with any statement that might be considered final. In San Juan de la Cruz this need to affirm and deny every affirmation and every negation is clear. "Dark Night" is a complete negation of the world outside ("My House at last completely quiet") and it is also an affirmation of an internal light by which the lover is guided "more directly than the midday sun," to "a place with no one in sight." And it is here, in that inner place, where the mystic reconciles his inner world:

> O night! O guide!
> O night more loving than the dawn!
> O night that joined
> Lover with beloved,
> Beloved in the lover transformed!

But what San Juan de la Cruz denies in "Dark Night" he affirms in "Spiritual Canticle." The whole external world is filled with the presence of the Beloved:

> Pouring a thousand graces
> He passed through these groves in haste,
> And, as he lent them his gaze
> By his figure alone
> He left them dressed with beauty.

The poet is now able to see those graces, not as traces of the Beloved, but as his real presence:

> My Beloved the mountains,
> The valleys' solitary groves,
> The sounding rivers and fountains,

The distant islands' soil,
The wind whistling love's song,

The calm night,
The twin of the rising dawn,
The silent music,
The sounding solitude,
The supper that kindles love and warms.

The poet might be content to stop here, having reached his esthetic goal. But the mystic, San Juan de la Cruz, is not concerned with esthetics as the primary intention of his poetry. Esthetics is a happy outcome, indirectly achieved, of a larger intention, the description in poetic form of his inner experience. And thus he continues. This beautiful world of the "Spiritual Canticle" must also be denied, for the Beloved is not really out there, he is not the manifestations, nor the memories. He is the flame, the light, the reality of the manifestations of fire, light, and memory.

O Love's living flame,
Tenderly you wound
My soul's deepest center!

The poem "Love's Living Flame" denies the world of the "Spiritual Canticle" in order to bring the soul back to its true origin and center:

O lamps of fiery lure,
In whose shining transparence
The deep cavern of the senses,
Blind and obscure,
Warmth and light, with strange flares,
Gives with the lover's caresses!

For in the end the poetic voice fails if it does not bring the reader back to the absolute source and place where it finds its own life.

It is therefore not surprising that so many great poets are present in the lines of San Juan de la Cruz. None is present, however, with the same intention and the same message as Juan himself. He lifts human experience to a higher or deeper level than esthetic feeling can account for, and while the lines might resemble other lines written by other poets, none of these poets is present at that level of experience. They did not care to write with the divine intention of San Juan de la Cruz, nor, in the end, did their poetry rise from the same experiential depths as his. And, as we have already suggested, none of them wrote poetry using Juan's mystical methods.

In the end the poetry of San Juan de la Cruz, his poetic voice, opens the horizons of poetry wider and farther than did any previous imagination. His imagination surpasses the coordinates of space and time, of past, present, and future, working on the assumption that those coordinates need to be denied and that the poetic voice must bring into the human coordinates of space and time a voice linked to an experience *outside* space and time, but nonetheless *real*. San Juan de la Cruz acts on the assumption that the experience he talks about in poetic form is an experience that has already happened and is present in the human experience, but whose origin is outside of time and space. This experience is for him that love, that union, that incarnation, that origin and manifestation inhabiting the original source of Christian life: the Trinity. In this light it is easy to see how his poems echo one another as a unity searching for that original experience, that original affirmation, mediation, negation, and union. It also explains some of the didactic poems like "*Super Flumina Babilonis*" and "Romance on the Gospel." They clearly indicate the direction of his poetic voice (as opposed to the prophetic imagination) and the memory points capable of building the temple of poetry San Juan de la Cruz left for us.

This message of the poetic voice is particularly needed in a society, like ours, which tends to romanticize nature, gaze to the future, or conceive religion as a purely theoretical, private, or symbolic activity. We believe, with Robert Frost, that

> The woods are lovely, dark, and deep
> But I have promises to keep. . . .

And yet it is the poetic voice that is capable of incarnating the actual multiple experience that today fills the American landscape. We are present on these shores not as theories, symbols, or isolated priva-

cies. We are here in communal bodies of experience which is accessible only as such, if we are going to believe that ours is a democracy
and live by that belief. We need to know the different ways of
creating experience so that we may make that experience accessible
to the rest of the community. But this will lead us onto the perilous
ground of communication and the politics of communication. It is,
therefore, important to examine how San Juan de la Cruz solves his
problem of communication, not in poetry, but in prose. Did he
solve it? Perhaps the answer is already in these lines of poetry:

> I entered not knowing where,
> And I remained not knowing,
> Beyond all science knowing. . . .

> It was peace, it was love,
> It was perfect knowledge,
> In deep loneliness
> I saw with wisdom; . . .

THE PROSE: WITHOUT FEAR OR HOPE

There is an intimidating quality to the prose writings of San Juan de
la Cruz. Where the reader feels so close to "that other experience"
reading the poetry, the prose intrudes on that intimacy and makes
the spiritual project seem distant and forbidding. San Juan de la
Cruz appears merciless and stiff, his writing meanders into repetition after repetition of the same ideas, and it is very difficult to see
the forest for the trees. The distance between reader and spiritual life
is so great, while reading the prose writings, that one is tempted to
discard them as archaeological curiosities, or give up on the spiritual
life and settle for the esthetic.

The reader, for several important reasons, should be encouraged to give the prose writings of San Juan de la Cruz another
chance.

Spiritual life is a life of faith—the movement of the soul toward
the closed horizons of life in the absence of beliefs. Life is a never-
ceasing effort to transcend the familiar, the comfortable, the self-

gratifying. Faith, not external sensations, should operate through our senses. This is the message of the poetry and also the message of the prose of San Juan de la Cruz. But while the poetry appears so close to us, the prose is distant, inflexible, dry. In fact it cannot be otherwise. The poetry is the result of will and imagination, the prose of discursive reasoning. It is the faculty of reason, not Juan himself, which creates the distances and inflexibilities while it operates. The inner landscape of reason is flat, wide, merciless in its demand that one step follow another, that stages be set, quotations brought out, verification of reason and authority introduced, the process repeated until it is time to go on to the next step and start over. The reader should be aware that these stutter-steps belong to the mental process chosen for communication, not to the process of spiritual life, nor to the way God operates on the soul. What takes so many books to set down, the soul and God may bring about in the closing and opening of one's eyes.

Public communication is necessary in spiritual life. It was even more so in the case of San Juan de la Cruz, with the Inquisition watching. Thus the spiritual soul ready to speak must be aware of the conditions of this communication, and San Juan de la Cruz was accomplished at this. He sold his program of spiritual practice to an ecclesiastical audience that would rather have seen him in jail than sainted. The Church Inquisitors of the time took it upon themselves to be God's watchdogs. Whatever passed by them had to be from God—sent by God or a member of the family. And this attitude worked in San Juan de la Cruz's favor. He not only passed the test, but became a saint and a Doctor of the same Church which, given the least pretext, would have condemned him. He had to be good at his explanations. His experience had to come from God.

It is obvious, therefore, that some of his prose writings are linked in context to their time. But San Juan de la Cruz managed to insert into other parts of his writings ideas that transcended his time and managed to introduce a paradigm, a way of communicating in prose, the authentic experience we feel in his poetry. And what is this paradigm?

Mystic experience is neither private nor totally subjective. It is carried out in the human body through embodied technologies, and both the technologies and the experience may be articulated as objectively verifiable and repeatable. The methodologies the mystic develops through meditation and the signs that result as a consequence of such practice in contemplation are objectively describable. Any inquisition will recognize them as either objective and accurate, or as false and deluded. It is to the credit of the Inquisition that it let the manifestation of God stand, even if the method of producing such a manifestation was contrary to the objective method of the Inquisition. It is to the credit of the Inquisition of those days that it allowed the manifestations of God to be recognized. It is not to the credit of contemporary inquisitions to deny even the possibility of such manifestations by denying the existence of objective signs, or human faculties capable of receiving those signs, and by demanding that all manifestation be in agreement with the scientific mode.

In his prose, San Juan de la Cruz gave us the most lucid and accurate description of the *itinerary of the soul* through the night of the senses and of the spirit, the bereavement of love, to the fullness of the senses when they allow faith to operate through them, in a constant effort to empty themselves of themselves. Where Ignatius de Loyola remains the master of the exercise of meditation, San Juan de la Cruz stands almost alone in the West in his description of the vicissitudes of contemplation. His descriptions provide a needed bridge, along with other extra-biblical traditions, so that revelation is again present in the public domain.

However, the reader should be aware that the way of description is not the way of spiritual practice. The intimidation of thought is not the closeness nor the warmth of the will in action. He must realize that where the mind only sees divisions and stages, the soul is immersed in consolations and desolations, light and darkness, all signs of living movement and participation in the game of love.

It is for this reason that I have edited the prose to say only what is needed for an objective description of its itinerary towards *love's living flame*. I have used only the critical editions of the prose writings, and kept the style and erotic phrasing of the original. It is sad that the few English translations available change the prose to say something else which seems less erotic while they leave out the most important descriptions of how the senses, one by one, are made fluid and erotic through meditation, and constitute sheer eroticism in contemplation.

It is sad, and it does not say much for our human condition, that the writings of San Juan de la Cruz, like the man himself, have to be rescued from so many prisons before he is able to speak for himself. This sad state of affairs appears all the more wasteful when we observe the best minds clamoring for "models" of rationality against which we can measure our own, and declare ourselves rational rather than arbitrary, or the users of some arbitrary power. Philosophy, in particular, has been proposing abstract models of rationality in the name of "deconstruction," "authenticity," "unveiling of being," and "difference," while all the while we have had with us actual models of how these rational impasses were solved. Had we heeded these models, the relation between language and experience, determining context and liberating context, immanence and transcendence, freedom and determinism, material datum and image, Being and beings, identity and difference, and a host of others would not have forced us into doing philosophy by inertia. These are important problems and their solutions have been worked out, at least theoretically, in history. Neither phenomenology nor language analysis has been able to provide a better and more accurate description of the acts of the mind than San Juan de la Cruz provides in his prose. It is no wonder that San Juan de la Cruz's sensorium is as fluid and as movable as it sounds, while ours repeats only the inertia of our intellectual movements. It is also true that no one may force us into the realization of freedom; unless we learn which faculty to use in order to perform free acts we may find ourselves, once more, singing songs of slavery while using the rhetoric of freedom. Ours is a culture expert in appropriating meanings. It is time we started manufacturing our own.

PART TWO

The Poetry
(Bilingual)

LETRILLAS

I.   Del Verbo divino
la Virgen preñada
viene de camino:
¡si le dais posada!

LA SUMA DE LA PERFECCIÓN

2.   Olvido de lo criado,
memoria del Criador,
atención a lo interior
y estarse amando al Amado.

SUPER FLUMINA BABILONIS

SALMO 136

Encima de las corrientes
que en Babilonia hallaba,
allí me sente llorando,
allí la tierra regaba,

5   Acordándome de ti,
¡oh Sión!, a quien amaba.
Era dulce tu memoria,
y con ella más lloraba.

Dexé los trajes de fiesta,
10   los de trabajo tomaba,
y colqué en los verdes sauces
la música que llevaba,

Poniendola en esperanza
de aquello que en ti esperaba.

LULLABY★

1.
By the divine Word
The Virgin is made pregnant
And is on her way:
Give her a place to stay!

THE SUM OF PERFECTION

2.
Forgetting all creatures,
Remembering the Creator,
Focusing on the interior
And loving the Beloved.

★ First published with "*Cautelas*" ("Precautions") in 1667.

BY THE WATERS OF BABYLON★

PSALM 136

Over the flowing streams
That in Babylon I found
There I sat and wept
There I watered the ground,

5 Remembering you
O Zion! whom I loved,
The sweeter your memory
The more it made me cry.

I cast off my festive clothes,
10 Donned my working garments,
And hung upon a green willow
The music of my laments,

In exchange for the hope
Of all I hoped was in you.

15   Allí me hirió el amor,
     y el corazón me sacaba.

     Díxele que me matase,
     pues de tal suerte llagaba.
     Yo me metía en su fuego,
20   sabiendo que me abrasaba,

     Desculpando al avecica
     que en el fuego se acababa.
     Estábame en mí muriendo,
     y en ti solo respiraba.

25   En mí por ti me moría,
     y por ti resucitaba,
     que la memoria de ti
     daba vida y la quitaba.

     [Moríame por morirme
30   y mi vida me mataba,
     porque ella perseverando
     de tu vista me privaba.]

     Gozábanse los extraños
     entre quien cautivo estaba.
35   [Miraba como no vían
     que el gozo los engañaba.]

     Preguntábanme cantares
     de lo que en Sión cantaba:
     —Canta de Sión un himno;
40   veamos cómo sonaba.

     —Decid: ¿Cómo en tierra ajena,
     donde por Sión lloraba,
     contaré yo el alegría
     que en Sión se me quedaba?
45   Echaríala en olvido
     si en la ajena me gozaba.

     Con mi paladar se junte
     la lengua con que hablaba,

15   There love wounded me,
And there my heart was lost.

I begged love to kill me,
Since he wounded me so deeply.
And I leaped into the fire,
20   Knowing I would burn completely,

Thus excusing the little moth
For burning in the flame.
To myself I was thus dying,
While inhaling from you new breath.

25   For you in me I was dying
And for you once more I revived,
For by remembering you
Life was given and taken away.

(I was dying to die
30   This my life was killing me,
For as long as it would last
It deprived me of your sight.)†

Strangers were glad while
They were my captors.
35   (I wondered if they were blind,
Deceived by their joy.)‡

They would ask me for songs
I used to sing in Zion:
"Sing a song from Zion,
40   Let's hear how it sounds."

"Tell me how, in exile,
Where I cry for Zion,
Can I sing the joy
That in Zion I left?"
45   I would be forgetting
If made happy in a strange land.

May the tongue of my speech
Cling to my palate,

si de ti yo me olvidare
50 en la tierra do moraba.

Sión, por los verdes ramos
que Babilonia me daba,
de mí se olvide mi diestra,
que es lo que en ti mas amaba,

55 Si de ti no me acordare,
en lo que más me gozaba,
y si yo tuviere fiesta
y sin ti la festejaba.

¡Oh hija de Babilonia,
60 mísera y desventurada!
Bienaventurado era
aquel en quien confiaba,
que te ha de dar el castigo,
que de tu mano llevaba.

65 Y juntará sus pequeños
y a mí, porque en ti lloraba,
a la piedra, que era Cristo,
por el cual yo te dexaba.

Debetur soli gloria vera Deo.

ROMANCE SOBRE EL EVANGELIO: *IN PRINCIPIO ERAT VERBUM,* ACERCA DE LA SANTÍSIMA TRINIDAD

[1]

En el principio moraba
el Vervo, y en Dios vivía,
en quien su felicidad
infinita poseía.

If I ever forget you
50 In this land where I suffer.

Zion, by the green branches
That Babylon gave me,
Let my right arm forget me,
I loved them most when free,

55 If I would not remember you,
In what I enjoyed most,
And if I celebrate a feast day
Without memory of you.

O daughter of Babylon,
60 Miserable, doomed!
He was blessed
In whom I set my trust,
And you will receive the punishment,
He received at your hand.

65 He will gather the little ones
And me, those you forced to weep,
Around the rock, who is Christ
And for whom I had to leave.

Debetur soli gloria vera Deo.

★ Composed 1578, while in jail, Sanlúcar ms.
† From the Jaen ms.
‡ Ibid.

ROMANCE ON THE GOSPEL:
IN PRINCIPIO ERAT VERBUM, REGARDING
THE MOST HOLY TRINITY★

[1]

In the beginning dwelt
The Word, and in God He lived,
In whom He had
His infinite happiness.

 5 El mismo Verbo Dios era,
    que el principio se decía.
    El moraba en el principio,
    y principio no tenía.

    El era el mesmo principio;
10 por eso de él carecía.
    El Verbo se llama Hijo,
    que de él principio nacía.

    Hale siempre concebido,
    y siempre le concebía.
15 Dale siempre su substancia,
    y siempre se la tenía.

    Y así, la gloria del Hijo
    es la que en el Padre había;
    y toda su gloria el Padre
20 en el Hijo poseía.

    Como amado en el amante
    uno en otro residía,
    y aquese amor que los une,
    en lo mismo convenía

25 Con el uno y con el otro
    en igualdad y valía.
    Tres Personas y un amado
    entre todos tres había;

    Y un amor en todas ellas
30 y un amante las hacía,
    y el amante es el amado
    en que cada cual vivía;

    Que el ser que los tres poseen,
    cada cual le poseía,
35 y cada cual de ellos ama
    a la que este ser tenía.

    Este ser es cada una,
    y éste sólo las unía

5   The very Word was God,
And He was called the beginning,
He dwelt in the beginning,
But He had no beginning.

He himself was the beginning;
10 And therefore He had none.
The Word was called the Son,
Born from that same beginning.

He was forever conceived,
And forever is He conceived.
15 He gives Him always his substance,
And he always retains it.

Thus, the glory of the Son
Is the same as in the Father;
And all His glory the Father
20 In the Son has placed.

One in the other lived
As the beloved in the lover,
And the love joining them,
On this point made them agree

25 That the one and the other
Match equality and worth.
Three Persons and one love
Among the Three they are;

One love in all Three
30 Makes of them one lover,
The lover being the beloved
In whom each one lives;

For the Being the Three share,
Each one has fully,
35 And each one loves
The other with this Being.

This Being is each one of them,
This Being alone unites them

en un inefable *nudo* [modo]
40 que decir no se sabía.

Por lo cual era infinito
el amor que las unía,
porque un solo amor tres tienen,
que su esencia se decía;
45 que el amor, cuanto más uno,
tanto más amor hacía.

DE LA COMMUNICACION DE LAS
TRES PERSONAS

[2]

En aquel amor inmenso
que de los dos procedía,
palabras de gran regalo
el Padre al Hijo decía

5 De tan profundo deleite,
que nadie las entendía;
solo el Hijo lo gozaba,
que es a quien pertenecía.

Pero aquello que se entiende,
10 de esta manera decía:
—Nada me contenta, Hijo,
fuera de tu compañía.

Y si algo me contenta,
en ti mismo lo quería.
15 El que a ti más se parece,
a mi mas satisfacía;

Y el que en nada te semeja,
en mí nada hallaría.
En ti solo me he agradado,
20 ¡oh vida de vida mía!

In an ineffable knot
40 That cannot be explained.

For this reason, the love
Uniting them is infinite,
For three have only one love,
That is called their Essence;
45 For love, the more it becomes one,
The more it is able to love.

ON THE COMMUNION OF THE
THREE PERSONS

[2]

Out of this immense love
Rising from both of them,
Words of great joy
The Father said to the Son

5 Of such deep delight,
That no one understood them;
The Son alone rejoiced in them,
And to Him they were meant.

But what of them can be understood,
10 In this manner was said:
—"Nothing, my Son, pleases me
Except your company.

And if anything else is pleasing
In you, my Son, I love it.
15 For the more anyone resembles You,
The more he makes me happy;

Who does not resemble You,
Will find nothing in me.
For You are the life of my life!
20 And in You alone I find delight.

Eres lumbre de mi lumbre.
Eres mi sabiduría;
figura de mi substancia,
en quien bien me complacía.

25 Al que a ti te amare, Hijo,
a mi mismo le daría,
y el amor que yo en ti tengo,
ese mismo en el pondría,
en razon de haber amado
30 a quien yo tanto quería.

DE LA CREACIÓN

[3]

Una esposa que te ame,
mi Hijo, darte quería,
que por tu valor merezca
tener nuestra compañía,

5 Y comer pan a una mesa
de el mesmo que yo comía,
por que conozca los bienes
que en tal Hijo yo tenía.

Y se congracie conmigo
10 de tu gracia y lozanía.
—Mucho lo agradezco, Padre—
el Hijo le respondía.

—A la esposa que me dieres.
yo mi claridad daría,

15 Para que por ella vea
cuánto mi Padre valía
y como el ser que poseo
de su ser le recibía.

Reclinarla he yo en mi brazo,
20 y en tu amor se abrasaría,

You are the fire of my fire.
You are my wisdom's power;
And the shape of my substance,
In You I am fully expressed.

25 Whoever loves You, my Son,
To him I would give myself,
And the love that I have for You,
In him I would place,
Just for having loved the one
30 Whom I myself love so deeply."

ON CREATION

[3]

I wish to give you, my Son,
A bride who will love You,
Who will merit our company
Because of your worth,

5 And eat my own bread
At my own table
And share the gifts
That with my Son I share.

Let her rejoice with me
10 In your grace and youth.
"I am very grateful, Father,"
Replied the Son,

"To the Bride You will give me
I would give my fire,
15 That by it she may see
The greatness of my Father
And how the Being I have
Had its birth in his Being.

I will cover her with my arms,
20 So that she may burn in your love,

y con eterno deleite
to bondad sublimaría.—

[4]

 —Hágase, pues—dixo el Padre,
 —que tu amor lo merecía.—
₂₅ Y en este dicho que dixo,
 el mundo criado había;

 Palacio para la esposa,
 hecho en gran sabiduría;
 el cual en dos aposentos,
₃₀ alto y bajo, dividía.

 El bajo de diferencias
 infinitas componía;
 mas el alto hermoseaba
 de admirable pedrería,

₃₅ Por que conozca la esposa
 el Esposo que tenía.
 En el alto colocaba
 la angélica jerarquía;

 Pero la natura humana
₄₀ en el bajo la ponía,
 por ser en su compostura
 algo de menor valía.

 Y aunque el ser y los lugares
 de esta suerte los partía;
₄₅ pero todos son un cuerpo
 de la esposa que decía;

 Que el amor de un mesmo Esposo
 una Esposa los hacía.
 Los de arriba poseían
₅₀ el Esposo en alegría,

 Los de abajo en esperanza
 de fe que les infundía,

And she will exalt your goodness
With eternal joy."

[4]

    —"And so it be, then," said the Father,
    "For your love deserves it."
25 And as soon as this was said,
    The Earth came into existence;

    A palace He built for the bride,
    Designed with love and wisdom;
    Divided into two quarters,
30 One high, one low.

    The lower was built
    With infinite variety;
    While the higher was covered
    With precious stones shining with beauty,

35 So that the bride might know
    The Bridegroom she had married.
    In the higher one He placed
    The angelic hierarchy;

    And humans were given
40 The lower part to inhabit,
    For the human condition
    Is of less worth than the angelic.

    Though beings and places
    He divided in this manner;
45 All formed one single body
    Of the Bride just betrothed;

    For the love of one single Bridegroom
    One bride made of them.
    Those above enjoyed
50 The Bridegroom in gladness and song,

    Those below had hope in Him
    Through the Faith He bestowed,

diciéndoles que algun tiempo
él los engrandecería,

55 Y que aquella su baxeza
él se la levantaría,
de manera que ninguno
ya la vituperaría;

Porque en todo semajante
60 él a ellos se haría,
y se vendría con ellos,
y con ellos moraría;

Y que Dios sería hombre,
y que el hombre Dios sería,
65 y [que] trataría con ellos,
comería y bebería;

Y que con ellos contino
él mismo so quedaría,
hasta que se consumase
70 este siglo que corría.

Cuando se gozaran juntos
en eterna melodía.
Porque el era la cabeza
de la esposa que tenía.

75 A la cual todos los miembros
de los justos juntaría,
que son cuerpo de la esposa,
a la cual él tomaría

En sus brazos tiernamente,
80 y allí su amor la daría;
y que así juntos en uno
al Padre la llevaría.

Donde de el mesmo deleite
que Dios goza, gozaría.
85 Que como el Padre y el Hijo,
y el que dellos procedía,

Promising that in time
He would exalt them,

55   And would raise their low condition
To a much higher grade,
So that no one could
Despise it as base;

For He would become in everything
60   Equal to them,
He would descend among them,
And live among them;

For God would become man,
And man would become God,
65   He would mingle with men freely,
And eat and drink with them;

And He would remain
Among them forever,
Till the end of this cycle
70   And the end of time.

They would march together in joy
In eternal melody.
For He is the head and crown
Of the bride He found.

75   He would grace all the just
With her beauty,
For they are the body of the bride,
He was about to embrace

In His arms tenderly,
80   And there He would give her
His love; and together return
As one to the home of the Father.

There the same joy
God enjoys would be her delight.
85   For as the Father and the Son,
And the One proceeding from them,

El uno vive en el otro,
así la esposa sería,
que, dentro de Dios absorta,
90   vida de Dios viviría.

[5]

Con esta buena esperanza
que de arriba les venía,
el tedio de sus trabajos
más leve se les hacía;

95   Pero la esperanza larga
y el deseo que crecía
de gozarse con su Esposo
continuo les afligía.

Por lo cual con oraciones,
100   con sospiros y agonía,
con lágrimas y gemidos
le rogaban noche y día

Que ya se determinase
a les dar su compañía.
105   Unos decían:—¡Oh si fuese
en mi tiempo el alegría!—

Otros:—¡Acaba, Señor¡
al que has de enviar, envía.—
Otros: ¡Oh si ya rompieses
110   esos cielos, y vería

Con mis ojos que bajases,
y mi llanto cesaría!
Regad, nubes de lo alto,
que la tierra lo pedía.

115   Y abrase ya la tierra,
que espinas nos producía,
y produzga aquella flor,
con que ella florecería.—

Each one in the other dwells,
Thus the Bride would live in joy
Absorbed forever in God,
90   Living the life of God.

[5]

With this high hope
Coming to them from above,
The tediousness of their work
Seemed to be lightened;

95   But the long wait
And the growing desire
To enjoy the Bridegroom
Burned them like fire.

So they kept up endless prayers,
100   With sighs and agony,
Tears and moaning
Pleading night and day

That He would consent
To share at last His company.
105   Some would say: "O, if such joy
Were to come in my time!"

Others: "Put an end, Lord!
The One you have to send, send now."
And others: "O, if the heavens
110   Would at last break and allow my eyes

To see the wonder of your descent,
My weeping would at last cease!
Lofty clouds, rain, rain down upon us
For the Earth's thirst to find release.

115   Let the Earth at last be open,
For it gave us thorns and gloom,
And let her produce that Flower,
The seed of her own bloom."

Otros decían:—¡Oh dischoso
120 el que en tal tiempo sería,
que merezca ver a Dios
con los ojos que tenía,

y tratarle con sus manos,
y andar en su compañía,
125 y gozar de los misterios
que entonces ordenaría!—

[6]

En aquestos y otros ruegos
gran tiempo pasado había;
pero en los postreros años
130 el fervor mucho crecía,

Cuando el viejo Simeón,
en deseo se encendía,
rogando a Dios que quisiese
dexalle ver este día.

135 Y así el Espíritu Santo
al buen viejo respondía:
Que le daba su palabra
que la muerte no vería

Hasta que la vida viese
140 que de arriba descendía,
y que él en sus mismas manos
al mismo Dios tomaría,
y le tendría en sus brazos,
y consigo abrazaría.

[7]

145 Ya que el tiempo era llegado
en que hacerse convenía,
el rescate de la esposa
que en duro yugo servía

Others would say: "O, blessed is he
120   Who at that time will be alive,
For he is worthy of seeing God
With his own eyes when He arrives,

And will touch Him with his hands,
And walk by His side,
125   And rejoice in the mysteries
He will then provide!"

[6]

In these and other prayers
A long time went slowly by;
But in later years
130   Their fervor grew so strong,

That the old man Simeon,
Burning with desire, would pray
For God to let him
See that wonderful day.

135   And the Holy Spirit
Answering the old man:
Gave him His word
That before his death

He would see the life
140   Descending from above,
And that in his own hands
God Himself would place Him,
And he would hold Him in his arms,
And keep Him close in his own embrace.

[7]

145   The time at last came
For the old order to be revoked,
To rescue the young Bride
Serving under the hard yoke

Debajo de aquella ley
150 que Moisés dado le había.
El Padre con amor tierno
de esta manera decía:

—Ya ves, Hijo, que a tu esposa
a tu imagen hecho había,
155 y en lo que a ti se parece,
contigo bien convenía.

Pero difiere en la carne,
que en tu simple ser no había.
En los amores perfectos
160 esta ley se requería:

Que se haga semejante
el amante a quien quería,
que la mayor semejanza
más deleite contenía;

165 El cual, sin duda, en tu esposa
grandemente crecería
si te viere semejante
en la carne que tenía.—

—Mi voluntad es la tuya,—
170 el Hijo la respondía,
—y la gloria que yo tengo
es tu voluntad ser mía.

Y a mi me conviene, Padre,
lo que tu Alteza decía,
175 porque por esta manera
tu bondad mas se vería;

Verase tu gran potencia,
justicia y sabiduría;
irélo a decir al mundo
180 y noticia le daría

De tu belleza y dulzura
y de tu soberanía.

Of the Law
150 That Moses had laid on her.
The Father with tender love
In this manner addressed His Son:

"You see, my Son, that your bride
In your image has been made,
155 And in that she resembles You,
With You she fits as mate.

Yet she is different in the flesh,
Which your simple Being does not possess.
And between perfect loves
160 This law must be upheld:

That the lover be made
In all similar to the beloved,
And the greatest similarity
Contains the greatest delight;

165 And your Bride, no doubt,
Would feel this love more
If she saw you alike
Invested in the flesh."

"My will is Yours,"
170 Answered the Son,
"And the glory I seek
Is to make Your will mine.

It is fitting, Father,
For me to do as You say,
175 For in this manner Your goodness
Will be made even more clear;

Your great power will show,
With Your justice and wisdom;
And I will so tell the world
180 Spreading the word to Your kingdom

Of Your beauty and sweetness
And of Your sovereignty.

Iré a buscar a mi esposa,
y sobre mi tomaría

185 Sus fatigas y trabajos,
en que tanto padescía;

Y por que ella vida tenga,
yo por ella moriría,
y sacándola del lago,
190 a ti te la volvería.—

[8]

Entonces llamó a un arcangel,
que San Gabriel se decía,
y envióle a una doncella
que se llamaba María,

195 De cuyo consentimiento
el misterio se hacía;
en la cual la Trinidad
de carne al Verbo vestía.

Y aunque tres hacen la obra,
200 en el uno se hacía;
y quedó el Verbo encarnado
en el vientre de María.

Y el que tenia sólo Padre,
ya también Madre tenía,
205 aunque no como cualquiera
que de varón concebía;

Que de las entrañas de ella
él su carne recebía;
por lo cual Hijo de Dios
210 y de el hombre se decía.

I will go and seek the bride,
And upon me will I take the dignity

186 Of her fatigue and labors,
So that she may love even more;
I myself will die for her,
And rescue her from the lake,
190 And return her to You."

[8]

He called then an Archangel
By the name of Saint Gabriel,
And sent him to a virgin
Whose name was Mary,

195 On whose consent
The mystery was pending;
For in her the Trinity
Dressed the Word in human flesh.

Though this was the work of Three,
200 Only One became a man;
Thus the Word became incarnate
In the womb of a woman.

And so He who had only one Father,
Had now also a Mother,
205 But not as any other
That through man became pregnant;

Of Mary's own flesh
He received His human flesh;
And so the Son of God
210 Is called also the son of man.

DEL NACIMIENTO

[9]

Ya que era llegado el tiempo
en que de nacer había,
así como desposado
de su tálamo salía,

5 Abrazado con su esposa,
que en sus brazos la traía;
al cual la graciosa Madre
en un pesebre ponía

Entre unos animales
10 que a la sazón allí había.
Los hombres decían cantares,
los angeles melodía,

Festejando el desposario
que entre tales dos había.
15 Pero Dios en el pesebre
allí lloraba y gemía;

Que eran joyas que la esposa
al desposorio traía.
Y la Madre estaba en pasmo
20 el que tal trueque veía:

El llanto de el hombre en Dios,
y en el hombre la alegría;
lo cual de el uno y de el otro
tan ajeno ser solía. —Fin.

THE NATIVITY

[9]

As the time arrived
For Him to be born,
As if newly wed
From the bridal chamber came forth,

5 Embraced to his bride,
Carrying Him in her arms;
The beautiful mother
Laid Him in a manger

Among the animals
10 That were at that time there.
Men sang songs,
The angels melodies,

Celebrating the wedding
That joined the two forever.
15 But God in the manger
Cried and whimpered;

The only jewels the wife
Had raised for the wedding.
The mother was amazed
20 At seeing such a change:

The tears of man in God,
And in man only joy;
A transformation so strange
In the laws of the earth—Finis.

*Composed 1578, while in jail.

NOCHE OSCURA

(En que cuenta el alma la dichosa ventura que tuvo en pasar por la
oscura Noche de la Fe, en desnudez y purgación suya
a la unión del Amado.)

1.   En una noche oscura,
    con ansias, en amores inflamada,
    ¡oh dichosa ventura!,
    salí sin ser notada,
5   estando ya mi casa sosegada.

2.   A escuras, y segura,
    por la secreta escala, disfrazada,
    ¡oh dichosa ventura!,
    a escuras y en celada,
10   estando ya mi casa sosegada.

3.   En la noche dichosa
    en secreto, que naide me veía,
    ni yo miraba cosa,
    sin otra luz y guía,
15   sino la que en el corazón ardía.

4.   Aquésta me guiaba
    más cierto que la luz del mediodía,
    adonde me esperaba
    quien yo bien me sabía,
20   en parte donde naide parescía.

5.   ¡Oh noche que guiaste!
    ¡Oh noche amable más que el alborada!
    ¡Oh noche que juntaste
    Amado con amada,
25   amada en el Amado transformada!

6.   En mi pecho florido,
    que entero para él solo se guardaba,
    allí quedó dormido,
    y yo le regalaba,
30   y el ventalle de cedros aire daba.

DARK NIGHT

(Songs of the soul delighted at having reached the high state of perfection, the union with God, by way of spiritual negation.)

1.   On a dark night,
Anxious, by love inflamed,
—O joyous chance!—
I left not seen or discovered,
5 My house at last completely quiet.

2.   In the darkness, with light,
By the secret ladder, disguised,
—O joyous chance!—
I left in the darkness, covered,
10 My house at last completely quiet.

3.   On that joyous night,
In secret, seen by no one,
Nor with anything in sight,
I had no other light or mark,
15 Than the one burning in my heart.

4.   This light guided me
More directly than the midday sun,
Where waiting for me
Was the One I knew so well, my delight,
20 In a place with no one in sight.

5.   O night! O guide!
O night more loving than the dawn!
O night that joined
Lover with beloved,
25 Beloved in the lover transformed!

6.   Upon my flowering breasts,
Which I had saved for him alone,
There he slept,
While I caressed his hair,
30 And the cedars' breeze gave us air.

7. El aire del almena,
cuando yo sus cabellos esparcía,
con su mano serena
en mi cuello hería,
35 y todos mis sentidos suspendía.

8. Quedéme y olvidéme,
el rostro recliné sobre el Amado;
cesó todo y dejéme,
dejando mi cuidado
40 entre las azucenas olvidado.

CANTICO ESPIRITUAL

(*Primera redacción, manuscrito de Sanlucar de Barrameda.*)

ESPOSA:
1. ¿Adónde te escondiste,
Amado, y me dexaste con gemido?
Como el ciervo huiste,
5 habiéndome herido;
salí tras ti clamando, y eras ido.

2. Pastores, los que fuerdes
allá, por las majadas, al otero,
si por ventura vierdes
10 aquel que yo más quiero,
decidle que adolezco, peno y muero.

3. Buscando mis amores
iré por esos montes y riberas;
ni cogeré las flores
15 ni temeré las fieras;
y pasaré los fuertes y fronteras.

PREGUNTA A LAS CRIATURAS:
4. ¿Oh bosques y espesuras
plantadas por la mano del Amado;
20 oh prado de verduras
de flores esmaltado;
decid si por vosotros ha pasado?

7.   As I spread his tresses,
     The fresh wind from the turret,
     Wounds me in the neck as it presses
     With its serene hand,
  35 Suspending all my senses with its caresses.

8.   I lose myself and remain,
     With my face on the Beloved inclined;
     All has come to rest,
     I abandon all my cares
  40 There, among the lilies, to die.

SPIRITUAL CANTICLE★
I. A.

BRIDE:
1.   Where did you hide,
     My Love, leaving me thus to moan?
     Like the stag, you fled,
   5 Leaving in me this wound;
     I ran calling loud, but you were gone.

2.   Shepherds who wander
     From the valleys to the hills,
     If by chance you encounter
  10 The one I love so deeply,
     Tell him I die, I languish and grieve.

3.   Searching after my love
     I'll cross shores and mountains;
     I will not gather flowers
  15 Nor fear beasts;
     I will pass forts and boundaries.

HE ASKS ALL CREATURES:
4.   O forests and woods
     Seeded by the hand of the Beloved;
  20 O green meadows
     Framed with flowers;
     Did he pass through you?

RESPUESTA DE LAS CRIATURAS:

5.   Mil gracias derramando
25   pasó por estos sotos con presura,
y, yéndolos mirando,
con sola su figura
vestidos los dexó de hermosura.

ESPOSA:

6. 30   ¡Ay! ¿quién podrá sanarme?
Acaba de entregarte ya de vero.   •
No quieras enviarme
de hoy más ya mensajero;
que no saben decirme lo que quiero.

7. 35   Y todos cuantos vagan
de ti me van mil gracias refiriendo,
y todos más me llagan,
y déjame muriendo
un no sé qué que quedan balbuciendo.

8. 40   Mas ¿cómo perseveras,
¡oh vida! no viviendo donde vives,
y haciendo por que mueras
las flechas que recibes
de lo que del Amado en ti concibes?

9. 45   ¿Por qué, pues has llagado
aqueste corazón, no le sanaste?
Y, pues me le has robado,
¿por qué así le dejaste,
y no tomas el robo que robaste?

10. 50   Apaga mis enojos,
pues que ninguno basta a deshacellos,
y véante mis ojos,
pues eres lumbre dellos,
y sólo para ti quiero tenellos.

11. 55   ¡Oh christalina fuente,
si en esos tus semblantes plateados
formases de repente

THE CREATURES RESPOND:

5. Pouring a thousand graces
25 He passed through these groves in haste,
And, as he lent them his gaze
By his figure alone
He left them dressed with beauty.

BRIDE:

6. 30 O! who can now end my grief?
Come, to me, at last surrender.
From now on
Do not send messengers;
They fail to say what I want to hear.

7. 35 And all those around me
Speak of you a thousand graces,
And wound me even more,
Babbling I know not what;
I am at the door of death.

8. 40 How can you endure,
O life! not living where your life is,
Being forced to die
Through the arrows you receive
By what of the Beloved you conceive?

9. 45 Why, then, if you so broke
My heart, do you refuse to make it heal?
And, since you have stolen it
Why did you abandon it,
Refusing to steal what you already stole?

10. 50 Put an end to all my troubles,
No one else can undo them,
Let my eyes see you,
For you are their flame,
And I need them only for you.

11. 55 O crystalline fountain,
If in your silvery faces
You would form of a sudden

los ojos deseados
que tengo en mis entrañas dibujados!

12.   60   ¡Apártalos, Amado,
que voy de vuelo!

ESPOSO:
Vuélvete, paloma,
que el ciervo vulnerado
65   por el otero asoma
al aire de tu vuelo, y fresco toma.

ESPOSA:
13.   Mi Amado las montañas,
los valles solitarios nemorosos,
70   las ínsulas extrañas,
los ríos sonorosos,
el silbo de los aires amorosos,

14.   la noche sosegada,
en par de los levantes de la aurora,
75   la música callada,
la soledad sonora,
la cena que recrea y enamora.

15.   Nuestro lecho florido,
de cuevas de leones enlazado,
80   en púrpura tendido,
de paz edificado,
de mil escudos de oro coronado.

16.   A zaga de tu huella
las jóvenes discurren al camino.
85   Al toque de centella,
al adobado vino,
emisiones de bálsamo divino.

17.   En la interior bodega
de mi Amado bebí, y cuando salía
90   por toda aquesta vega
ya cosa no sabía,
y el ganado perdí que antes seguía.

The desired eyes
I have pictured in my inner places!

12. 60 Turn them aside, my Love
For I take flight!

BRIDEGROOM:
Return, my dove,
For the wounded stag
65 Rises over the horizon's light
Refreshed by the air of your flight.

BRIDE:
13. My Beloved the mountains,
The valleys' solitary groves,
70 The sounding rivers and fountains,
The distant islands' soil,
The wind whistling love's songs,

14. The calm night,
The twin of the rising dawn,
75 The silent music,
The sounding solitude,
The supper that kindles love and warms.

15. There lies our flowery bed,
Surrounded by dens of lions,
80 Covered in purple,
Grounded in peace,
Guarded by a thousand golden shields.

16. Chasing after your footprints
Young women take to the roads.
85 The touch of a spark,
The taste of scented wine,
Are in them a divine balm.

17. In the inner wine cellar
Of my Beloved I drank, and when I left
90 I found that in this world's fair
I felt for no thing or place,
I even lost the flock I once chased.

18.   Allí me dió su pecho,
           allí me enseñó ciencia muy sobrosa,
95   y yo le dí de hecho
           a mi, sin dejar cosa,
           allí le prometí de ser su esposa.

19.   Mi alma se ha empleado
           y todo mi caudal en su servicio.
100   Ya no guardo ganado
           ni ya tengo otro oficio,
           que ya sólo en amar es mi ejercicio.

20.   Pues ya si en el ejido
           de hoy más no fuere vista ni hallada,
105   diréis que me he perdido;
           que, andando enamorada,
           me hice perdidiza, y fuí ganada.

21.   De flores y esmeraldas,
           en las frescas mañanas escogidas,
110   haremos las guirnaldas,
           en tu amor florecidas,
           y en un cabello mío entretejidas.

22.   En solo aquel cabello
           que en mi cuello volar consideraste,
115   mirástele en mi cuello,
           y en él preso quedaste,
           y en uno de mis ojos te llagaste.

23.   Cuando tú me mirabas,
           su gracia en mí tus ojos imprimían;
120   por eso me adamabas,
           y en eso merecían
           los míos adorar lo que en ti vían.

24.   No quieras despreciarme,
           que, si color moreno en mí hallaste,
125   ya bien puedes mirarme,
           después que me miraste,
           que gracia y hermosura en mí dejaste.

18.   There he gives me his chest,
           There sweet science he uncovers,
   95 There I give him in return
           All of me, with nothing to recover,
           And there I become the bride of my lover.

19.   My whole soul has now surrendered
           With all its gifts to his dominion.
  100 I have no flock to tend
           Nor any other preoccupation,
           For his love alone is now my occupation.

20.   So if I am no longer seen or found
           In the pastures or squares,
  105 Say that I lost my bounds;
           That roaming with love's cares.
           I lost myself, but found my share,

21.   Of flowers and emeralds,
           Gathered in the morning sun,
  110 We'll make up garlands,
           Bloomed in love for love to entwine,
           And we'll braid in them one hair of mine.

22.   In just that lock of hair
           That on my neck you saw move,
  115 As you looked upon it there,
           A prisoner it made of you,
           And in my eyes you received a wound.

23.   When you looked upon me,
           The grace of your eyes in me you printed;
  120 For this you adored me,
           And for this my eyes deserved
           To love what in you they beheld.

24.   Despise not my humble ways,
           For even if my color is brown,
  125 On me you may well gaze,
           For your look is the crown,
           Of every grace and beauty I have.

25. Cogednos las raposas,
que está ya florecida nuestra viña,
130 en tanto que de rosas
hacemos una piña,
y no parezca nadie en la montiña.

26. Detente, cierzo muerto;
ven, austro, que recuerdas los amores,
135 aspira por mi huerto,
y corran sus olores,
y pacerá el Amado entre las flores.

ESPOSO:
27. Entrado se ha la esposa
140 en el ameno huerto deseado,
y a su sabor reposa,
el cuello reclinado
sobre los dulces brazos del Amado.

28. Debajo del manzano,
145 allí conmigo fuiste desposada,
allí te di la mano,
y fuiste reparada
donde tu madre fuera violada.

29. A las aves ligeras,
150 leones, ciervos, gamos saltadores,
montes, valles, riberas,
aguas, aires, ardores
y miedos de las noches veladores:

30. Por las amenas liras
155 y canto de sírenas os conjuro
que cesen vuestras iras,
y no toquéis al muro,
por que la esposa duerma más seguro.

ESPOSA:
31. 160 ¡Oh ninfas de Judea!
en tanto que en las flores y rosales
el ámbar perfumea,

25.   Catch us the little foxes,
             Our vineyard is now in bloom,
130   And while of roses
             We make a fistful,
             Let no one appear on the hilltop.

26.   Stop, dead wind;
             Come, warm wind with love's memories,
135   Breathe through my garden,
             The scent of your caresses,
             For the Beloved to graze among the flowers.

            BRIDEGROOM:
27.   The bride now enters
140   The pleasant orchard so desired,
             And to her content she lingers,
             Her neck gently inclined
             Upon the sweet arm of the Beloved.

28.   Under the apple tree,
145   You and I were wedded,
             There I took your hand in mine,
             There you were recreated
             Where your mother was violated.

29.   And to the light birds of the air,
150   Lions, deer, leaping does,
             Mountains, valleys, and lairs,
             Water, air, burning foes
             And fears of wakeful night's moans:

30.   By the pleasant lyres
155   Of the songs of sirens, I conjure you all
             To put a stop to your ires,
             Do not touch the wall,
             That the bride may fall into deeper sleep.

            BRIDE:
31. 160 O nymphs of Judea!
             While the scent of amber
             Lingers in the roses and flowers,

morá en los arrabales,
y no queráis tocar nuestros umbrales.

32. 165   Escóndente, Carillo,
y mira con tu haz a las montanas,
y no quieras decillo,
mas mira las compañas
de la que va por ínsulas extrañas.

170   ESPOSO:
33.   La blanca palomica
al arca con el ramo se ha tornado;
y ya la tortolica
al socio deseado
175   en las riberas verdes ha hallado.

34.   En soledad vivía,
y en soledad ha puesto ya su nido,
y en soledad la guía
a solas su Querido,
180   también en soledad de amor herido.

ESPOSA:
35.   Gocémonos, Amado,
y vámonos a ver en tu hermosura
al monte u al collado,
185   do mana el aqua pura;
entremos más adentro en la espesura.

36.   Y luego a las subidas
cavernas de la piedra nos iremos,
que están bien escondidas,
190   y allí nos entraremos,
y el mosto de granadas gustaremos.

37.   Allí me mostrarías
aquello que mi alma pretendía,
y luego me darías
195   allí tú, vida mía,
aquello que me diste el otro día:

Delay in the periphery,
Do not dare touch our chamber.

32. 165 My love, hide from view,
To the mountains turn your face,
Do not try to speak,
But look at the company you keep
When traveling to islands so strange.

170 BRIDEGROOM:
33. The white, tiny dove
Has returned to the ark with an olive branch;
And thus the turtledove
Has found her match
175 On the green shores of the riverbank.

34. In solitude she lived,
In solitude she built her nest,
In solitude she is led
All alone by her love's zest,
180 To the wound of solitude love knows best.

BRIDE:
35. Rejoice, my Beloved, with me,
And to see ourselves in your beauty
Let us go to the mountains or the hills,
185 Where water flows with purity;
Let us go deeper into the valley.

36. Then we shall climb higher
To the lofty caverns of stone,
Which are all well hidden,
190 And there we shall go,
And pour the sweet wine of pomegranates.

37. There you will show
The things my soul desired,
And there you will bestow,
195 My love, what my life required,
What to me, the other day, you uncovered:

38.   El aspirar del aire,
             el canto de la dulce filomena,
             el soto y su donaire
200   en la noche serena,
             con llama que consume y no da pena.

39.   Que nadie lo miraba . . .
             Aminabad tampoco parecía;
             y el cerco sosegaba,
205   y la caballería
             a vista de las aguas descendía.—Fin.

CANTICO ESPIRITUAL

(Segunda redacción, manuscrito de Jaen.)

ESPOSA:

I.   ¿Adónde te escondiste,
             Amado, y me dejaste con gemido?
             Como el cievo huiste,
5   habiéndome herido;
             salí tras ti clamando, y eras ido.

2.   Pastores, los que fuerdes
             allá, por las majadas, al otero,
             si por ventura vierdes
10   aquel que yo más quiero,
             decilde que adolezco, peno y muero.

3.   Buscando mis amores
             iré por esos montes y riberas;
             ni cogeré las flores
15   ni temeré las fieras;
             y pasaré los fuertes y fronteras.

38.   The breathing of the air,
             The song of the tender nightingale,
             The grove without cares
        200 In the serene night, and the flame
             That consumes but gives no pain.

39.   No one was watching . . .
             Aminabad did not appear;
             The siege was lifted when
        205 At the sight of water so clear
             The cavalry began to disappear.—Finis.

> *Stanza eleven (verses 53–57 of Spiritual Canticle II. B.) have been deleted in this first redaction, codex of Sanlúcar de Barrameda ms.

SPIRITUAL CANTICLE★
II. B.

(Exposition of the songs dealing with the exercise of love between the soul and her spouse Christ. In it certain points and effects of prayer are touched upon and explained, at the request of Mother Ana de Jesús, Prioress of the Discalced at San José de Granada, in the year 1584.)

BRIDE:
1.   Where did you hide,
           My Love, and left me thus to moan?
           Like the stag, you fled,
      5   Leaving in me this wound;
           I ran calling loud, but you were gone.

2.   Shepherds who might wander
           From the valleys to the hills,
           If by chance you encounter
      10   The one I love so deeply,
           Tell him I die, languish and grieve.

3.   Searching after my loves
           I'll cross shores and mountains;
           I will not gather flowers
      15   Nor fear beasts;
           I will cross forts and boundaries.

4.   ¿Oh bosques y espesuras
        plantadas por la mano del Amado;
        oh prado de verduras
   20   de flores esmaltado;
        decid si por vosotros ha pasado?

5.   Mil gracias derramando
        pasó por estos sotos con presura,
        y, yéndolos mirando,
   25   con sola su figura
        vestidos los dejó de hermosura.

6.   ¡Ay!, ¿quién podrá sanarme?
        Acaba de entregarte ya de vero.
        No quieras enviarme
   30   de hoy más ya mensajero;
        que no saben decierme lo que quiero.

7.   Y todos cuantos vagan
        de ti me van mil gracias refiriendo,
        y todos más me llagan,
   35   y déjame muriendo
        un no sé qué que quedan balbuciendo.

8.   Mas ¿cómo perseveras,
        ¡oh vida! no viviendo donde vives,
        y haciendo por que mueras
   40   las flechas que recibes
        de lo que del Amado en ti concibes?

9.   ¿Por qué, pues has llagado
        aqueste corazón, no le sanaste?
        Y, pues me le has robado,
   45   ¿por qué así le dejaste,
        y no tomas el robo que robaste?

10.   Apaga mis enojos,
        pues que ninguno basta a deshacellos,
        y véante mis ojos,
   50   pues eres lumbre dellos,
        y sólo para ti quiero tenellos.

4.   O forests and woods
      Seeded by the hand of the Beloved;
      O green meadows
20   Framed with flowers;
      Did he pass through you?

5.   Pouring a thousand graces
      He passed through these groves in haste,
      And, as he lent them his gaze
25   By his figure alone
      He left them dressed with beauty.

6.   O! who can now end my grief?
      Come, to me, at last surrender.
      From now on
30   Do not send messengers;
      They fail to say what I want to hear.

7.   And all those around me
      Speak of you a thousand graces,
      And wound me even more,
35   Babbling I know not what;
      I am at the door of death.

8.   How can you endure,
      O life! not living where your life is,
      Being forced to die
40   Through the arrows you receive
      By what of the Beloved you conceive?

9.   Why, then, if you so broke
      My heart, do you refuse to make it heal?
      And since you already stole it
45   Why did you abandon it,
      Refusing to steal what you already stole?

10.   Put an end to all my troubles,
      No one else can undo them,
      Let my eyes see you,
50   For you are their flame
      And I need them only for you.

11.   Descubre tu presencia,
       y máteme tu vista y hermosura.
       Mira que lo dolencia
   55 de amor, que no se cura
       sino con la presencia y la figura.

12.   ¡Oh cristalina fuente,
       si en esos tus semblantes plateados
       formases de repente
   60 los ojos deseados
       que tengo en mis entrañas dibujados!

13.   ¡Apártalos, Amado,
       que voy de vuelo!

       ESPOSO:
   65 Vuélvete, paloma,
       que el ciervo vulnerado
       por el otero asoma
       al aire de tu vuelo, y fresco toma.

14.   Mi Amado las montañas,
   70 los valles solitarios nemorosos,
       las ínsulas extrañas,
       los ríos sonorosos,
       el silbo de los aires amorosos;

15.   la noche sosegada,
   75 en par de los levantes del aurora,
       la música callada,
       la soledad sonora,
       la cena que recrea y enamora.

16.   Cogednos las raposas,
   80 que está ya florecida nuestra viña,
       en tanto que de rosas
       hacemos una piña,
       y no parezca nadie en la montiña.

17.   Detènte, cierzo muerto;
   85 ven, austro, que recuerdas los amores,
       aspira por mi huerto,

11.   Reveal your presence,
      Let your sight and beauty be my killer.
      Remember that for the pains of love
  55 There is no other cure
      But the lover's presence and figure.

12.   O crystalline fountain,
      If in those your silvery faces
      You would form of a sudden
  60 The desired eyes
      I have pictured in my inner places!

13.   Turn them aside, my Love,
      For I take flight!

      BRIDEGROOM:
  65 Return, my dove,
      For the wounded stag
      Rises over the horizon's light
      Refreshed by the air of your flight.

14.   My Beloved the mountains,
  70 The valleys' solitary groves,
      The sounding rivers and fountains,
      The distant islands' soil,
      The wind whistling love's songs,

15.   The calm night,
  75 The twin of the rising dawn,
      The silent music,
      The sounding solitude,
      The supper that kindles love and warms.

16.   Catch us the little foxes,
  80 Our vineyard is now in bloom,
      And while of roses
      We make a fistful,
      Let no one appear on the hilltop.

17.   Stop, dead wind;
  85 Come, warm wind with love's memories,
      Breathe through my garden,

y corran sus olores,
y pacerá el Amado entre las flores.

18. ¡Oh ninfas de Judea!
90 en tanto que en las flores y rosales
el ámbar perfumea,
morá en los arrabales,
y no queráis tocar nuestros umbrales.

19. Escóndete, Carillo,
95 y mira con tu haz a las montañas,
y no quieras decillo,
mas mira las compañas
de la que va por ínsulas extrañas.

20. A las aves ligeras,
100 leones, ciervos, gamos saltadores,
montes, valles, riberas,
aguas, aires, ardores
y miedos de las noches veladores:

21. Por las amenas liras
105 y canto de sirenas os conjuro
que cesen vuestras iras,
y no toquéis al muro,
por que la esposa duerma más seguro.

22. Entrado se ha la esposa
110 en el ameno huerto deseado,
y a su sabor reposa,
el cuello reclinado
sobre los dulces brazos del Amado.

23. Debajo del manzano,
115 allí conmigo fuiste desposada,
allí te di la mano,
y fuiste reparada
donde tu madre fuera violada.

24. Nuestro lecho florido,
120 de cuevas de leones enlazado,
en púrpura tendido,

The scent of your caresses,
For the Beloved to graze among the flowers.

18.   O nymphs of Judea!
90   While the scent of amber
Lingers in the roses and flowers,
Delay in the periphery,
Do not dare touch our chamber.

19.   My love, hide from view,
95   To the mountains turn your face,
Do not try to speak,
But look at the company you keep
When traveling to islands so strange.

20.   And to the light birds of the air,
100   Lions, deer, leaping does,
Mountains, valleys, and lairs,
Water, air, burning foes
And fears of the wakeful night's moans:

21.   By the pleasant lyres
105   Of the songs of sirens, I conjure you all
To put a stop to your ires,
Do not touch the wall,
That the bride may fall into deeper sleep.

22.   The bride now enters
110   The pleasant orchard so desired,
And to her content she lingers,
Her neck gently inclined
Upon the sweet arm of the Beloved.

23.   Under the apple tree
115   You and I were wedded,
There I took your hand in mine,
There you were recreated
Where your mother was once violated.

24.   There lies our flowery bed,
120   Surrounded by dens of lions,
Covered in purple,

de paz edificado,
de mil escudos de oro coronado.

25. A zaga de tu huella
125   las jóvenes discurren al camino.
Al toque de centella,
al adobado vino,
emisiones de bálsamo divino.

26. En la interior bodega
130   de mi Amado bebí, y cuando salía
por toda aquesta vega
ya cosa no sabía,
y el ganado perdí que antes seguía.

27. Allí me dió su pecho,
135   allí me enseñó ciencia muy sabrosa,
y yo le dí de hecho
a mi, sin dejar cosa,
allí le prometí de ser su esposa.

28. Mi alma se ha empleado
140   y todo mi caudal en su servicio.
Ya no guardo ganado
ni ya tengo otro oficio,
que ya sólo en amar es mi ejercicio.

29. Pues ya si en el ejido
145   de hoy más no fuere vista ni hallada,
diréis que me he perdido;
que, andando enamorada,
me hice perdidiza, y fuí ganada.

30. De flores y esmeraldas,
150   en las frescas mañanas escogidas,
haremos las guirnaldas,
en tu amor florecidas,
y en un cabello mío entretejidas.

31. En solo aquel cabello
155   que en mi cuello volar consideraste,
mirástele en mi cuello,

Grounded in peace,
Guarded by a thousand golden shields.

25.   Chasing after your footprints
125   Young women take to the roads.
The touch of a spark,
The taste of scented wine,
Are in them a divine balm.

26.   In the inner wine cellar
130   Of my Beloved I drank, and when I left
I found that of this world's fair
I felt for no thing or place,
I even lost the flock I once chased.

27.   There he gives me his chest,
135   There sweet science he uncovers,
There I give him in return
All of me, with nothing to recover,
And there I become the bride of my lover.

28.   My whole soul has now surrendered
140   With all its gifts to his dominion.
I have no flock to tend
Nor any other preoccupation,
For his love alone is now my occupation.

29.   So if I am no longer seen or found
145   In the pastures or squares,
Say that I lost by bounds;
That roaming about with love's cares,
I lost myself, but found my share.

30.   Of flowers and emeralds,
150   Gathered in the morning sun,
We'll make up garlands,
Bloomed in love for love to entwine,
And we'll braid in them one hair of mine.

31.   In just that lock of hair
155   That in my neck you saw move,
As you looked upon it there,

y en él preso quedaste,
y en uno de mis ojos te llagaste.

32.   Cuando tú me mirabas,
160   su gracia en mi tus ojos imprimían;
por eso me adamabas,
y en eso merecían
los míos adorar lo que en ti vían.

33.   No quieras despreciarme,
165   que, si color moreno en mí hallaste,
ya bien puedes mirarme,
después que me miraste,
que gracia y hermosura en mí dejaste.

34.   La blanca palomica
170   al arca con el ramo se ha tornado;
y ya la tortolica
al socio deseado
en las riberas verdes ha hallado.

35.   En soledad vivía,
175   y en soledad ha puesto ya su nido,
y en soledad le guía
a solas su Querido,
también en soledad de amor herido.

36.   Gocémonos, Amado,
180   y vámonos a ver en tu hermosura
al monte y al collado,
do mana el agua pura;
entremos más adentro en la espesura.

37.   Y luego a las subidas
185   cavernas de la piedra nos iremos,
que están bien escondidas,
y allí nos entraremos,
y el mosto de granadas gustaremos.

38.   Allí me mostrarías
190   aquello que mi alma pretendía,
y luego me darías

A prisoner it made of you,
And in my eyes you received a wound.

32.   When you looked upon me,
160   The grace of your eyes in me you printed;
For this you adored me,
And for this my eyes deserved
To love what in you they beheld.

33.   Despise not my humble ways,
165   For if my color is brown,
On me you may well gaze,
For your look is the crown,
Of every grace and beauty I have.

34.   The white, tiny dove
170   Has returned to the ark with an olive branch;
And thus the turtledove
Has found her match
On the green shores of the riverbank.

35.   In solitude she lived,
175   In solitude she built her nest,
In solitude she is led
All alone by her love's zest,
To the wound of solitude love knows best.

36.   Rejoice, my Beloved, with me,
180   And to see ourselves in your beauty
Let's go to the mountains or the hills,
Where water flows with purity;
Let us go deeper into the valley.

37.   Then we shall climb higher
185   To the lofty caverns of stone,
Which are all well hidden,
And there we shall go,
And pour the sweet wine of pomegranates.

38.   There you will show
190   The things my soul desired,
And there you will bestow,

allí tú, vida mía,
aquello que me diste el otro día:

39.
     195   El aspira del aire,
el canto de la dulce filomena,
el soto y su donaire
en la noche serena,
con llama que consume y no da pena.

40.
     200   Que nadie lo miraba . . .
Aminabad tampoco parecía;
y el cerco sosegaba,
y la caballería
a vista de las aguas descendía.

OH LLAMA DE AMOR VIVA

*(Canciones que hace el alma en la íntima unión
en Dios, su esposo Amado.)*

1.
    ¡Oh llama de amor viva,
que tiernamente hieres
de mi alma en el más profundo centro!
Pues ya no eres esquiva,
    5   acaba ya, si quieres:
¡rompe la tela de este dulce encuentro!

2.
    ¡Oh cauterio sauve!
¡Oh regalada llaga!
¡Oh mano blanda! ¡Oh toque delicado,
    10   que a vida eterna sabe
y toda deuda paga!
¡Matando, muerte en vida la has trocado!

3.
    ¡Oh lámparas de fuego,
en cuyos resplandores

My love, what my life required,
What to me, the other day, you uncovered:

39.   The breathing of the air,
195   The song of the tender nightingale,
The groves without cares
In the serene night, and the flame
That consumes but gives no pain.

40.   No one was watching . . .
200   Aminabad did not appear;
The siege was lifted when
At the sight of water so clear
The cavalry began to disappear.

*This is the second version of the Spiritual Canticle [Jaen ms.]. The first redaction is considered by the critics the best of the two versions of this poem. Verses 53–57 are taken from the second redaction, the Jaen ms., and were not included in the first version. The poem was composed in prison, at least in part.

LOVE'S LIVING FLAME

(Songs that the soul sings in her intimate union with God, her beloved Bridegroom.)

1.   O Love's living flame,
Tenderly you wound
My soul's deepest center!
Since you no longer evade me,
5   Will you, please, at last conclude:
Rend the veil of this sweet encounter!

2.   O cautery so tender!
O pampered wound!
O soft hand! O touch so delicately strange,
10   Tasting of eternal life
And canceling all debts!
Killing, death into life you change!

3.   O lamps of fiery lure,
In whose shining transparence

15   las profundas cavernas del sentido,
    que estaba oscuro y ciego,
    con extraños primores
    calor y luz dan junto a su Querido!

4.   ¡Cuán manso y amoroso
20   recuerdas en mi seno,
    donde secretamente solo moras:
    y en tu aspirar sabroso,
    de bien y gloria lleno,
    cuán delicadamente me enamoras!

CANTAR DE LA ALMA QUE SE HUELGA DE CONOCER A DIOS POR FE

¡Qué bien se yo la fonte que mana y corre,
aunque es de noche!

1.   Aquella eterna fonte está escondida,
    ¡qué bien sé yo do tiene su manida,
5   aunque es de noche!

2.   [En esta noche oscura desta vida,
    ¡qué bien sé yo por fe la fonte frida,
    aunque es de noche!]

3.   Su origen no le sé, pues no le tiene,
10   mas sé que todo origen de ella viene,
    ¡aunque es de noche!

4.   Sé que no pueda ser cosa tan bella,
    y que cielos y tierra beben della,
    ¡aunque es de noche!

5. 15 Bien sé que suelo en ella no se halla,
    y que ninguno pueda vadealla,
    ¡aunque es de noche!

6.   Su claridad nunca es escurecida,
    y sé que toda luz de ella es venida,
20   ¡aunque es de noche!

₁₅ The deep cavern of the senses,
Blind and obscure,
Warmth and light, with strange flares,
Gives with the lover's caresses!

4. How tame and loving
₂₀ Your memory rises in my breast,
Where secretly only you live,
And in your fragrant breathing,
Full of goodness and grace,
How delicately in love you make me feel!

SONG OF THE SOUL THAT DELIGHTS IN KNOWING GOD BY FAITH*

*Well I know the fountain that runs and flows,
though it is night!*

1. This eternal fountain is hidden deep,
Well I know where it has its spring,
₅ Though it is night!

2. [In this life's dark night,
Faith has taught where this cold fountain lies,
Though it is night!]

3. Its origin I cannot know, it has none,
₁₀ And I know all origins come from it,
Though it is night!

4. And I know there can be nothing more fair,
The heavens and earth drink there,
Though it is night!

5. ₁₅ And I know it has no bed,
And I know no one can cross its depths,
Though it is night!

6. Its clarity is never clouded,
And I know all light shines from it,
₂₀ Though it is night!

7.   Sé ser tan caudalosos sus corrientes,
      que infiernos, cielos riegan, y las gentes,
      ¡aunque es de noche!

8.   El corriente que nace desta fuente
   25 bien sé que es tan capaz y omnipotente,
      ¡aunque es de noche!

9.   El corriente que de estas dos procede,
      sé que ninguna de ellas le precede,
      ¡aunque es de noche!

10. 30 [Bien sé que tres en sola una agua viva
      residen, y una de otra se deriva,
      ¡aunque es de noche!]

11.   Aquesta eterna fonte está escondida
      en este vivo pan por darnos vida,
   35 ¡aunque es de noche!

12.   Aquí se está llamando a las criaturas,
      y de esta agua se hartan, aunque a escuras,
      ¡aunque es de noche!

13.   Aquesta viva fuente que desco,
   40 en este pan de vida yo la veo,
      ¡aunque es de noche!

OTRAS CANCIONES A LO DIVINO: DE CRISTO Y EL ALMA

1.   Un pastorcico, solo, está penado,
      ajeno de placer y de contento,
      y en su pastora puesto el pensamiento,
      y el pecho del amor muy lastimado.

2.   5 No llora por haberle amor llagado,
      que no le pena verse así afligido,

7.   I know her streams swell so abundantly,
       They water people, heaven and even hell,
       Though it is night!

8.   The current born of this fountain
    25 I know to be wide and mighty,
       Though it is night!

9.   And from these two another stream flows,
       And I know neither comes before,
       Though it is night!

10.   30 [I know Three in only one water live,
       And each the other feeds,
       Though it is night!]

11.   This eternal fountain is hiding from sight
       Within this living bread to give us life,
    35 Though it is night!

12.   He calls all creatures to this light,
       And of this water they drink, though in the dark,
       Though it is night!

13.   This living fountain I desire,
    40 I see it here within this living bread,
       Though it is night!

*This poem is found in the Sanlúcar ms. It was composed in prison, December 1577–
August 1578. The verses within brackets are found in another ms. at Sacro Monte and
are considered authentic.

MORE SONGS ABOUT SPIRITUAL MATTERS: OF CHRIST AND THE SOUL*

1.   A young shepherd is alone pining,
       Bereft of pleasure and happiness,
       His thoughts fixed upon his shepherdess,
       His chest with love deeply hurting.

2.   5 He does not weep that love has pierced him,
       He does not grieve at being so afflicted,

aunque en el corazón está herido;
mas llora por pensar que está olvidado.

3.   Que sólo de pensar que está olvidado
10 de su bella pastora, con gran pena
se dexa maltratar en tierra ajena,
el pecho de el amor muy lastimado.

4.   Y dice el pastorcico:—Ay, desdichado
de anquel que de mi amor ha hecho ausencia,
15 y no quiere gozar la mi presencia,—
y el pecho por su amor muy lastimado.

5.   Y a cabo de un gran rato se ha encumbrado
sobre un arbol, do abrió sus brazos bellos;
y muerto se ha quedado asido dellos,
20 el pecho de el amor muy lastimado.

ENTRÉME DONDE NO SUPE

(Coplas del mismo hechas sobre un estasis de harta contemplación.)

Entréme donde no supe,
y quedéme no sabiendo,
toda ciencia trascendiendo.

1.   Yo no supe dónde entraba,
5 pero, cuando allí me ví,
sin saber dónde me estaba,
grandes cosas entendí;
no diré lo que sentí,
que me quedé no sabiendo,
10 *toda ciencia trascendiendo.*

2.   De paz y de piedad,
era le ciencia perfecta,
en profunda soledad
entendida (via recta);

Though his heart is still bleeding;
He cries, thinking he is forgotten.

3. By just thinking he is forgotten
10   By his beautiful shepherdess, in deep pain
He lets himself be wounded in a foreign land,
His chest deeply hurting with love.

4. "Alas for him," the young shepherd cries,
"Who lets me feel of my love only the absence,
15   Refusing to enjoy my presence,"
His chest with love deeply hurting.

5. After a while he begins to climb
To the top of a tree to open his beautiful arms;
And there he dies hanging by a branch,
20   His chest hurts deeply with love.

*Date uncertain, Sanlúcar de Barrameda ms.

I ENTERED NOT KNOWING WHERE*

(Song by the same author on an ecstasy of high contemplation.)

I entered not knowing where,
And I remained not knowing,
Beyond all science knowing.

1. I did not know where I entered,
5   But when I saw myself there,
Not knowing where I entered,
Many things I suddenly learned;
I will not say what these things were,
For I remained not knowing,
10   *Beyond all science knowing.*

2. It was peace, it was love,
It was the perfect knowledge,
In deep loneliness
I saw with wisdom;

15 era cosa tan secreta
que me quedé balbuciendo,
toda ciencia trascendiendo.

3. Estaba tan embebido,
tan absorto y ajenado,
20 que se quedó mi sentido
de todo sentir privado;
y el espíritu dotado
de un entender no entendiendo,
toda ciencia trascendiendo.

4. 25 El que allí llega de vero,
de sí mismo desfallesce;
cuanto sabía primero
mucho baxo le paresce;
y su ciencia tanto cresce,
30 que se queda no sabiendo,
toda ciencia trascendiendo.

5. Cuanto más alto se sube,
tanto menos entendía,
que es la tenebrosa nube
35 que a la noche esclarecía;
por eso quien la sabía
queda siempre no sabiendo,
toda ciencia trascendiendo.

6. Este saber no sabiendo
40 es de tan alto poder,
que los sabios arguyendo
jamás le pueden vencer;
que no llega su saber
a no entender entendiendo,
45 *toda ciencia trascendiendo.*

7. Y es de tan alta excelencia
aqueste sumo saber,
que no hay facultad ni ciencia
que le puedan emprender;
50 quien se supiere vencer

15 It was a thing so secret
   I was left babbling and trembling,
   Beyond all science knowing.

3.   I was so far beyond,
     So lost and absorbed,
20   I lost all my senses
     I was of all sensing dispossessed;
     And my spirit was filled
     With knowledge not knowing,
     Beyond all science knowing.

4. 25 Whoever truly reaches there,
        To himself he is lost;
        All he knew before
        Now appears very base;
        But his knowledge grows,
30   And he remains not knowing,
        Beyond all science knowing.

5.   The higher he climbs,
     The less he understands,
     For this is the dark cloud
35   That brings light to the night;
     And whoever has this light
     Always remains not knowing,
     Beyond all science knowing.

6.   This knowing by not knowing,
40   Is of such high power,
     That the arguments of the wise
     Are unable to grasp it;
     For their knowledge does not explain
     Not to know knowing,
45   *Beyond all science knowing.*

7.   And this exalted wisdom
     Is of such excellence,
     That no faculty or science
     Can hope to reach it;
50   But he who learns to conquer himself

con un no saber sabiendo,
irá siempre trascendiendo.

8.   Y si lo queréis oir,
consiste esta suma ciencia
55 en un subido sentir
de la divinal Esencia;
es obra de su clemencia
hacer quedar no entendiendo,
toda ciencia trascendiendo.

VIVO SIN VIVIR EN MI

(Coplas del alma que pena por ver a Dios, de el mismo autor.)

Vivo sin vivir en mí,
y de tal manera espero,
que muero porque no muero.

1.   En mí yo no vivo ya,
5 y sin Dios vivir no puedo;
pues sin él y sin mí quedo,
este vivi, ¿qué será?
Mil muertes se me hará,
pues mi misma vida espero,
10 *muriendo porque no muero.*

2.   Esta vida que yo vivo
es privación de vivir;
y así, es contino morir
hasta que viva contigo.
15 Oye, mi Dios, lo que digo,
que esta vida no la quiero;
que muero porque no muero.

3.   Estando absente de ti,
¿qué vida puedo tener,
20 sino muerte padescer,

With this knowledge of not knowing,
Will always go beyond all science knowing.

8.   And if you want to hear it,
          This highest science consists
    55   In a most sublime sensing
          Of the Divine Essence;
          It is an act of clemency
          Which leaves us not knowing,
          Beyond all science knowing.

★Date uncertain, Sanlúcar ms.

NOT LIVING IN MYSELF I LIVE★

(Songs by the same soul suffering from her desire to see God.)

    Not living in myself I live,
    and so painful is my wait,
    I die because I do not die.

1.   No longer do I live in myself,
    5   And without God I cannot live;
          Without Him, without myself I am left,
          How can I call this life?
          I will live a thousand deaths,
          Waiting for my own life,
    10   *Dying because I do not die.*

2.   This life I now live
          Is rather a lack of living;
          It is a continuous dying
          If with You I do not make my living.
    15   Listen, my God, to what I say,
          I do not want this life of mine;
          For I die because I do not die.

3.   Being removed from You,
          How can I make life,
    20   And not suffer the worst death

la mayor que nunca vi?
Lástima tengo de mí,
pues de suerte persevero,
que muero porque no muero.

4. 25 El pez que del agua sale,
aun de alivio no caresce,
que en la muerte que padesce,
al fin la muerte le vale;
¿Qué muerte habrá que se iguale
30 a mi vivir lastimero,
pues si más vivo, más muero?

5.   Cuando me pienso aliviar
de verte en el Sacramento,
háceme más sentimiento
35 el no te poder gozar;
todo es para más penar,
por no verte como quiero,
y muero porque no muero.

6.   Y si me gozo, Señor,
40 con esperanza de verte,
en ver *que* puedo perderte
se me dobla mi dolor;
viviendo en tanto pavor
y esperando como espero,
45 *muérome porque no muero.*

7.   Sácame de aquesta muerte,
mi Dios, y dame la vida,
no me tengas impedida
en este lazo tan fuerte;
50 mira que peno por verte,
y mi mal es tan entero,
que muero porque no muero.

8.   Lloraré mi muerte ya
y lamentaré mi vida
55 en tanto que detenida
por mis pecados está.

I could ever have?
I feel sorry for myself,
For I keep living this lie,
And die because I do not die.

4.   25   The fish leaving the water,
Does not lack relief,
For his death is brief,
And his death is his reward;
What type of death may equal
30   This pitiful life,
If the more I live the more I die?

5.   When I hope to find relief
Seeing You in the Sacrament,
Deeper becomes my pain
35   Not becoming lost in You;
It all adds to my grief,
Not seeing You as I wish,
And die because I do not die.

6.   If I rejoice, O Lord,
40   In hope of seeing You,
Thinking I may lose You
I double my pain;
Living in such dread
And waiting as I wait,
45   *I die because I do not die.*

7.   Release me from this dying,
And give me life, my God,
Do not hold me down
With such a strong weight;
50   I am pining for your sight,
And this illness is so fatal,
That I die because I do not die.

8.   Let me cry at my own death
And mourn my life now
55   As long as it is the crown
By my many sins and crimes.

¡Oh mi Dios!, ¿cuándo será
cuando yo diga de vero:
vivo ya porque no muero?

SIN ARRIMO Y CON ARRIMO
GLOSA DEL MISMO

Sin arrimo y con arrimo,
sin luz y a oscuras viviendo,
todo me voy consumiendo.

1.   Mi alma esta desasida
5   de toda cosa criada,
y sobre sí levantada,
y en una sabrosa vida,
sólo en su Dios arrimada.
Por eso ya se dirá
10   lo cosa que mas estimo,
que mi alma se ve ya
sin arrimo y con arrimo.

2.   Y, aunque tinieblas padezco
en esta vida mortal,
15   no es tan crecido mi mal,
porque, si de luz carezco,
tengo vida celestial;
porque el amor (da) tal vida,
cuando más ciego va siendo,
20   que tiene al alma rendida,
sin luz y a oscuras viviendo.

3.   Hace tal obra el amor
después que le conoci,

O my God! When will it be true
That I will say without lying
Now I live because I am not dying?

*The probable date of composition is before 1578, in Avila. There is a strong similarity
between this poem and others written by St. Teresa de Avila which, according to Yepes,
were written in 1573. It is commonly held that the two saints often challenged one
another to this kind of poetic and spiritual contest. San Juan de la Cruz was St. Teresa's
confessor from 1572 to December 1577 [Sanlúcar ms.].

WITHOUT FEELING OR WITH FEELING*
COMMENTARY, BY THE SAME*

*Without feeling or with feeling,
without light and in darkness living,
all of me is slowly burning.*

1.
     My soul is so detached
5 From these creatures of the world
And upon itself so raised,
Tasting a life so delicate,
That only her God is felt.
This will then clarify
10 What I love the most,
For my soul is not lost
Without feeling or with feeling.

2.
And, though I suffer the dark
In this mortal life
15 My pain is not so keen,
For, if I lack this light,
I have heavenly life;
For love grants such a life,
The more blind it becomes,
20 And it keeps the soul alive,
Without feeling and with feeling.

3.
Love worked such wonders
After I came to know it,

que, si hay bien o mal en mí,
25   todo lo hace de un sabor,
y al alma transforma en sí;
y así, en su llama sabrosa,
la cual en mí estoy sintiendo,
apriesa, sin quedar cosa,
30   *todo me voy consumiendo.*

TRAS DE UN AMOROSO LANCE
OTRAS DEL MISMO A LO DIVINO

Tras de un amoroso lance,
y no de esperanza falto,
volé tan alto, tan alto,
que le dí a la caza alcance.

1.   5   Para que yo alcance diese
a aqueste lance divino,
tanto volar me convino
que de vista me perdiese;
y, con todo, en este trance
10   en el vuelo quedé falto;
mas el amor fué tan alto,
que le dí a la caza alcance.

2.   Cuando más alto subía
deslumbróseme la vista,
15   y la más fuerte conquista
en escuro se hacía;
mas, por ser de amor el lance,
dí un ciego y oscuro salto,
y fuí tan alto, tan alto,
20   *que le dí a la caza alcance.*

3.   Cuanto más alto llegaba
de este lance tan subido,
tanto más bajo y rendido

That if there is good or evil in me,
25 It makes everything taste the same,
Turning the soul to itself;
And thus within its savory flame,
The fire I am now feeling,
Quickly, sparing no pain
30 *All of me is slowly burning.*

*Date uncertain, Jaen ms.

CHASING AFTER LOVE'S HIGH GAME*
OTHER SONGS WITH A DIVINE INTENTION

Chasing after love's high game,
and not lacking in hope,
so high, so high I soared,
that the hunt became my prey.

1. 5 To follow that flight
In chase of the divine,
I had to fly so high
I was lost from sight;
Even then, in this game
10 I fell short in my flight;
But my love flew yet so high,
That the hunt became my prey.

2. The higher I climbed
The more my eyes became blind,
15 My greatest conquest was won
In the deepest black of night;
But to be this love's game,
I gave a blind leap in the dark,
And I flew so high, so high,
20 *That the hunt became my prey.*

3. The higher I climbed
In this high game of love,
The more tired and low,

y abatido me hallaba;
25 dixe:—No habrá quien alcance!—
y abatíme tanto, tanto,
que le dí a la caza alcance.

4.   Por una extraña manera
mil vuelos pasé de un vuelo,
30 porque esperanza del cielo
tanto alcanza cuanto espera;
esperé solo este lance
y en esperar no fuí falto,
pues fuí tan alto, tan alto,
35 *que le dí a la caza alcance.*

POR TODO LA HERMOSURA
GLOSA A LO DIVINO

Por toda la hermosura
nunca yo me perderé,
sino por un no sé qué
que se alcanza por ventura.

1.   5 Sabor de bien que es finito,
lo más que puede llegar
es cansar el apetito
y estragar el paladar;
y así, por toda dulzura
10 nunca yo me perderé,
sino por un no sé qué
que se halla por ventura.

2.   El corazón generoso
nunca cura de parar
15 donde se puede pasar,
sino en más dificultoso;
nada le causa hartura,

The more beaten was my downward plunge;
25   I said: "No one can seize the prey!"
This cast me down so low, so low
That higher and higher I soared,
And the hunt became my prey.

4.   Following a strange course
30   I flew a thousand flights as one,
For the hope of heaven's door
Reaches as high as it hopes;
All my hope is in this love's game
And my hope did not fall short,
35   For so high, so high I soared,
That the hunt became my prey.

★Date uncertain, Sanlúcar ms.

NOT FOR ALL THE BEAUTY★
POEM WITH A DIVINE INTENTION★

Not for all the beauty
will I ever be lost,
but for I-know-not-what
that by fortune I may reach.

1.   5   The taste of what is finite,
Goes only as far
As to weary the appetite
And destroy the taste;
Thus not for sweetness
10   Will I ever be lost,
But for I-know-not-what
That by fortune I may reach.

2.   The generous heart
Never cares to stop
15   Where it is easy to cross,
But tries where it is hard;
Nothing satisfies him,

y sube tanto su fe,
que gusta de un no sé qué
20 *que se halla por ventura.*

3. El que de amor adolesce,
del divino ser tocado,
tiene el gusto tan trocado
que a los gustos desfalle(s)ce;
25 como el que con calentura
fastidia el manjar que ve,
y apetece un no sé qué
que se halla por ventura.

4. No os maravilléis de aquesto,
30 que el gusto se quede tal,
porque es la causa del mal
ajena de todo el resto;
y así, toda criatura
enajenada se ve,
35 y gusta de un no sé qué
que se halla por ventura.

5. Que estando la voluntad
de Divinidad tocada,
no puede quedar pagada
40 sino con Divinidad;
mas, por ser tal su hermosura
que solo se ve por fe,
gústala en un no sé qué
que se halla por ventura.

6. 45 Pues, de tal enamorado,
decidme si habréis dolor,
pues que no tiene sabor
entre todo lo criado;
solo, sin forma y figura,
50 sin hallar arrimo y pie,
gustando allá un no sé qué
que se halla por ventura.

And with faith he climbs so high,
That he tastes I-know-not-what
20 *That by fortune I may reach.*

3.   He who is pierced by love,
        Or touched by the divine,
        Has his taste so changed
        That to all taste he is dead;
25   As someone may leave
        The food he sees when sick,
        And craves for I-know-not-what
        That by fortune I may reach.

4.   Do not be surprised
30   That taste be thus changed,
        For the cause of this evil
        Is alien to all the rest;
        Thus every creature
        Sees itself estranged,
35   And tastes I-know-not-what
        That by fortune I may reach.

5.   For as soon as the will
        Is touched from above,
        It cannot be satisfied
40   But with the divine;
        Its beauty being such
        That only faith may show it,
        For it tastes of I-know-not-what
        That by fortune I may reach.

6.   45   Tell me if for such a lover,
        You will feel any pain,
        For he finds no pleasure
        Among created things;
        Alone, with no figure or shape,
50   Without company or even memory,
        Except the taste of I-know-not-what
        That by fortune I may reach.

7.   No penséis que el interior,
        que es de mucha más valía,
   55   halla gozo y alegría
        en lo que acá da sabor;
        mas sobre toda hermosura,
        y lo que es y será y fué,
        gusta de allá un no sé qué
   60   *que se halla por ventura.*

8.   Mas emplea su cuidado
        quien se quiere aventajar
        en lo que está por ganar
        que en lo que tiene ganado;
   65   y así, para más altura,
        yo siempre me inclinaré
        sobre todo a un no sé qué
        que se halla por ventura.

9.   Por lo que por el sentido
   70   puede acá comprehenderse
        y todo lo que entenderse,
        aunque sea muy subido,
        ni por gracia y hermosura
        yo nunca me perderé,
   75   sino por un no sé qué
        que se halla por ventura.—Fin.

7.   Do not think that the soul,
That is worth much more,
  55 Finds joy and happiness
In what on earth gives taste;
It is beyond beauty,
In what is, was or will be,
That it tastes I-know-not-what
  60 *That by fortune I may reach.*

8.   Whoever wants to advance
Would better use care
In what is left to gain
Than in what he has already won;
  65 And thus aiming for the heights,
I will always try
For that I-know-not-what
That by fortune I may reach.

9.   What comes through the senses
  70 And may here be understood
And whatever may be learned,
Even though very high,
Not for all that beauty
Will I ever be lost,
  75 But for that I-know-not-what
That by fortune I may reach.—Finis.

*Date uncertain, Jaen ms.

PART THREE

The Prose (Excerpts and Commentary)

PRAYER OF THE SOUL IN LOVE

Lord, God, my love! If You still remember my sins, and thus avoid granting what I ask of You, perform in them, my God, your will, for this is what I want most. Practice your goodness and compassion and You will be known through them. But if it is my works You are waiting for to grant my prayer, then give them to me, work them out Yourself with all the sufferings You can bear, and let it be done so. But if it is not my works You are waiting for, what is it, my most clement Lord? Why are You taking so long? If, in the end, it is grace and compassion I need, as I ask You through your Son (2 Tim. 1:2), then take my "penny," since You want it, and grant me those gifts for You also want them. Who can get rid of this base life if You do not raise him to You in purity of love, my God? How can the man conceived and raised in the lowest form of life climb up to You, if You do not raise him, Lord, by the hand You created yourself? (Ps. 118:73) You will not be able to take away from me, my Lord, what you once gave me in your only Son Jesus Christ, in whom You gave me all I want (Rom. 8:22; Pet. 1:3–4). Thus I am assured You will not take long, if I wait. Oh soul, what excuses do you use to wait, for, after all, you may love God in your heart? Mine are the heavens, and mine is the earth; mine are the people; mine are the just and the sinners; the angels are mine, the Mother of God, and all things are mine; God himself is mine and for me, for Christ is mine and He is all things for me. Therefore, what are you looking for, soul? All this belongs to you, and all this is for you (Luke 15:31; 1 Cor. 3:22–23). Do not think of yourself as worth little, or be content with the crumbs from your father's table. Come out and enjoy your own glory. Hide within it, relish it, thus you will attain the prayers of your heart (Ps. 36:4).[1]

from *Sayings of Light and Love*

THE ASCENT
OF
MOUNT CARMEL

This treatise deals with the way a soul should ready itself to reach divine union in a short time. It presents very valuable instruction and doctrine for beginners and proficients alike, that they may learn to rid themselves of all temporal things and not become burdened with spiritual attachments in order to be able to reach that complete nakedness and freedom of spirit needed for divine union.

THEME

The whole doctrine I intend to discuss in this treatise, "The Ascent of Mount Carmel," is summarized in the following stanzas. They describe the way to climb to the top of this mountain—that high state of perfection we here call union of the soul with God. Since my way of proceeding is to use these stanzas as a basis for all I shall say, I am going to write them down here in full, so that at a glance they may be seen and understood as a summary of what I am about to write; I will quote each stanza separately before its explanation, and give the verses of each stanza separately, as the subject and explanations so require.

PROLOGUE TO
"THE ASCENT OF MOUNT CARMEL" AND
"DARK NIGHT"

A greater light of knowledge and experience than mine is needed to make understood this dark night through which the soul journeys to reach that divine light of perfect union with the love of God, as it can be experienced in this life. The sufferings and trials, as much spiritual as temporal, ordinarily befalling those fortunate souls that they may reach this high state of perfection are so many and deep that no amount of human knowledge is sufficient to understand them, nor is there sufficient experience to be able to talk about them. And those who go through this experience may feel it, but not talk about it adequately.

I will not trust, therefore, experience or science when saying something about this dark night, for they may fall short and deceive us. But I will not neglect to make use of both in whatever way I may find useful. And in those matters that are important and most obscure I will help myself to the Sacred Scripture to be able to say what, with divine favor, I ought to say. Taking Scripture as our guide we cannot err, for the Holy Spirit speaks to us through it. And if I should fall into error by not being able to understand well what I speak about either quoting the Scripture or not quoting it, be it understood that it is not my intention to deviate from the holy meaning and doctrine of the Holy Mother the Catholic Church. And if that be the case, I subject and resign myself totally to its command, and even to that of anyone who may judge more competently of this matter than I.

In setting all this down in writing, I have not been moved by my own capacity to achieve something so difficult, but by my trust in God. He will help me explain this matter because of the great need many souls have of it. For though these souls have started on the road of virtue, and our Lord desires to place them in the dark night so they may move on to divine union, they do not advance. At times these souls do not wish to enter the dark night or allow themselves to be ushered in, perhaps for lack of understanding or suitable and alert guides to lead them to the top of the mountain. Thus, it is a pity to see so many souls to whom God has given talents and favors to advance further, content to deal with God in a lowly method of communion, either because they do not wish it to be otherwise, or because they do not know better, or are not helped through guidance to break away from earlier ways, for if these souls wanted to proceed further they would reach this high state of perfection. For even if our Lord comes to their rescue by depriving them of this or that consolation and makes them advance, they arrive much later, with much more effort, and with less merit, for they have failed to adapt themselves to God by allowing Him to place them freely on the true and pure path of union. For even if God leads them—for He can do so without their cooperation—they fight his lead. Thus, they travel less road by resisting the one carrying them, and gain less merit by not applying their will, and thus they suffer even more. There are souls who, instead of abandoning themselves to God and thus helping themselves, hamper Him by indiscreet actions or lack of actions, resembling children who kick and cry when their mothers want to carry them in their arms; they protest demanding to walk on their own feet when they can hardly walk, or can only do so at a child's pace.[2]

With God's help, therefore, we will offer doctrine and advice both to beginners and those more proficient, to help them understand or at least to allow themselves to be carried by God when His Majesty wishes thus to make them advance. Some spiritual directors, lacking light and experience of these paths, are more likely to be a hindrance than a help to these souls when placing them on the path. They are like the builders of the Tower of Babel (Gen. 11:1–9), unable to provide the proper materials for its construction because they failed to understand the language spoken to them, and thus nothing was built. It is hard for a soul facing such decisions not to be able to understand herself, nor find anyone who can understand her. For God may take a soul by the highest way of dark contemplation and spiritual dryness where the soul finds herself lost and, while in this state of darkness and sufferings, of trials and temptations, someone will approach, in the style of Job's consolers (Job 4:8–11), and proclaim that all this is the result of melancholy, depression, temperament, or perhaps some hidden sin, and that God has abandoned her. Thus their private judgment is that this soul must have been wicked, since she is afflicted with such sufferings.

There will be others who will tell these souls they are sliding backward, for they find no comfort and taste, as they previously did, in their spiritual practice. Thus, they double the effort of the poor soul, for the soul's greatest suffering is caused by knowing her own miseries; it is at these times that the soul sees with more clarity than the light of day that she is full of evil and sin, for God himself provides this light of knowledge in the night of contemplation (as I shall show later). When a soul in such a condition finds someone who agrees that all her troubles are her own fault, then her sufferings and distress grow without bound, and she feels, then, worse than death. These spiritual directors, in judging these trials to be the result of sin, force such poor souls to rummage through their lives and make many general confessions, and thus they crucify these souls once again. They do not understand that this is not the time to stir things up, but to let those poor souls experience the purgation God is working on them, giving them comfort and encouragement to endure their sufferings for as long as God wills it, for there is not much those souls can do or the director can say under such circumstances.

We will with divine help talk of these things, and also how these souls should behave under such circumstances; and how the spiritual director should deal with those souls; also of the signs that appear to be able to be known if we are dealing with this purgation of the soul; and if this purgation is of the senses or of the spirit, what we call the dark night of the spirit; and also how to know if we are dealing with melancholy or some other imperfection of the senses or the spirit. For there are always souls*—or their confessors—who think that God is leading them along this road of the dark night of spiritual purgation, when in fact it is only some imperfection in those souls. Likewise, many people think they are lacking in prayer, when in fact they are not; while others think highly of their prayer while in fact they have none.

It is also sad to see so many souls work and struggle so much to end by sliding backward; they set the goal of their improvement and yet there is no improvement, but rather a hindrance to improvement. There are other souls who profit greatly in rest and quiet. There are some souls who allow themselves to be encumbered by the very presents and favors God grants them to proceed forward, and go nowhere.

There are, besides, many other signs coming to those traveling on this road—joy, sorrow, hope, pain; some coming from perfection, some from imperfection. We will try, with divine help, to say something about all these points, so that those reading this book may see, in some fashion, the road they themselves travel, and the one they ought to, if they intend to reach the top of this mountain.

The doctrine I am explaining here—how the soul must go to God through a dark night—may itself be obscure to the reader, and this is no surprise. This, I believe, will be the case at the beginning of the reading, but as soon as the reader proceeds further it will be easier to understand, for by understanding his own soul he will understand what it is meant by the dark night. Then, if the work is read a second time, the subject will seem clearer and the doctrine sounder. If some people, however, still find difficulty in understanding this doctrine, it will be the fault of my lack of knowledge and poor style, for the subject in itself is good and very necessary. It seems to me that even if it were written with greater perfection and completeness than it is here, only a few would profit by it, for we are not writing here on moral and pleasing subjects addressed to the type of spiritual person who likes to reach God by tasting sweet and pleasing things. We are dealing here with a substantial and solid doctrine applicable to everyone who wishes to reach this nakedness of the spirit about which I am writing.

My main intention is not to address everyone, but only some of the people of our holy order of the primitive observance of Mount Carmel, both friars and nuns. It is at their request that I am writing, for God has already chosen them and put them on the path leading to this mountain. Since these people are already removed from the temporal things of this world they will more easily understand this doctrine of the nakedness of the spirit.[3]

SECTION ONE:
A PHENOMENOLOGY OF HUMAN APPETITES

How they bind and cause anguish in the soul, and how they must be purified through the dark night—excerpts

Chapter Six

For the sake of gaining a clearer and fuller understanding of what it is being said, it will be to everyone's good to write down how these appetites[4] cause two main harms in the soul: The first is that they deprive the soul of God's Spirit, and the second, that they tire, torment, cover with shadows, dirty, and weaken the soul. Jeremiah says as much when he writes: *Duo mala fecit populus meus, derelinquerunt fontem aquae vivae, et foderunt sibi cisternas dissipatas, quae con-*

tinere non valent aquas They have forsaken Me, the fountain of living water, and dug for themselves leaking cisterns that hold no water (Jer. 2:13). These two evils, privation and its positive contrary, are caused by any inordinate act of the appetites. It is obvious, referring to privation, that to the same degree that the soul is attached to anything pertaining to creatures of this earth, and to the degree this appetite gains substance in the soul, to that same degree the capacity of the soul to love God is diminished. . . .

Let us speak now of the second effect the appetites have on the soul—this being, as mentioned, that they tire, torture, darken, dirty, and weaken the soul. There are five things I wish to mention.

It is obvious the appetites tire and exhaust the soul. They are like ill-bred little children always asking from their mother, but never satisfied. . . . The soul becomes tired and exhausted by her appetites, for she is wounded, moved, and disturbed by them like water by the winds, and thus remains in continual agitation, not being allowed to rest in any one place or in any one thing. Isaiah wrote: *Cor impii quasi mare fervens* The heart of the evil man is like the boiling sea (Isa. 57:20). Evil is the man who does not conquer his appetites. The soul grows tired and exhausted when chasing her appetites. It is like being hungry and opening one's mouth to fill one self with air, rather than its proper food. Jeremiah says in this regard: *In desiderio animae suae attraxit ventum amoris sui* In the appetite of its soul it brought to itself the wind of its own affection (Jer. 2:24). . . .

Chapter Seven

As a second consequence the appetites cause the soul harm through torture and anguish. It is like someone tied by ropes to a post, suffering a torture that will not end until he is freed from those ropes. David said: *Funes peccatorum circumplexi sunt me* The ropes of my sins [that is, my appetites] have me bound all over (Ps. 119:61). Something similar happens when one lies naked over thorns and nails, which is the case of the afflicted and tormented soul when she lies over her appetites; they wound, lacerate, scratch, hurt the soul like thorns. David also writes of these souls: *Circumdederunt me sicut apes, et exarserunt sicut ignis in spinis* They surrounded me like bees, stinging me, and turned against me like fire on thorns (Ps. 117:12); for the fire of anguish and torment grows through the appetites. . . .

Chapter Eight

The third consequence of the appetites on the soul is to blind and darken her. It is like fog darkening the air and not letting the clear sun through, or like fog on a mirror not letting a face be seen clearly, or like water mixed with slime which does not allow the face looking at it to be clearly reflected; thus in the soul taken over by the appetites, her intellect is darkened and makes no room for the sun of natural reason nor the sun of God's supernatural wisdom to come through and spread clarity. . . .

Appetites darken and blind the soul because they are blind. They lack understanding in themselves, for reason is to them like the blind leading the blind. . . . Of little use are the eyes to the tiny moth, for its appetite for the beauty of the light drives her unthinkingly to burn in the fire. We may also say that those feeding their own appetites are like unknowing fish; their enchantment is like darkness to them, for it does not enable them to see the harms fishermen are preparing at their expense. . . .

. . . This is exactly what appetites do to the soul. They light up concupiscence and enchant the intellect so that no light is visible. The reason for this enchantment of the soul is that it sets another light in front of the eyes; our sense of sight feeds on it and forgets all other lights. The appetites appear to the soul to be as close as if they were inside of her, thus the soul stumbles on this first light and feeds on it; no other light is visible from the intellect or anywhere else, nor will it be seen until the soul removes from in front the fatuous lights of the appetites.[5]

It is, therefore, sad to see the ignorance of those who burden themselves with extraordinary penances and many voluntary exercises; they think this ought to be sufficient to bring them to union with divine Wisdom, even if they do not try to deny their appetites with diligence. . . .[6]

Chapter Nine

The appetites cause a fourth harm to the soul: they defile and dirty her. As it is said in Scripture: *Qui tetigerit picem, inquinabitur ab ea.* Whoever touches tar will get dirty by it (Eccles. 13:1). Whenever we touch another creature to fill the appetite of our will, we touch tar. And notice how Scripture compares creatures to tar. . . . ; if we were to place warmed-up gold or diamonds on tar, they would also become ugly and smeared as a result of the attraction of heat, and in the same manner would the soul warm by the heat of appetite toward any creature; all it brings away from such contact is dirt and stains.[7] There is, however, an even greater difference between the soul and other corporal creatures than between a very clear liquid and very dirty slime; were we to mix the slime with such clear liquid it would become dirty, as happens with the soul when it becomes dirty through contact with creatures, for in such contact it becomes similar to that creature. . . .

Chapter Ten

The fifth point concerning the way souls are dirtied by the appetites is that they weaken the soul and make her flaccid, removing any strength to continue and persevere on the path of virtue. It is the case that the power of appetites becomes divided among the many things it desires, and is less strong than if it remained whole addressing one single thing. The more it shares its power with many things, the less there remains for each. Philosophers say that a united virtue is stronger than a dispersed one.[8] . . . Just as when hot water not contained in a covered pot loses its heat, and just as perfumes from within open bottles lose their strength of fragrance, so the soul when not gathered within the one and only appetite for God loses its heat and vigor toward virtue. . . .

SECTION TWO:
THE DARK NIGHT

Excerpts from "The Ascent of Mount Carmel," giving a description of the dark night; its nature, its movements in the lower and higher parts of the soul.

Chapter One

> On a dark night,
> Anxious, by love inflamed,
> —O Joyous chance!—
> I left not seen or discovered,
> My house at last completely quiet.

The soul sings in this first stanza of her joyous chance and good fortune when leaving all things behind to emerge, rid of her appetites and imperfections. . . . To understand how this comes about, it is necessary to know that for a soul to reach the state of perfection she must pass through two different types of "nights." Spiritual fathers call these nights purgations or purifications of the soul. I call them both "nights" because the soul must travel through both in the dark, as if by night.

The first night, or purgation, to which this stanza refers, and which is also the theme of the first part of this book, is the sensory part of the soul. The second night, referred to in the stanza that follows, is the spiritual part of the soul. We will comment on it in the second and third sections of this book, speaking of it in its active phase. In the fourth section we will discuss this night in its passive phase.[9]

The first night belongs to beginners, at the time when God introduces them to the state of contemplation. We will explain in due time how this night extends also to the spirit. The second night or purification belongs to those already advanced in contemplation, at the time when God introduces them to the state of divine union. This purgation is more obscure, darker, and more frightening, as we will in due course point out.

COMMENTARY ON THE STANZA

The soul wishes to declare in summary, in this stanza, that she emerged—that God brought her out[10]—only on account of her love for Him. She is inflamed with his love on a dark night. This is the privation and purgation of all sensuous appetites for all external things of this world, and of those that were pleasurable to the flesh, and of all the desires of the will. All this happens in this purgation of the senses; for this reason the poem claims that the soul was leaving "when my house was at last completely quiet." It refers here to the sensory part of the soul, all her appetites quiet and asleep, and the soul with them; for the soul is not freed from the sufferings and anguish of the appetites until they are silenced and asleep. . . .

It was a "joyous chance" to be placed by God in this night that produced so much good. The soul would have never found the door to this night by herself, as no soul by herself may find the way to empty herself of all appetites in order to reach God.

Chapter Two

Describes what kind of "night" this is through which the soul passes to reach union with God.

On a dark night,

There are three reasons for calling this journey to union with God a *night*. The first refers to the point of origin, the point from which the soul comes, for it must deprive itself of appetites (taste) for the things of this world, thus denying them. This negation and privation is like night for the senses. The second refers to the means or road taken for the soul to journey to this divine union. This road is faith, and this faith is like dark night to the intellect. The third reason refers to the point of arrival, namely God. And He is actually dark night for the soul in this life. . . .

We find these three nights in the Book of Tobias (Tb. 6:18–22) where we read how the angel asked the young Tobias to wait three nights before union with his wife. On the first night he was asked to burn the fish heart on the fire. This signifies the human heart that is attached to the things of this world. . . .

On the second night Tobias was told that he would enter the company of the holy patriarchs, the fathers of the faith. For as soon as the soul passes through the first night . . . it enters the second night, living by faith alone . . . with no relation to the senses.

On the third night the angel promised that he would "receive the blessing," which means God. God operates through the second night, that is faith, by communicating to the soul secretly and intimately, and this is another night for the soul since communication is more obscure than it was previously. . . . After this third night, that is, when God has finished his communication to the spirit in the deepest darkness, comes the union with the spouse, that is, God's wisdom. The angel told Tobias that "after the third night he would join his wife with the fear of the Lord. . . .

These three parts of the night are but one night; but, like the real night, it is divided into three parts. The first one, the night of the senses, is the early part of the night when the soul is deprived of the attraction of things; the second part, faith, is like midnight, totally in the dark; and the third, towards the early morning hours, is God, when the light is about to arrive. . . .

Chapter Three

Here we call *night* the privation of taste in the appetite for things of the world. Night is no more than the privation of day and, by extension, of all objects that may be seen by light. . . . We can also say that mortifying our appetites is like night for the soul, for through privation of taste in the appetite for things the soul remains in the dark and empty. . . .

. . . This is the reason we call this nakedness night for the soul. We are not dealing here, however, with the actual privation of things—this would not make the soul naked, for the appetite for them would still cover it. We are dealing with the nakedness of the taste and appetite for things. Only this nakedness leaves the soul free and empty of things, even when surrounded by things. The soul, in fact, is not busy with the things of this world, nor do they cause the soul any harm, for the only thing that enters the soul is the will and appetite for them.[11]

THE DARK NIGHT: PASSIVE NIGHT
OF THE SENSES

Chapter Eight

On a dark night,

This night, which we call contemplation, is the source of two kinds of darkness or purgation in spiritual people, according to the two parts of the soul, the sensory and the spiritual. . . .

The first purgation or night is bitterly frightening to the senses, as we shall soon see. This, however, is nothing in comparison to the second, which is horrible and even more frightening to the spirit. . . .

Beginners conduct themselves in a lowly way when dealing with the path of God, too close to their own self-love and willfulness (as earlier explained). It is these people God wishes to draw forth from this low way of love and lead to a higher state of love. . . . Thus, He leaves them in such darkness that they do not know which way to turn with the faculty of discursive imaginings. They are unable to advance one step through their meditation, as they used to before, now that the inner faculty is flooded with these nights. This leaves them in such inner dryness that they not only do not taste and enjoy spiritual matters and spiritual practice as they used to, but they find these practices distasteful and bitter. For, as I have said, when God sees that they have grown a little, He weans them so that they gain in strength and leave behind their swaddling clothes; He puts them down from His arms so that they grow accustomed to walking on their feet. This sudden change disorients these souls, for now their whole world seems to be running backward. . . .[12]

The reason for this dryness is that God changes His gifts and strength from the senses to the spirit. Since the senses are not capable of tasting the gifts of the spirit, they are left famished, dry, and empty. The senses have no sensing power for the things of the pure spirit; thus, while the spirit is sensitized, the flesh is starved and turns weak in its activities. But the spirit so sensitized grows stronger and more alert, and becomes more careful than before about not failing God. . . .

Yet, as I have just said, when this aridity is the outcome of the purgative way on the sensory appetite, even though the spirit may not in the beginning have any feeling, it feels the strength and vigor to work through the sustenance provided by the inner food; this inner food is the beginning of dark and dry contemplation for the senses. This contemplation, though secret and hidden to the one receiving it (as it happens in most cases), together with the dryness and emptiness it bestows on the senses, produces a desire in the soul to remain alone and in quiet; the soul is then unable to think of any particular thing, and even the desire to do so is absent. It is then that if those to whom this happens are able to remain quiet, if they do not care to perform any interior or exterior act, or feel the need to do anything, that in this abandonment and leisure they will feel a consistent inner nourishment. This nourishment is so delicate that if anyone wishes to try to experience it, ordinarily he cannot, for, as I said, it operates when the soul is most at rest and abandoned; it is like air, it escapes as soon as we try to grasp it within our hand.

Chapter Twelve

The Benefits This Night Causes in the Soul.

. . . The truth is that the soul did not know of her own misery. When she was walking about as on a cloud, finding great joy, consolation, and comfort in God, she believed she was serving God somehow . . . but as soon as the soul dons these other working clothes of dryness and desolation, and her former lights have been darkened, she becomes richer with those very same lights in the most excellent and necessary virtue of self-knowledge. She considers herself to be nothing, and finds no satisfaction in herself, for it is obvious the soul cannot by herself act, is not able to do anything. . . .

. . . Job was not readied to speak with Him out of the delights and joys he was accustomed to experience in His presence, as he narrates (Job 1:1–8), but was readied by being kept naked in a pigsty, abandoned and even persecuted by his friends, full of anguish, bitterness, the soil about him covered with worms (Job 2:8, 30:17–18). It is only under these circumstances that He who raises the poor from the dunghill (Ps. 113:7), the most high God, was

pleased to descend and speak face to face with him, and reveal the
high mysteries of His Wisdom, to a degree never before done in the
time of Job's prosperity (Job? 38–41) . . . .

. . . We conclude, therefore, that self-knowledge flows first
from this dry night. It is from this knowledge, as a foundation, that
the other knowledge, that of God, proceeds. . . .

. . . In a desert land, without water, dry and without a way, I
appeared before You to be able to see Your virtue and Your glory
(Ps. 63:2–3). David's teaching is here very fitting, for the means to
the knowledge of the glory of God were not the many spiritual
consolations and gratifications he was accustomed to but the dryness
and aridity of his senses, as indicated by the expression "In a desert
land, without water." As in the previous instance, David does not
clearly explain that the experience and vision of the virtue of God
does not come through concepts, not even through walking the
discursive road of imagination, of which he had made extensive
use—this is what is meant in the quotation "land without a way." To
know both God and oneself, this dark night with its dryness and
emptiness is the way, though not with the fullness and power of the
other night of the spirit, for this knowledge is only the beginning of
that other.

Chapter Fourteen

. . . Such is the night and purgation of the *senses* in the soul. And for
those who are to proceed to that other, more grave night of the *spirit*
(for only the few rather than the many carry on), toward divine
union, this night is accompanied by heavy burdens and sensual
temptations, lasting a long time, for some more than for others. For
some have constantly present the angel of Satan (2 Cor. 12:7), that is,
the spirit of fornication, to stir their senses with abominable and
strong temptations, stirring their spirit with dirty suggestions and
representations vividly imprinted in the imagination to the point of
causing more pain to those souls than death itself.

At other times the spirit of blasphemy makes itself present in
this night. There is no thought or idea not accompanied by intolerable blasphemies, and they are at times so vividly suggested to the
imagination that these people are almost forced to say them, and this

causes them grave torment. Other times these souls are visited by another spirit which Isaiah calls the *spiritum vertiginis* (spirit of confusion) (Isa. 19:14), not because it brings those souls down but because it keeps them in activity. This spirit so blinds the senses that the souls are filled with scruples and indecisions; these seem so intricate that such people find no way to reach satisfaction in the soul, nor to make judgments about any advice or concept. This is one of the most burdensome stimuli and horrors of this night, very similar to what happens in the night of the spirit. . . .[13]

BOOK TWO

Excerpts dealing with the more intimate purgation, which is the second (passive) night of the spirit.

Chapter One

Those souls God plans to carry further in the spiritual life, are not immediately placed by Him in this *night of the spirit* as soon as they have left the dryness and obstacles of the first purgation or *night of the senses*. Rather, they usually spend a long time, even years, exercising in this state of proficiency after having emerged from the state of the beginners. These souls feel as if they had just come out of a very narrow jail and walk about the things of God with more ease, feeling more satisfaction and interior joy in the soul than they did at the beginning of the journey, before they entered this dark night. Their discursive faculties and imagination are no longer bound, and feel as free as they used to. Very soon, they find in their souls a very serene and loving contemplation full of spiritual relish, with no effort whatsoever from the faculties. Nonetheless, since the purgation of the soul is not complete (the purgation of the main part, the spirit, is still lacking, and without it the purgation of the senses, however strong it may have been, is incomplete because of the union between these two parts of the soul which form one single whole), some desires, aridities, darkness, and conflicts are felt. These are at times far more intense than those of the past, and appear as omens or messengers of the coming night of the spirit. . . .

God purges some souls in this manner, for they are not destined to climb to so lofty a degree of love as other souls. He seems to alternate the night of contemplation and the night of purgation in these souls, where as often as the dawn rises it becomes dark night. This is as David said: "He sends *His crystal,*" meaning contemplation, "in tiny bites" (Ps. 147:17). These tiny bites of dark contemplation are never as intense as that frightful night of contemplation we are about to speak of, into which God purposely places the soul in order to be able to carry her to divine union. . . .

Chapter Three

. . . For God wishes in fact to strip these souls of the habits of the *old* man and clothe them with the habits of the *new*. The Apostle wrote (Col. 3:9–10) that God strips their faculties, affections, and senses, both spiritual and sensuous, interior and exterior; He leaves the intellect in the dark, the will dry, the memory empty, and the affections of the soul in deep affliction, bitterness, and indecision, by depriving the soul of the feeling and satisfaction she previously experienced from spiritual practice. This privation thus becomes one of the required conditions for the soul, so that the form of the spirit, which is the union of love, may enter the soul and be united with her. The Lord works all this in the soul through pure and dark contemplation, as is indicated in the poem's first stanza. . . .[14]

Chapter Four
The First Stanza

On a dark night,
Anxious, by love inflamed,
—O joyous chance!—
I left not seen or discovered,
My house at last completely quiet.

COMMENTARY

We must understand this stanza now to refer to contemplative purgation, or nakedness and poverty of spirit (these being about the same). We may now comment on it, hearing the soul speak thus:

In poverty, abandoned, without any help from the perceptions of my soul (my intellect in darkness, my will undecided, my memory in affliction and anguish), left in the dark with only pure faith, (for this is *dark night* for these natural faculties), with only my will touched by pain and anguish, and *anxious for love* of God, I came out of *myself* (my low manner of understanding, my feeble way of loving, and my poor and limited way of savoring God), and I did this unhindered either by my own sensuality or the devil.

This was a great *joy* and my good *chance,* for as soon as the operations of my faculties stopped, and the affections of my passions, appetites, and desires quieted down (upon which I based in a low manner my feeling and taste for God) I came out of my human way of operating and acting and began to operate and act with God. That is, my intellect left itself, turning from human and natural to divine, for being united to God through this purgation, it no longer understood by its own natural light and power, but through the divine wisdom to which it was joined. My will left itself and became divine; united with divine love it no longer loves in a low manner through its natural power, but with the power and purity of the Holy Spirit; thus the will set next to God does not operate in a human way. In the same manner, my memory is now touched by eternal perceptions of glory. . . .

Chapter Five

Yet a question arises: why, if this is a divine light (for, as we claim, it lights up and purges the soul from her ignorance), is it called here a *dark night*? Two reasons may be given as to why this wisdom is not only night and darkness to the soul, but also pain and torture. First, because of the height of divine wisdom—far in excess of the ability of the soul. Second, because of the low state and impurity of the soul—this is painful, afflictive, and is darkness to the soul.

. . . When this light of contemplation enters a soul not yet entirely enlightened, it produces in her spiritual darkness, for not only does this light overpower the soul, but it deprives and darkens its own power to act from its natural intelligence. This is the reason St. Dionysius and other mystical theologians call this infused contemplation a *ray of darkness;* that is, for the soul not yet purged and enlightened. This great supernatural light overcomes and deprives the intellect of its natural power. David said something similar: Clouds and darkness are near God and surround Him (Ps. 18:12)— and not because this is how it is in reality. . . .

The second way in which the soul suffers is caused by her natural, moral, and spiritual weakness. For this divine contemplation enters the soul with a certain force in order to strengthen and subdue her; and the soul suffers so much in feeling her own weakness that she almost collapses, particularly at times when the divine contemplation enters with greater power. Both the sensory and spiritual parts of the soul, feeling as if they were under a heavy and threatening load, agonize to such a degree that the soul would take death as a relief and choice. . . .

Chapter Six

. . . Divine light enters the soul to cook her [*sic*] and make her divine by this transformation, stripping her of the habitual acts and properties of the old man to which she is so united, attached, and reduced. The spiritual substance of the soul is so cut up and boiled down, she is so deeply absorbed in a mysterious and deep darkness at the sight of her own dissolution and her own melting down in the face of these miseries, that she experiences a cruel spiritual death. It feels as if a large beast had swallowed her and she were being digested in its belly; her anguish is comparable to Jonah's in the belly of the whale (Jon. 2:1–3). It is necessary for the soul to lie in this tomb of dark death so that her spiritual resurrection may take place.

David describes this passion and pain, though in truth it is beyond description, when he says: The sighs of death encircled me, the sorrows of hell surrounded me, in my tribulation I cried out (Ps. 17:5–7). But what causes the most pain to the soul is the conviction that God has rejected her, and that out of contempt she has been cast into darkness. This thought that God has abandoned the soul is a heavy and painful suffering . . . for when this purgative contemplation lays siege to the soul, she feels in the raw the shadow and sighs of death and the pains of hell. This translates for the soul into feeling abandoned by God, punished, rejected, and unworthy, and she also feels as if God were annoyed. All this is felt inside, and the soul feels it will last forever.

God accomplishes all this by means of dark contemplation. The soul not only suffers the emptiness and privation of these natural aids and sensations, which is a terrible anguish (like hanging in midair, unable to breathe), but she is also purged by this contemplation. This contemplation destroys, empties, consumes in the soul all the affections and imperfect habits she has acquired throughout its life, just as fire consumes the tarnish and rust of metals. Since these habits and affections are so deeply embedded in the substance of the soul, she feels deep bereavement and inner torments on top of the privation and spiritual emptiness. Ezechiel's authority is here verified when he said: Heap together the bones, and I shall burn them in the fire, the flesh shall be consumed, and the whole composition burned, and the bones destroyed (Ezek. 24:10).[15] He refers here to the pain felt at the emptiness and privation of the soul, in both her parts, the sensuous and the spiritual. And he adds: Place it also thus empty on the embers that its metal may become hot and melt and its uncleanness be taken away from it and its rust consumed (*Ezek.* 24:11). This spells out clearly the heavy affliction the soul suffers from the purgation caused by the fire of contemplation. As the prophet says, to get rid of the rust of the affections the soul must, in a certain way, destroy and undo herself in the same measure that her passions and imperfections are embodied in her.

Chapter Eleven

Anxious, by love inflamed,

In the above line the soul speaks of the fire of love which, like fire on wood, burns up the soul in this night of painful contemplation. . . .
. . . This fire of love burns in the spirit so that the soul caught in the midst of dark indecisions feels itself deeply wounded by a strong, divine love, with a certain feeling and inkling of God. . . .
All the appetites and energies of the soul are gathered together in this inflamation of love, while the soul herself is wounded, and becomes touched and passionate with the collected power of all; what will be the movements of all these energies and appetites as soon as the soul realizes she is inflamed and wounded by divine love, and yet not able to gain possession and satisfaction of this love in her

state of doubt and darkness? No doubt they will suffer hunger, like a dog, as David says: The dogs surrounded the city and, not being filled with this love, they are left howling and sighing (Ps. 59:6, 14). For the touch of this divine love so dries up the spirit,[16] and simultaneously kindles the soul's appetites to quench the thirst she feels for this divine love, that the soul turns herself around a thousand times and turns to God equally often with the greed and desire of her appetites. David makes this understandable when he says: My soul thirsts for You; in how many ways does my flesh long for You (Ps. 62:2)—that is, in its desires. Another translation puts it this way: My soul thirsts for You; my soul loses itself or dies for You.

. . . Yet, it is in the midst of these dark pains of love that the soul feels a certain company and energy inside her. This gives the soul so much support and strength that if this burden of the dark night were removed the soul would feel, as often happens, alone, empty and weak. The reason for this is that the power and efficacy of the dark fire of love entering the soul produces these effects; as soon as this fire stops so does the darkness and the strength and warmth of love in the soul.

SECOND STANZA

> In the darkness, with light,
> By the secret ladder, disguised,
> —O joyous chance!—
> I left in the darkness, covered,
> My house at last completely quiet.

Chapter Sixteen

In the darkness, with light,

This *darkness* of which the soul speaks relates to the appetites, and to the sensory, spiritual, and interior faculties. All these faculties become dark with respect to their natural light in this night, and by purging them they may receive the supernatural light. All sensuous and spiritual appetites fall asleep, and are silenced, unable to taste the divine or the human; the affections of the soul remain oppressed and deadened, unable to move closer or find consolation in anything; the imagination remains bound and unable to proceed; memory is emptied; the intellect is dark, unable to understand anything; and the will dries up and feels bound. All the faculties feel empty and useless. And over all this hangs a thick and heavy cloud on the soul, making her feel anguished and separated from God. Thus, the soul proclaims here that in the dark she moved with light. . . .[17]

Therefore, if spiritual communion does not come from above, from the Father of lights (James 1:17), from above human free will and appetites, the soul will not taste this communion in a divine and spiritual manner, but humanly and naturally, regardless of how much her human faculties are turned to God and how much satisfaction the soul finds in this exercise. Spiritual communion does not proceed from man to God, but from God to man. Perhaps this is the place to explain how many people derive great affections and consolations by applying their faculties to God or to spiritual matters and how they think their actions are supernatural and spiritual, while in fact they are the consequence of merely natural and human appetites. These people are naturally gifted at moving their natural and human faculties towards anything, and in the same manner they move them toward spiritual matters.

The other reason why the soul walks with light when she walks thus in the dark, and why she keeps on improving and gaining, is because ordinarily all this happens where the soul least expects it, and thus does not understand; the soul usually feels she is losing her way. For the soul has never had this new experience which forces her to come out, blinded and lost with regard to her previous manner of procedure. Thus she thinks she is lost rather than gaining and advancing, for the soul feels a real loss about what she previously knew and liked, and finds herself in a place she does not know or like. This is similar to the traveler going to places not previously known, and walking paths that are not only new but unknown to others previously. He walks on these paths not guided by what he previously knew, but in doubt and counting on the words of others. It is obvious this traveler could not travel in new lands or learn more than he previously knew were he not able to leave aside the paths he knows already. It is the same in any task or art: as one keeps on learning more details through practice, one travels in the dark, not because of what one previously knew, but because on advancing one must leave behind what one knew at first. Thus the more the soul advances, the more she walks in the dark and not knowing.

Chapter Seventeen

By the secret ladder, disguised

The inability to understand this spiritual communion is not the only reason why it is called "secret"; it is also on account of the effects produced on the soul. When this wisdom of love purges the soul with darkness and predicaments, it is secret because the soul does not know what to say about it. Even after enlightenment, when this wisdom is clearly known, it is still so secret to the soul that it is unable to speak about it or give it names; and it is also true that the soul does not feel like talking about it at all, for she is unable to find any means, any metaphor, adequate to it or able to signify such a high means of knowing and such delicate spiritual feeling. Thus, regardless how much one desires to make it public, or the great variety of metaphors one might use to conjure up meaning, it would always remain secret and unsaid. The interior wisdom is so simple, so overwhelming, so spiritual that it could not reach the intellect with any image or concept derived from the senses, and therefore, the senses or the imagination are unable to account for it or imagine it in order to talk about it, since this wisdom did not originate in them. . . .

Another reason it is called secret is that this mystical wisdom has the power to hide the soul within itself; for, besides its ordinary effects, it has the power to absorb the soul in such a way, hiding it in its secret abyss, that the soul sees at once that it is placed at the most remote location from any creature. Thus the soul feels itself to be within the deepest loneliness and isolation, where no human may reach. It is like a vast desert with no limits to the eye, but which is the more delightful, joyful, and lovable, the deeper, wider and more solitary it is. Here the soul feels herself secret, as she feels raised above all temporal creatures. . . .

SECTION THREE:
DENIAL OF THE ACTIVITIES OF THE FACULTIES

Concerning the active procedure to deny the activity of the faculties: (a) to cancel the different motions of the intellect; and (b) to reveal the negative character of faith and virtues in general. Excerpts from Book Two, *The Ascent of Mount Carmel,* Active Night of the Spirit.

Chapter One

SECOND STANZA

In the darkness, with light,
By the secret ladder, disguised,
—O joyous chance!—
I left in the darkness, covered,
My house at last completely quiet.

This second stanza is the song of the soul at its realization of the joyous chance which overcame her when the spirit became naked of all spiritual imperfections and appetites. This joyous chance is even greater than before, for the difficulty involved is greater when trying to quiet this house of all spiritual acts, when trying to enter the darkness inside, the spiritual nudity of all things, spiritual and material, by leaning on pure faith alone, and climbing by it to God. For this reason it is here called a *secret ladder,* for all the rungs and articles of faith it represents are secret and hidden to the senses and the intellect. Thus the soul is left climbing in the dark, without the light of the senses or intellect, beyond the fences of all rationality and natural powers, by the divine ladder of faith that leads up to and enters the deep realm of God. For this reason the soul says it was disguised, for its garments and natural faculties were changed from natural to divine, for her climb was only by faith. . . .

 . . . The soul also says that she came out on this night when her house was *at last completely quiet*—that is, the spiritual and rational parts were quiet. For when the soul reaches this union with God, her natural appetites—the faculties, desires, and sensuous inclinations of her spirit—are also quiet. This is the reason it is not written here that she left "anxious," as she did in the first night of the senses. In order to walk the night of the senses, to rid oneself of the sensual, it is necessary to feel "anxious for love" before one can emerge; but in order to quiet the house of the spirit one needs only to base all faculties, appetites, and spiritual inclinations on pure faith. This done, the soul joins the Beloved in a simple and pure union of love and likeness.[18]

It is worth noting that in the first stanza, referring to the sensual aspect, the poem says that the soul left on *a dark night*—while here, referring to the spiritual aspect, it asserts that it left *in the darkness*. The darkness of the spiritual part is deeper, as darkness is more obscure than night; no matter how dark a night may be, something can still be seen, but in actual darkness nothing is seen. . . .

Chapter Three

Theologians define faith as a certain obscure habit of soul. The reason it is an obscure habit is that it enables belief in truths revealed by God himself, truths above any natural light and far beyond all human understanding. As a result this excessive light given to the soul in faith is a deep darkness to her; the brighter light cancels the lesser ones, as the sun cancels lesser lights in such a way that even when burning they scarcely resemble light at all. . . .

Such is faith to the soul; it imprints on us things we never saw or understood before, either in themselves or in their likeness, for they lack any reference. We have no natural lights to show us these things. Our senses are not capable of receiving what faith teaches, though we know of it through hearing, by believing what faith teaches us, binding and blinding our natural lights. St. Paul teaches that *Fides ex auditu* (Rom. 10:17) faith is not knowledge derived from the senses but an assent of the soul to what enters through hearing.

In addition, faith far exceeds what these examples suggest to us, for not only does it fail to create information and knowledge but, as we said, it deprives and blinds the soul to any other information and knowledge, so that she may stand on her own and be the judge of information and knowledge. . . . It is therefore clear that faith is a dark night in the soul. In this manner it provides light to the soul, and the darker it becomes in the soul the more light it provides, for through blinding it sheds light. . . . Thus was faith foreshadowed in the cloud that separated the children of Israel from the Egyptians as they were about to cross the Red Sea, as the Scripture says: It was a dark cloud and it illumined the night (Exod. 14:19–20).

Chapter Six

We must deal, first, with the way to include the three faculties of the soul—intellect, memory, and will—in this spiritual night—the way to divine union. It is necessary first to clarify in this chapter how the three theological virtues, faith, hope, and charity . . . perform the same emptiness and darkness, each on its own faculty: faith on the intellect, hope on the memory, and charity on the will. . . .

These virtues void the faculties, as we have said: Faith empties the intellect and causes darkness of understanding; hope empties the memory of all its possessions; and charity empties the will, detaching it from all affection and joy in anything that is not God. Faith communicates what cannot be understood by the intellect, as we know. For this reason Paul (Heb. 11:1) says *Fides est sperandarum substantia rerum, argumentum non apparentium* (paraphrasing) that faith is the substance of the things we hope for. The intellect may with certitude and firmness assent to them, but these things are not discovered by the intellect, for if they were, there would be no faith. Faith may bring certitude to the intellect—not clarity, however, but darkness.

Hope, also, without doubt, voids memory and covers it with darkness concerning the matters of here and beyond. Hope is always about the things we do not have, for if we had them, there would be no necessity for hope. Thus St. Paul states: *Spes, quae videtur, non est spes; nam quod videt quis, quis sperat?* (Rom. 8:24) Hope when seen, is not hope, for what one sees this is what he has, therefore, how can he hope? Thus this virtue voids its faculty, too, for hope is of what we do not have and not of what we have.

Charity, too, empties the will of all things, for it forces us to love God above all things. This is not possible unless we remove all our affection from things and put it entirely in God. . . . In this manner these three virtues cause darkness in the soul and empty it of all things.

Chapter Nine

We may gather from what has been said that the soul must remain clean and empty of whatever may fall on the senses, and nude and detached from everything that may strike the intellect, she must remain intimately at peace and silence, standing on faith alone, if she is to proceed to divine union. Faith is the only proximate and proportionate means for the soul to join God. . . . And just as God is darkness to our intellect, so faith blinds and dazzles it. . . . As David said: He set darkness under His feet. And He rose above the cherubim and flew on the wings of the wind. He made darkness and the dark water His hiding place (Ps. 17:10–12).

This *darkness under God's feet,* and the phrases *He made of the dark water his hiding place,* and *He was all surrounded by darkness,* signify the darkness of faith surrounding God. When it is said that *He rose above the cherubim and flew on the wings of the wind,* it is to be understood that God flies above all thought, for *cherubim* means those who think or contemplate, and *the wings of the wind* refer to the subtle and high informations and concepts of the spirit. His Being is above all of these, and no one can reach it through his own efforts alone.

We read something similar in Scripture when Solomon had finished the temple and God descended in darkness and filled it so that the children of Israel were unable to see. Solomon then said: The Lord has promised to dwell in darkness (1 Kings 8:12). God was also covered in darkness when He appeared to Moses on the mountain (Exod. 24:16), and often when God communicated with someone He appeared covered in darkness. This may be seen in the Book of Job, where it is said that God spoke to Job from the dark air (Job 38:1, 40:1). All of this refers to the darkness of faith in which the Divinity is covered while communicating itself to the soul. . . .

It is therefore clear that for the soul to come to union with God in this life and come in direct communion with Him, it must join itself to the darkness of which Solomon spoke, where God had promised to dwell, and join the darkness of air where God revealed His secrets to Job . . .[19]

Chapter Eleven

The type of knowledge we have spoken about in the previous chapter is knowledge achieved by natural means. Of this we have already spoken in Book One, where we guided the soul on the *night of the senses,* and therefore we will mention nothing here. There we presented the proper doctrine about this knowledge. Our present discussion will cover only the supernatural knowledge (be it in the form of information or touches) that reaches the intellect by way of the exterior bodily senses: sight, hearing, smell, taste, touch. It is possible and common for spiritual persons to receive, through these senses, supernatural representations and objects. As for sight, they may have visions or images of persons from the other life: saints, good and bad angels, unusual lights and displays. Through hearing they may listen to extraordinary words which come from visions, or at other times from unseen persons. They may sometimes smell the sweetest fragrances without knowing their origin, or experience the most exquisite flavors through taste. Through touch they may feel extreme delight, at times so intense they rejoice in their bones and marrow, as they bloom and bathe in it. This delight is sometimes called *spiritual unction,* because in pure souls it passes from the spirit to the senses, and it is common with spiritual persons. . . .

Warning should be given that though all these signs may fall on the senses from God, we should never rely on them nor accept them. We must rather avoid them and flee them, without stopping to examine whether they are good or bad. For the more exterior and corporal they are the less certain is their origin in God. It is more common and easier for God to commune with the spirit, where the soul finds more security and profit, than with the senses. . . .[20]

Chapter Twelve

Before discussing those visions achieved through imagining, which are usually imparted supernaturally to the inner faculty (the power of fantasy and imagination), we will discuss here the natural workings of this same inner faculty, so that we may proceed in logical order. . . .

The first point to consider here is the inner corporal faculty, the power of fantasy and imagining. This faculty needs also to be emptied of all the forms and signs of imagining that might naturally occupy it. . . .

We are dealing here with two inner bodily senses: imagination and fantasy. They serve each other consecutively, for one presents images discursively while the other fashions them. For our purpose there is no need to speak of their differences, which must be remembered even if they are not explicitly mentioned. These senses can build only imaginations and phantasms. These are forms represented to the inner senses through material images and figures. There are two kinds of representations, the supernatural and the natural. The supernatural take place passively, without the work of the senses. These are called supernatural imaginative visions, and will be discussed later. The natural are those the soul may actively construct by its own power, through images, forms, and figures. What we call meditation is the province of these two faculties or inner senses, for meditation is a discursive act carried out through images, forms, and figures, fabricated and imagined by the senses. Thus we may imagine Christ crucified, or at the pillar, or in some other scene; or God seated on a throne in resplendent majesty; or we may imagine heaven as a beautiful light, and so on. In the same way we may consider other things, human or divine, as long as they are imaginable. But all these imaginings need to be emptied from the soul, leaving it in darkness as far as this faculty goes, in order to reach divine union. There can be no use made of these imaginings as a means to reach God, just as there can be no use made of the five exterior senses.[21]. . .

. . . Let the soul learn to stay with attention and loving presence in God with total quietude, achieving nothing through imaginings or through its workings; for here, as we have said, the faculties are at rest and do not operate actively, but passively, receiving what God works in them.[22]. . .

Chapter Fourteen

. . . What the soul was previously acquiring in installments through its own labor of meditating on particular signs has now been converted into one habitual and substantial, loving, general sign, rather than different or particular ones, as previously. Thus as soon as the soul enters meditation, it is as if someone with water were ready by her mouth—she drinks peacefully with no labor, with no need to fetch the water through the channels of past experiences, forms, and figures. The moment she collects herself in the presence of God she places herself in an act of general, loving, peaceful, and quiet signing; though confused, it allows the soul to drink wisdom, love, and joy.[23]

Chapter Twenty-Three

. . . We shall now deal with those other four signs of the intellect, which in chapter ten we called *purely spiritual,* that is: revelations, locutions, visions, and spiritual consolations. We call these purely spiritual because, contrary to corporal imaginings, they come to the intellect through means other than the corporal senses. They come to the intellect without the means of any external or internal corporal sense, and appear to it clearly and distinctly by way of a supernatural passivity, while the soul contributes nothing of itself in any active manner. . . .

As we did previously with imaginative corporal signs, we must disengage the intellect from these spiritual signs, guiding and directing the soul past them into the spiritual night of faith, to the divine and substantial union with God. For the soul may become so busy with and used to them that it may be shut out of the path of solitude and detachment required of all things in this spiritual path. . . .

Chapter Twenty-Four

Concerning the two types of spiritual visions.

To speak properly, now, of spiritual visions, those excluding the bodily senses, we state that there are two types of visions that can enter the intellect: one is related to corporeal substances, the other to separate, or incorporeal, substances. Corporeal visions are about material things as they may be found in heaven or upon the earth. These the soul may see, even while in the body, by means of a supernatural light provided by God, in Whom all absent objects of the earth or heaven may be seen. . . .

The other visions, those of incorporeal substances, are not attained through this derived light we speak about here, but through another much higher light called the *light of glory*. These visions of incorporeal substances, such as angels or souls, are not of this life, nor may they be seen while in a mortal body. For if God desired to communicate them to the soul as they essentially are, the soul would untie its bonds of flesh and leave its mortal life. . . .

These visions are not the daily occurrence of this life, except at times in passing, and this only with the help of God who sustains the human condition and natural life by removing the spirit from it totally. It is only with his favor that the natural functions of the soul toward the body are preserved. For this reason St. Paul exclaimed: He was carried up to them, and what he saw, he says, he did not know if it was in or out of the body, for only God knows (2 Cor. 12:2,4). It is clear his natural life was changed, with God effecting the manner of this transformation. . . .

Although these visions of spiritual substances cannot be made present and seen clearly in this life with our intellect, they may be felt in the substance of the soul as a very soft touch, and so with all the other signs. This belongs to the realm of what is called spiritual feelings, and of these we shall speak later. We take aim at them, for they are the union of the soul with the divine Substance. . . .

We will now concern ourselves with the visions of corporeal substances that are received spiritually in the soul, for they are like corporeal visions. . . .

. . . It is, at times, as if a door were opened and through it we can see a bolt of lightning, as when on a dark night the lightning suddenly brightens the sky and makes things clear and visible and then returns them to the darkness, after which the forms of those things remain in the imagination. This same thing happens in the soul but with greater perfection, for the things seen by the spirit remain so imprinted in the soul by that light, that forever the soul keeps seeing them as it saw them previously, the way we see images on the mirror each time we look in it. Never will the soul forget those impressions it received through these visions, even with passage of a long time.[24]

These visions cannot serve the intellect as means for union with God, for they belong to creatures with whom God shares no proportion or essential likeness. The soul must respond negatively toward them, as we said about all other signs, in order to progress by the only proximate means, which is faith.

BOOK THREE:
ACTIVE NIGHT OF THE SPIRIT
ON MEMORY AND WILL

Concerning the purgation of the active night of memory and will.

Chapter One

We have already dealt with the first faculty of the soul, namely the intellect, through all its perceptions of faith, the first theological virtue. . . . We must now do the same with the other two faculties of the soul—memory and will. They must also undergo purification of all their sensations, so that through these two faculties the soul may reach union with God in perfect hope and charity. . . .

Chapter Two

Let us start, then, with natural signs. I call natural signs of memory all those images that may be formed by memory of objects perceived by means of the five senses: hearing, seeing, smelling, tasting, and touching, as well as everything memory can fashion and shape based on these perceptions and signs. Now, memory must cancel and empty itself of all these signs and shapes; it must also lose the imaginary impresssion of those signs in such a manner that no sign or vestige is left printed in memory. Memory must be left bold and empty as if nothing whatsoever had passed through it; it must remain forgotten to itself, excluding all sensation from objects.

. . . Since God has no form or image that memory may apprehend or form, when memory is united with God, it is left without form or shape. Imagination is lost, and memory is drunk with the highest taste; memory has lost everything and remembers nothing, for the divine union empties fantasy completely—all forms and signs are swept away, and taken up to a higher supernatural plane.

It is worth mentioning what at times happens to memory. When God touches memory with His union, memory suddenly somersaults in the brain, where it is located. As a result one feels as if one has lost one's head, and with it one's consciousness and sensations. This may be experienced with greater or lesser power, depending on the power of the touch of union. It is then that due to this union, memory is made empty of all signs, lost to itself, at times so lost it is necessary to make a great effort and work very hard to remember anything.

This emptiness of memory and the suspension of imagination is at times so complete, when the soul is united to God, that one may spend a long time trying to retrace the things one did, or even noticing their absence. Because imagination is also withheld, even when one's body is subject to pain, one does not feel it, for without imagination there is no sensation; and the same is true of thinking, for no thought occurs. . . .

Some people may object that this doctrine appears to be good, but the truth is that this doctrine proclaims the destruction of the natural activity and use of the faculties; in this state people are left like animals, without memory, or worse, not able to use their reason or remember their natural activities and needs. They will argue that God does not destroy nature, but rather perfects it, and will claim that the above description hints at its destruction, saying that in order to follow this path people must forget what is moral, rational, and natural, for in that state all this is forgotten since none of the signs and forms of memory are present.

To this I answer by saying that they are right . . . for when memory is united to God, no signs or shapes of things may be imprinted on it. Therefore, the operations of memory and of the other faculties in such a state are only divine, for by God possessing them as Lord of them all, and by having transformed them to Himself, it is He himself who moves them and orders them in His divine manner according to His divine spirit and will. As a result these operations are not different from God's, for what appears in the soul belongs then to God and His divine operations. . . .

I will give an example of these operations: someone might ask a soul in this state to pray for him or her. This soul will not remember to carry out this request out of any sign or remembrance of such a person, but if it were convenient for such a person to be prayed for (that is, if God wishes this person to be commended to Him) God himself will move the will of such a soul for the prayer to take place. . . .[25]

Chapter Six

From the different kinds of harm caused by the signs of memory, we can also determine the opposite—that is, the benefits that come to it from the void and forgetfulness of memory. . . . The soul enjoys peace and tranquility, for it lacks the disturbances and changes that come from thinking and the signs of memory. . . .

. . . Even if no benefit would come to those dedicated to meditation other than this forgetfulness and void of memory to be rid of anxieties and pains, this alone would be a great advantage and blessing to them. For the anxieties and pains borne in the soul out of adversity are of no use or profit in remedying those adversities. It is but ordinary experience that these things make the soul feel worse and harm it. Thus David said: *Indeed every person is disturbed in vain* (Ps. 39:7). It is clear it is always in vain to be disturbed, for it brings no profit whatsoever. Thus if the whole world came to an end, and everything turned out the opposite of our expectations and against us, it would be in vain to be disturbed. . . .

Chapter Sixteen

(a) Reorientation of the will;
(b) Degrees of mutations.

Concerning the dark night of the Will: the different motions of the will.

We would have worked for nothing in purging the intellect to ground it on the virtue of faith, or memory on that of hope, if we did not also purge the will to ground it on the third virtue, charity.

Through charity, works done in faith are alive and of great value;
without it they are dead and worth nothing, as St. James testifies:
Without works of charity, faith is dead (James. 2:20). I have found
no better passage for a treatise on the active night and purging of this
faculty, with the aim of guiding and instructing the soul in this
virtue of the love of God, than that in *Deuteronomy* Chapter 6, where
Moses commands: *You shall love the Lord your God with all your heart,
and with all your soul, and with all your strength* (Deut. 6:5). This
passage contains all that the spiritual person must do and what I
must teach them here for them to reach God by union of the will
through charity. . . .

    The strength of the soul is no more than its faculties and desires.
All of them are ruled by the will. When the will directs these
faculties, passions, and appetites to God and takes them away from
what is not God, then the will gathers the strength of the soul only
for God. Thus the soul comes to love God with all her strength. For
the soul to be able to achieve this, we shall deal here with how to
purge the soul of all her inordinate affections, for they engender
appetites, emotions, and activities contrary to God, and the failure
to preserve one's strength so it can be directed to God. These
affections or passions are four: joy, hope, sorrow, and fear. These
passions, directed toward God by rejoicing only in what is to God's
glory and honor, by not hoping in anything but God, nor feeling
sorrow about anything else but this goal, and by not feeling any fear
but the fear of God, manifestly direct and guard the strength of the
soul and its ability to love God. . . .

Chapter Nineteen

The harm caused to the soul by enjoyment of temporal goods.

This harm . . . has four degrees, each worse than the other. When
the soul reaches the fourth it has reached all the evils and harms that
can be mentioned in this matter. Moses mentions these four degrees
in Deuteronomy: The beloved was surfeited and hobbled backwards; he was surfeited, grew fat, and spread out. He forsook God
his Maker, and departed from God his Savior (Deut. 32:15).

To surfeit the soul that was loved before it began to stuff itself with the joy of creatures is to dwell in this joy. From here springs the first degree of this harm. The soul darkens the mind about God, thus concealing the goods of God, as the mist darkens the air and does not receive the rays of the sun. . . .

The second degree of this harm is caused by the first one; as it is said above: *surfeited, grew fat, and spread out*. In this second degree the will expands with greater freedom among temporal things; and this consists in neither sorrowing as much, nor feeling so much joy in the goods of this world. This is caused by first allowing the soul to get drunk with joy, thus allowing her to become fat with it; and that fatness of joy and appetite allows her to become wider and spread out among creatures. . . .

The third degree . . . is summarized in the words: *he forsook God, his Maker.* This degree refers to all those who have so lost the faculties of their souls among the things, customs and tastes of this world that they think nothing of obligations to the law of God. They are totally lost and forgetful about their salvation, and are more alert and open to the things of the world. Christ calls them in the Gospel *children of this century,* and He says of them that they are more prudent and sharp in their dealings than the *children of the light* in theirs (Luke 16:8). Thus, these people are all to the world and nothing to God. These people are the greedy. Their appetite and joy is already so spread over everything of this world and so bound to these things in their affections that they never have enough. Their appetite grows as much as their thirst, in the same proportion as they are separated from the only fountain that could stop them from thirsting, and that is God. God speaks of these people through Jeremiah: *They have abandoned Me, the fountain of living water, and they dig for themselves broken wells that can hold no water* (Jer. 2:13). This is simply because the greedy can find nothing in creatures of this world to quench their thirst, but rather they increase it. . . .

The fourth degree is mentioned in the last phrase: *and departed from God his Savior.* . . .

. . . For this person has built for himself a god out of money and temporal goods, as St. Paul mentions: greed is a form of idolatry (Col. 3:5). For the people in this last degree forget God and set their heart, which should belong to God, on money, as if they had no other God.

Those belonging to this fourth degree subordinate the supernatural to the natural, making of it a god. . . .

. . . Many today belong in various ways to this fourth degree,
their reason in spiritual matters darkened through greed, and
thus they serve money and not God, they act for money and not for
God, they set a higher esteem on price than on the values and
rewards of God; to them, money, in many ways, is their main end
and god, giving it priority over the last end, which is God.

Chapter Twenty

. . . By removing the enjoyment of temporal goods the soul ac-
quires the virtue of liberality, one of the main conditions of reaching
union with God. This virtue cannot be gained through greed. The
soul, besides, gains freedom of spirit, clarity of reason, peace,
tranquillity, and confidence. . . .

. . . The soul gains more joy in creatures by being detached
from them. This could not be achieved if the soul viewed those
creatures with any type of possessiveness, for this attitude would tie
the soul to the earth and deprive her of freedom. Through detachment, the soul gains better knowledge of creatures, either naturally
or supernaturally; in this manner the soul enjoys creatures in a
different way than the one who is attached to them. This other way
is all to its advantage and brings with it great depth; for the soul that
is detached loves creatures according to their truth, the attached
person according to their falsity; the one according to their best, the
other their worst; the one according to their substance, the other
their accidents; for the senses only penetrate as far as the accidents,
but the spirit purged from clouds and the sensations of the surface
penetrates into the truth and value of things, for this is its goal. . . .

The detached soul, then, enjoys all things, her joy not attached
to them, as if they belonged to her. On the other hand, as soon as she
attaches herself to anything she loses at once the joy of all things in
general. When none of them rests on the heart, the soul has all of
them *in great freedom,* as St. Paul said (2 Cor. 6, 10). When it is
attached to things it does not truly possess anything, for it is things
that possess the soul through the heart. For this reason, because she
is captive, the soul suffers. And so the more joys she wishes to have

from creatures, of necessity the more sufferings and sorrows will come upon her. The detached soul does not suffer any care. . . .

Chapter Twenty-Seven

The fourth degree, in which the soul may rejoice, is that of moral goods. By moral goods we mean here virtue and the habits derived from them, insofar as they are moral, and the exercise of virtue: acts of mercy, keeping the law of God, of the state, and all those exercises of good manners and inclination. . . .

. . . Virtue deserves to be loved by itself, both on account of being familiar with its practice (being present in us) and the good it brings to people in a human and temporal manner. . . .

But though Christians may rejoice in this manner by observing the good virtue brings, morally or temporally, they should not stop here . . . but, guided by the light of faith . . . they must principally rejoice in the exercise and possession of these moral goods according to the second manner, and that is by performing their works only for the love of God. . . .

. . . There were many in the past, among them many Christians, who possessed and exercised many virtues, but these virtues and good works will not profit them in the least for eternal life, for in those works they did not have in mind the glory and honor of God alone.[26]

SPIRITUAL CANTICLE:
Beyond the Dark Night
I. A.

Commentary on the stanzas that deal with the exchange of love between the soul and its Bridegroom Christ, treating certain aspects and effects of prayer. Written at the request of Mother Ana de Jesús, prioress of the Discalced Carmelite nuns of St. Joseph's in Granada, 1584.

NOTE: Ana de Jesús (Lobera) (1545–1621) was born in Medina del Campo. She entered St. Joseph's in Avila in 1571. She became prioress of Beas, Granada, and Madrid. After 1604 she founded the Carmelite Order in France and Belgium. She died in Brussels. The cause of her beatification is in process.

PROLOGUE

Considering, Religious Mother, that these poems have been written with considerable love for our Lord, whose wisdom and love is so immense, as the Book of Wisdom states, reaching from end to end (Wis. 8:1), and considering that those moved and informed by it carry in themselves this same abundance and exuberance in their speech, it is beyond the scope of this commentary to cover the breadth of love that the words of these poems have received from the fullness of love of the spirit. It would also be foolish to expect that expressions of love uttered in a mystical trance, such as the present poems, may be explained with ordinary words. The Spirit of the Lord, as St. Paul says, *aids our weakness* by dwelling within us, and *pleads for us with unspeakable groanings* in order to manifest what we ourselves are hardly able to understand. Who can write down the knowledge He communicates to the loving soul where He lives? And who can express with words the sensations He makes them feel? Who, finally, can describe what He makes them long for? No one can, not even the souls sharing these experiences. Consequently, these people let something of their experiences overflow with metaphors and comparisons, and in the abundance of their spirit they pour out unintelligible secrets rather than rational explanations. If these metaphors are not read with the simplicity of the spirit of love and knowledge they contain, they sound like absurdities rather than reasonable explanations, as is the case with the divine Canticle of Solomon and other books of Sacred Scripture in which the Holy Spirit, unable to express the fullness of His meaning with common and ordinary words, utters mysteries using strange metaphors and comparisons. The same is true of the saintly Doctors of the Church, for no matter how much they have said or will say, they can never provide all the words needed, for it was not in words that it was said to begin with. Thus the explanations and commentaries are the least of what is contained in the experience.

Since these poems, then, have been written within the love of abundant mystical understanding, I cannot be exact in commenting on them, nor is that my intention. I only wish to shed some general light on them, for this is what Your Reverence asked of me. I believe this course is the more suitable, for the sayings of love are better left in their broadest sense so that everyone may derive meaning from them according to their style and depth of spirit, rather than narrowed down to one single sense not suitable to every taste. Consequently, though I comment on these poems, no one should feel bound by this commentary. Mystical wisdom, which comes through love and is the subject of these poems, need not be understood clearly in order to cause results and keenness in the soul. It works in the manner of faith, through which we love God without understanding Him.

. . . Though Your Reverence lacks training in scholastic theology, by which the divine truths are understood, you are not lacking in mystical theology, learned through love, by which one not only knows the divine truths but also experiences them.

In order for my commentaries to be more believable (which I wish to submit to anyone with a better judgment than myself and certainly to Our Mother Church), I do not intend to affirm anything of myself or trust in any of my own experiences or that of other spiritual persons I have known, or heard of from them,

though I intend to use both, but not without the authority of Sacred
Scripture. . . .

THE COMMENTARY BEGINS

FIRST STANZA

Where did you hide,
My Love, leaving me thus to moan?
Like the stag, you fled,
Leaving in me this wound;
I ran calling loud, but you were gone.

COMMENTARY

The soul, in love with the Word, the Son of God, her Bridegroom, wishes to be united to Him in a clear and essential vision.[27]
She speaks out her deep desire for love chiding Him for His absence,
more so since she is wounded with love. It is for this love that she left
behind all things and even herself—why should she then still suffer
the absence of her Beloved? Why does not He untie her from her
mortal flesh so she may enjoy Him eternally, in glory? Thus she says:

"Where did you hide,"

This is as if she said: "Divine Word, my Groom, show me the
place where You hide"; and so she asks for the manifestation of His
divine essence. The place where the Son of God is hidden is, as St.
John says, *the womb of his Father* (John 1:18), and this is the divine
essence that is hidden and alien to the mortal eye and all human
intellect. Isaiah said as much: *You truly are the hidden God* (Isa. 45:15),
for regardless of the visions, communications, and great signs a soul
may receive from God in this life, they are not yet God, nor do they
refer to Him, for He always remains hidden to the soul, and it is
always better for the soul to have Him hidden and search for Him as
hidden,[28] despite all those great things. Thus the soul exclaims:
"Where did you hide," For the most sensible communications and
presence of such things are no greater testimony of His presence in
the soul than dryness and the absence of those communications. . . .

My Love, leaving me thus to moan?

. . . The absence of the Beloved is a continuous moan in the lover's heart, for since she loves nothings outside of Him, she cannot rest or receive relief. . . .

. . . It is within our heart, where we keep our token, that we feel what it is that hurts us, and this is His absence. This, then, is the moan the soul feels in the absence of the Beloved, the more so when, after having tasted some sweet and savory communication from Him, the soul is left dry and alone. . . .

Leaving in me this wound;

This is equivalent to saying: "It was bad enough to bear the pain and suffering I normally endure in your absence, but now, wounding me even deeper with your arrow of love, increasing my passion and desire for your sight, You take flight with the speed of a stag and leave not even a small trace."

A further comment about this verse is needed. God visits the soul in many ways to wound it and make it rise in love, but at times He barely grazes it with flaming touches of love. They wound and penetrate the soul like an arrow of fire and leave it cauterized with the fire of love. These are properly called love's wounds, and are here mentioned by the soul. They so inflame the will with desire that the soul burns with the fire and flame of love, so much so that the soul seems to be consumed by that flame, which forces the soul to come out of itself, all renewed, and transformed into a new form of being, like the phoenix that is born out of its own ashes. . . .

The appetites and feelings . . . become divine within that loving flare of the heart and the soul, out of love, feels inclined toward nothing, for she knows nothing but love. It is at this loving time that the imprisoned appetites of the will are exchanged for the torment and desire of seeing God. The soul then feels that the discipline used by love on it is unbearable, not because she feels wounded, for she previously considered these wounds to be her health, but because she was left wounded and yet not wounded enough to die of it, so that she could see herself finally united to Him in the revealed and clear sight of perfect love.[29]

It is for this reason . . . that the soul says "leaving in me this wound"; for this feeling is so deep because of the wound of love imprinted in it by God that it rises quickly to the possession of the Beloved. The soul felt Him nearby with the touch of love, and with the same quickness it feels the absence and the moan at once, for He appears and disappears at the same time, and the soul is left empty and with as much pain and moaning as the desire for union was deep. . . .[30]

I ran calling loud, but you were gone.

There is no medicine for the wounds of love, unless it is delivered by the one who caused them. Thus it is written "calling loud," that is, asking for medicine from the one who caused the wound, out of the strength of the fire raging in the wound. The expression "I ran" may be understood in two ways: first, "I ran out of all things," by despising and rejecting them; second, "I ran out of myself," by forgetting and abandoning myself, and this happens because of a holy loathing of oneself caused by the love of God. He so lifts the soul that He forces it to abandon itself, its habits and natural operations, calling after God.[31] . . .

"but you were gone." This is as if to say: "When I wanted to join your presence I did not find You, and I was left empty and detached from all things because of You, but was unable to catch up to You, pining in midair because of love, feeling neither your presence nor mine."

STANZA 7

And all those around me
Speak of you a thousand graces,
And wound me even more,
Babbling I know not what;
I am at the door of death.

COMMENTARY

The soul declared in the previous stanza that it was ill and and wounded by the love of the Groom, due to the information it received from irrational creatures. In this stanza the soul declares that it is "sore" with love, due to the higher form of information it has received from rational and nobler creatures, like angels and people. She also claims to be dying because of an admirable depth she fathoms through these creatures, though this depth never becomes fully uncovered. The soul calls this an "I know not what," for she is not able to say it; but the feeling is so intense that the soul is dying of love.

We may then infer that in this process of loving there are, for the Beloved, three ways of suffering, each caused by a different way of receiving information about Him: The first is called *wound*, and it is not very deep and lasts only a brief time; it is born of the information the soul receives from ordinary creatures, the lowest forms of God's work. . . .

The second is called *sore*, and this settles longer on the soul and lasts longer, for it feels like a wound turned into a sore, and makes the soul truly feel sore with love. This sore grows in the soul from the information received regarding the works of the Incarnation of the Word and the mysteries of faith. These hold greater dignity as works of God and show greater love than that revealed by creatures; thus, they cause in the soul deeper effects of love—so that, if the first feels like a wound, this second one feels more like a living sore that lasts. . . .

The third way of suffering of love feels like *death*. This is as if the living sore, even the whole soul, has become infected, living as if dying until, killed by love, it forces the soul to live the life of love, transforming it into love. This death of love is caused when the soul is touched by the highest information concerning the Divinity itself. This is the "I know not what" of which this stanza speaks and about which people continue to "babble." Such a touch of information is not continuous, for the soul would then have to leave the body, but ends in a short time. Thus the soul is left dying of love, and dies all the more seeing it does not die of love. . . .

STANZA 11

O crystalline fountain,
If in your silvery faces

You would form of a sudden
The desired eyes
I have pictured in my inner places!

COMMENTARY

Since the soul longs so vehemently for union with the Bride-groom and finds no consolation in any creature nor knows any way to proceed, she turns to faith, for it most vividly sheds light on the Beloved, and the soul takes it as the means toward this union. . . . She addresses faith with deep longings: "O faith of my Spouse, Christ, if you would but show me clearly now the truths of my Beloved, which you have infused in my soul with darkness and obscurely . . . so that what you now communicate to me in an obscure way you would show suddenly, clearly, and perfectly, trans-forming it into a manifestation of glory!"

O crystalline fountain,

Faith is called "crystalline" for two reasons: first, because it refers to Christ, the Spouse; and second, because it has the charac-teristics of crystal in that it is pure in its truths, and strong and clear because it is clean of errors and natural forms. . . . It is called "foun-tain" because from it, as from a spring, the waters of all spiritual gifts flow into the soul. . . .[32]

If in your silvery faces

The propositions and articles of faith are called "silvery faces." . . . Faith is compared to silver with respect to those propositions it teaches. The truths and substance they contain are compared to gold, for what we now believe and see covered and dressed in the silver of faith, we shall see and enjoy uncovered and naked in the next life as the gold of faith. . . . Faith, therefore, gives us God and communicates His signs, though they be covered by the silver of faith. Yet, it does not for this reason fail to give Him to us in truth, as when we receive a gold vase plated with silver we do not fail to receive gold because it is plated with silver. . . .

The desired eyes
I have pictured in my inner places!

"The eyes" mean here, as we have said, the light of divine truths. These speak to us in propositions that are inexplicit and obscure. It is as if the soul said: "O, if only the truths hiding in your propositions of faith, which you teach me in an obscure and inexact manner, were to be given to me in a clear and uncovered manner as it is my desire!" . . .

I have pictured in my inner places!

She speaks of the truths "I have pictured in my inner places!" This means in the soul, in the intellect and will. For these truths are infused by faith into her soul, but since the knowledge of them is imperfect, she says they are "pictured." In the same way that a drawing is not a perfect painting, the signs of faith are not perfect knowledge. Thus the infused truths of faith are present in the soul as a drawing, but if they appear in a clear vision they will be present in the soul as a perfect and finished painting. . . .

STANZA 13

Turn them aside, my Love
For I take flight!

BRIDEGROOM:
Return, my dove,
For the wounded stag
Rises over the horizon's light
Refreshed by the air of your flight.

COMMENTARY

. . . Since the soul has so desired the sight of the divine eyes (as she has just mentioned in the previous stanza), the Beloved now grants her some rays of His greatness and divinity, as she wished. He grants them with such depth and force that they cause the soul to come out of itself in rapture and ecstasy. In the beginning great pain and fear accompanies the natural sensations. . . .

Turn them aside, my Love

The torture experienced during these rapturous visits is at times so extreme that there is no other which so disjoints the bones and so threatens the natural sensations—were God not to provide, life would come to an end. And in truth this is how the soul feels, for it feels as if it has been cut loose from the flesh and is abandoning the body. And the reason is that such gifts cannot be received wholly in the flesh, for the spirit is raised to commune with the divine spirit which comes to the soul. Thus the soul must forcefully abandon the flesh in some fashion. The flesh must suffer, and consequently the soul in the flesh, because of their unity in one only *suppositum*. . . .

Yet, it should not be thought that just because the soul says "turn them aside," the soul desires for God to do so. She speaks out of natural fear, as we have said. Even if the cost were heavier, the soul would never want to lose these visits and gifts of the Beloved, for though the natural sensations suffer, the soul flies to the supernatural realm to enjoy the presence of the Beloved, just as she desired, and for which she prayed. Yet the soul would not want to receive the Spirit in the flesh, for He cannot be received there fully, but in small portions and through suffering. She would rather receive Him in the flight of the Spirit outside of the flesh, where one can freely rejoice. For this reason the soul exclaims: "Turn them aside, my Love"; that is, stop communicating to me in the flesh. . . .

For the wounded stag

Here the Bridegroom compares himself to a stag,[33] and with this name He refers to himself. It is in the character of the stag to climb to high places, to race quickly searching for coolness in fresh waters when wounded, and if he hears the cry of his wounded mate, he at once takes off with her, giving her comfort and caressing her. Thus acts the Bridegroom. On seeing that the bride is wounded with His love, He too becomes wounded at her moan of love, for among lovers the wound of one is shared by both, for both share the same feeling. . . .

This mutual love, then, makes the Bridegroom come running to drink in this fountain of love of the bride, just as fresh waters draw the wounded and thirsty stag to drink. Thus it is said, "refreshed."

As a breeze cools and refreshes a person worn out by heat, so this breeze of love cools and rests the person burning with the fire of love. The character of this fire of love is such that the breeze that cools and rests is also the fire of love. For in the lover, love is a flame burning with the desire to burn even more, like the flame of a natural fire. Thus when this desire to burn more in the heat of love of his bride is fulfilled, this is called "the air of your flight," and "refreshed." This is as much as to say: "The heat of your flight burns even more, for one love kindles another love." . . .[34]

STANZAS 14 AND 15

My Beloved the mountains,
The valleys' solitary groves,
The sounding rivers and fountains,
The distant islands' soil,
The wind whistling love's songs,

The calm night,
The twin of the rising dawn,
The silent music,
The sounding solitude,
The supper that kindles love and warms.

COMMENTARY ON THE TWO STANZAS.

Since the little dove was flying in the air of love above the waters of the flood of her fatigue and desire for love . . . and could find no place to alight, the compassionate father Noah extended his merciful hands on this last flight, caught her, and brought her inside the ark of his love and charity. This is the time when in [stanza 13] it is said: "Return, my dove."

And this is also the substance of what is said in the above two stanzas.

The bride says in these stanzas that the Beloved is all these things in Himself and for her. What God usually communicates in such excesses is what the soul feels and knows: the truth of St.

Francis, who says "My God and all things". . . . What is here described is in God in an eminent and infinite manner—or even better, each one of these things is God, and all together are God. Insofar as the soul joins God it feels that all these things are God in a simple being, as St. John felt when he said: *What was made, in Him it became life* (John 1:4). Thus it should not be understood that it is being said here that the soul sees things in the light or creatures in God, but rather that in that union all things are God. [35]

My Beloved the mountains,

Mountains are high, wide, beautiful, graceful, flowery, and give out beautiful smells. These mountains are my Beloved to me.

The valleys' solitary groves,

Solitary valleys are quiet, pleasant, cool, shady, full of sweet waters; a variety of groves and the pleasant song of birds provide recreation and delight to the senses; they provide freshness and rest in their solitude and silence. These valleys are my Beloved to me.

The distant islands' soil,

These distant islands are girded by the sea and are beyond the known seas, distant and apart from the communication of people. There are born, and made to grow, different things from the ones here, of different qualities never seen by humans, causing great wonder and admiration in those seeing them. On account of the different and admirable novelties and knowledge they provide, like the knowledge the soul experiences in God which is so uncommon to the general taste, they are called "distant islands' soil" . . . [36] But they are not strange or new to themselves.

The sounding rivers and fountains,

Rivers have these properties: first, that all they find they attack and level; second, they fill all the low and empty spaces they find; third, their sound is such that they cover up other sounds. . . .
. . . In the same manner does the soul feel itself attacked by the

torrent of the spirit of God, and become possessed of as much strength that she feels all the rivers of the world are riding over her, and she feels flooded by them as she feels all the actions and passions of the past disappear under its waters. . . .

. . . The second property is experienced by the soul when the divine waters feel the lower parts of her humility and fill the empty spaces of her appetites. . . . The third property is felt by the soul in these sounding rivers of the Beloved, and this is a sound and spiritual voice above any other sound and any other voice; this voice covers any other voice with its sound and its pitch exceeds all the sounds of this world. . . .[37]

. . . This spiritual voice and sound is what the Apostles heard when the Holy Spirit descended upon them like a flooding torrent, as it is said in the Acts of the Apostles. . . .

The wind whistling love's songs,

We feel two things from the air: a touch, and a sound or whistle. In this manner is the communication from the Bridegroom both a feeling of delight and an intelligence. And as the touch of the air is enjoyed by the sense of touch, and its whistle by the ear, in the same manner the touch of the virtues of the Beloved are felt and enjoyed in the touch of the soul, that is, in its substance; while the intelligence of such virtues of God is enjoyed in the ear of the soul, which is the intellect. It is then that it is said that the loving air arrives, wounding joyfully, and filling up the appetite of the one in need of such food. The sense of touch is then pampered, and in this pampering the sense of hearing feels great delight in the sound and whistle of the air, much more than touch with the contact of the air. . . .

. . . It is called "whistle" because in the same manner the whistle of the air enters sharply in the tube of the ear, in this same manner this subtle and sharp intelligence enters with deep flavor and delight in the intimate part of the substance of the soul. This is a greater delight than any of the others. The reason is that the soul perceives the intelligence of her own naked and known substance without accidents or phantasms. . . .[38]

The calm night,

While in this spiritual sleep the soul enjoys on the chest of the Beloved she also receives all the peace and rest of the quiet night, while she also receives from God a deep and obscure divine intelligence. . . .

The twin of the rising dawn,

This calm night, it is said, is not a dark night, but more like the twin of the rising dawn. The peace and quiet that comes to the soul in God is not obscure as in the dark night, but rather peace and quiet in the divine light of the knowledge of God where the spirit lies sweetly quiet, raised to the divine light. This divine light is here properly called "the twin of the rising dawn," which means the morning, for as the dawn closes out the night and uncovers the light of day, this quiet spirit resting in God is raised from the darkness of natural knowing to the matutinal light of the supernatural knowledge of God, not yet fully clear, but, as stated, like the "twin of the rising dawn." For dawn is neither fully night, nor fully day, but as people say, between two lights (twilight); and so is this solitude and peace of divine union. It is neither informed in full clarity by divine light, nor does it stop sharing in it.

The silent music,

It is within this peace and silence of the night, and within these signs of divine light, that the soul realizes an admirable adjustment and disposition of wisdom in the differences of all its creatures and works. Each has the capacity to respond to God, and each lets out its voice of what in it is God. It all sounds like a high harmony of very delicate music above all the music and melodies of this world. The poem calls this music "silent," for though this music is silent to the natural senses and faculties, it is also a sounding solitude for the spiritual faculties. For these spiritual faculties, being alone and empty of all natural forms and apprehensions, are then able to receive spiritual sounds in a deep and sounding voice in the spirit, singing of the excellence of God in Himself, and of all creatures. . . .

STANZA 17

Chasing after your footprints
Young women take to the roads.

The touch of a spark,
The taste of scented wine,
Are in them a divine balm.

These simple verses describe the inner exercise these souls accomplish in their wills, moved by two graces and inner visitations of the Beloved. These are called "touch of a spark," and "scented wine." The inner exercise of the will as the result of these two visitations is called here "a divine balm." As to the first, the "touch of a spark," this touch, through which the Beloved touches the soul even when the soul is most absent-minded, kindles the heart with a fire of love in such a manner that it resembles a spark that flies away from the fire and burns the soul. Then the soul suddenly remembers, and the will flames up with love and the desire to praise, be grateful, adore, appreciate, and pray to God with the deepest taste of love. It is for this reason that these signs are called "a divine balm," emanating from the divine love of the "touch of a spark," comforting and strengthening the soul with its odor and substance. . . .

The Bride speaks of this divine touch in the Canticle: (My Beloved entered his hand through my opening, and my stomach shook internally at his touch, [Canticle, 5:4]). The touch of the Beloved is the touch of love we have mentioned here and the effect He thus produces on the soul. The "opening" through which the hand enters is the way and degree of perfection the soul already possesses, for the touch is in proportion to the degree of perfection in the soul. It is said that her "stomach" shook internally, and this means her will, where the divine touch takes place. "She shook internally," refers to the rising of the appetites and affections toward God, such as desire, love, praise, and those others we have mentioned, and these are the "divine balm," the result of such a touch.

The taste of scented wine,

This scented wine is a greater gift which God sometimes grants to the more advanced souls. God inebriates them with the Holy Spirit as with a soft wine of love that is delicious and full-bodied, and for this reason it is called scented wine. For as the scented wine is warmed with many different fragrant and vigorous spices, so is this love God grants to those who are already perfect; for this love is already warm and settled on the soul, and scented with the virtues the soul has already gained. . . .

This gift of soft inebriation does not disappear as fast as the "touch of a spark." It is already settled on the soul. The spark touches and dissipates, though its effects linger on, and at times very much so; but the scented wine and its effects last a long time, and this is, as earlier stated, soft love in the soul. At times it lasts one, two, or many days. . . .

Since we have spoken of warm wine, it might be useful here to point out briefly the difference between the warm, cooked wine, (also called aged) and the new wine, for the difference will be the same as between aged and new lovers; and this will serve as spiritual doctrine. The new wine has not digested the dregs, nor has it settled, and thus it ferments on the outside, and we cannot know its goodness and worth until it has well fermented the dregs and bite. Unless this is done, the wine is in danger of turning sour; it tastes thick and rough, and harms those who drink too much of it. Aged wine has already digested the dregs and settled down; thus it does not ferment from the outside. Its goodness can be easily seen, and there is no danger it will go sour, for it has been able to control the furies and movements of the dregs, which could well have turned it sour. Thus a well-fermented wine hardly ever becomes sour; its taste is soft and not only the taste but the strength of the substance of wine is in it; thus to drink from this wine creates good feelings and gives strength to the drinker.

. . . This same comparison may be found in Ecclesiastes: New wine is like a new friend; it will age, drink it then softly (Eccles. 9:15). . . .

STANZA 18

In the inner wine cellar
Of my Beloved I drank, and when I left
I found that in this world's fair
I felt for no thing or place,
I even lost the flock I once chased.

COMMENTARY

The soul sings in this stanza of the extraordinary gift God granted her when she was taken into the intimacies of love, that is, into the union or transformation of love in God. She tells of two effects she encountered there, and these are forgetfulness and dispossession of all the things of this world, and the death of all her appetites and tastes.

In the inner wine cellar

It would take the Holy Spirit to move my hand and write down what my soul wishes here to be understood, or even say something about this inner wine cellar. The wine cellar the soul speaks of here is the last and deepest degree of love the soul may dwell in during this life. For this reason it is called "inner wine cellar," that is to say, the most interior part of the soul. . . .

There are many souls who arrive and even enter the first wine cellar, each according to the degree of perfection they hold. But few souls arrive in this last and most interior wine cellar during this life, for in this place the perfect union with God has already taken place. This is called spiritual marriage, as the soul describes it here. And what God communicates to the soul in this union cannot be spoken about, and there is nothing that can be said, as nothing can be said about God that in any way equals Him. It is God Himself who makes the communication, having transformed the soul from herself unto Him in admirable glory, remaining both one. . . .

Of my Beloved I drank,

In the same manner that drink spreads and overflows through all the members and veins of the body, in the same way does the communication of God substantially spread and overflow the whole soul. Or even better, the soul transforms itself into God, and in this transformation the soul drinks of God according to her substance and spiritual faculties. She drinks wisdom and science through the intellect, the softest love through the will, and enjoyment and delight through remembering and the feeling of glory. . . .

I felt for no thing or place,

The soul becomes so lost in God, her mind so raised to Him, that she feels as if she were robbed by Him, drunk with love, totally transformed in God; and thus she is unable to notice anything of this world. So she may well say, "I felt for no thing or place," for she not only becomes detached from everything, but also from herself; and she feels destroyed, as if transformed into love itself, which is no more than her passage from herself to the Beloved. . . .

It is not to be understood that the soul, in such a state, loses her habits of science and the information of the things she knew—though she remains as if not knowing. The soul loses the act and memory of things in that transformation of love. . . .

STANZA 23

In just that lock of hair
That on my neck you saw move,
As you looked upon it there,
A prisoner it made of you,
And in my eyes you received a wound.

COMMENTARY

The soul tries to say three things in this stanza. First, that the love in which virtues rest is a strong love, for such it must be to keep them. The second, that God was caught by this hair of love, seeing it alone and strong. The third, that God fell madly in love with the soul, on seeing her purity and integrity of faith. Thus she says:

In just that lock of hair
That on my neck you saw move,

The "neck" here means strength, upon which it is said the hair of love in which all her virtues are entwined is moving with strength. . . . Virtues are so strung and in such order in this hair of love that if one broke or were lost, all would be lost. Where one virtue is, there are all the others, and where one is missing, so are all the others missing. It is said that it "moved" on the neck, for in the strength of the soul, that is, on the neck of the soul, this love moves to God with great fortitude and agility, not stopping for anything; and as the air moves and makes the hair fly on the neck, in the same manner the air of the Holy Spirit moves and changes a strong love so that it may fly to God. Virtues do not achieve any effects by themselves unless this divine wind moves the faculties to exercise their love of God. . . .[39]

A prisoner it made of you,

Oh wonder of wonders, to see God prisoner of a hair! The reason for this, and for such expression as prisoner, is that God stops to look; that is, He stops to love our low being. For if God, in His great compassion, did not look at us and love us first, thus lowering Himself, as St. John says, He would never become prisoner of the hair of our low love. The soul cannot fly so high as to catch this high bird of the heavens. But since God descends to look at us and entice our own flight and spread our wings, He makes our love worth something. It is for this reason that He himself becomes a prisoner of the hair as it moves, that is, He pays Himself and pleases Himself, and thus He is caught. . . .

STANZA 26

Catch us the little foxes,
Our vineyard is now in bloom,
And while of roses
We make a fistful,
Let no one appear on the hilltop.

COMMENTARY

The soul, wishing therefore that this inner delight of love—for this is the flower of the vineyard—not be stopped, either by envious or malicious devils, or by the furious appetites of sensuality, or the comings and goings of imaginations, or by any other type of information or presence of things, she prays to the angels to catch all these things and keep them from interfering with the exercise of inner love; it is while delighting in them that virtues and graces are communicated and enjoyed between the soul and the Son of God. . . .

While the soul is thus enjoying the flower of the vineyard and taking rest upon the chest of the Beloved, the virtues of the soul appear, sharp and at the ready, totally fulfilled, showing themselves to the soul in this manner and giving her great delight and sweetness. The soul feels these virtues in herself and in God at the same time, and they seem to her like a very ripe vineyard, pleased with her and her Beloved, and where both delight and rest. . . .

STANZA 27

Stop, dead wind;
Come, warm wind with love's memories,
Breathe through my garden,
The scent of your caresses,
For the Beloved to graze among the flowers.

COMMENTARY

. . . Spiritual aridity may also stop the interior flow of sweetness of which the soul spoke above. Fearing this, the soul does two things in this stanza. First, she stops aridity by closing the door to it through continuous prayer and dedication. Second, she calls on the Holy Spirit, who is the one capable of dispelling this aridity of the soul, and of sustaining and increasing in her the love for the Beloved. He is the one to bring the soul to the inner exercise of virtue, so that the Son of God, the Beloved, may rejoice and delight more in her, since her entire aim is to please the Beloved.

STANZA 28

The bride now enters
The pleasant orchard so desired,
And to her content she lingers,
Her neck gently inclined
Upon the sweet arm of the Beloved.

COMMENTARY

Now that the bride has made the effort of catching the little foxes, stopping the dead wind, and calming the nymphs of Judea,

all of which were impediments to the full enjoyment of the state of
spiritual marriage; and now that she has also managed to call for and
bring close the wind of the Holy Spirit, as is described in the
preceding stanzas (for He is the proper disposition and instrument
for the perfection of such a state), we must now concern ourselves
more particularly with this subject by explaining this stanza, for it is
here that the Bridegroom speaks of the soul as His wife. Two things
are here accomplished. First, the soul, victorious, explains how she
has reached this delightful state of spiritual marriage, which both
had so greatly desired. Second, the properties of this state that the
soul now enjoys are described, as for example resting in its delight
and laying her neck on the sweet arms of the Beloved, as we will
now explain.

The bride now enters

To clarify the order of these stanzas and what the soul has to
undergo to reach this state of spiritual marriage (which is the highest and of which now, with divine help, we intend to speak), it must
be noted that before the soul reaches this state she must first participate in the practice and trials of mortification, and also in meditation
on spiritual matters. To this the soul referred beginning with the
first stanza and up to the point at which she says, "Pouring a
thousand graces." The soul then enters on the contemplative life.
She undergoes the trials and ways of love, as she explains in stanza
after stanza, until she reaches the one in which she says, "Turn them
aside, my love." Here the spiritual marriage takes place. The soul
then proceeds by the unitive path, where she receives many and
very deep communications, visits, gifts, and jewels from the Bridegroom and, like one newly married, she learns and improves her
love for Him. This the soul sings beginning with the said stanza in
which the marriage took place ("Turn them aside, my love") to the
present one, which says, "The bride now enters." This is the point
at which the spiritual marriage between the soul and the Son of God
is at last consummated. This consummation bears no comparison to
the spiritual wedding, for here a deep and total transformation takes
place. Both surrender to one another by taking possession of each
other; the consummation occurs in the union of love, where the soul

is divinized through participation in God, to the degree that is possible in this life. . . . This is the highest state that can be reached in this life. For, as in the consummation of a carnal marriage *two people become one flesh,* as the Scripture says (Gen. 2:24), so also in the spiritual marriage consummation takes place between the soul and God, two natures joined in one spirit and love of God; this is similar to the light of a candle or a star joining that of the sun, for then what gives light is not the candle or the star, but the sun, having absorbed the other lights into its own.

The pleasant orchard so desired

This is as if the soul were to say, "I have been transformed into my God," a state which is here called a "pleasant orchard," because of the delightful and sweet rest the soul finds in it. No one reaches this desired orchard of full transformation, which is the joy, delight, and glory of spiritual marriage, without first passing through the spiritual wedding, and the common and faithful love of married people. For after the soul has been for a time the spouse of the Son of God in total and soft love, God gives her the nod and places her in this flowering garden to consummate this most happy state of marriage to Him. In this union there is such joining of the two natures and such communication of the divine into the human, that without either changing his or her nature, each one appears to be God. . . .

STANZA 36

Rejoice, my Beloved, with me,
And to see ourselves in your beauty
Let us go to the mountains or the hills,
Where water flows with purity;
Let us go deeper into the valley.

COMMENTARY

Now that the perfect union of love between the soul and God has taken place, the soul wishes to exercise and dedicate herself to the virtues of love. Thus she speaks in this stanza with the Bridegroom, asking for three things. First, to receive the joy and taste of love, and this she does when she says: "Rejoice, my Beloved, with me." Her second request is that she wishes to become similar to the Beloved, and this she asks when she says, "And to see ourselves in your beauty"; and the third is to scrutinize and learn the things and secrets of the Beloved, and this she asks when she says, "Let us go deeper into the valley.". . .

And to see ourselves in your beauty

This means: Let us act in such a way that by this act of love we may be able to see ourselves in Your beauty. That is, let us be equal in beauty, and let it be such that looking at one another the beauty we see will be equal to Yours, and we will be seen in Your beauty; this will happen if You transform me into Your beauty, and I will see myself, then, in it. . . .

Let us go to the mountains or the hills,

The soul will not be able to see herself in God's beauty and resemble Him in that beauty if she is not first transformed into the wisdom of God. She needs to be transformed into what is seen and held from above. Thus the soul wishes to go to "the mountains or the hills."

This stanza also speaks of the trials and tribulations the soul wishes to undergo. She says, "Let us go deeper into the valley." These trials and tribulations are the means of entering the "valley" of the delightful wisdom of God, for the purest suffering brings with it the purest wisdom, and also the purest and highest joy, for it comes from deeper inside. Thus, the soul, not satisfied with any form of suffering, asks, "Let us go deeper into the valley.". . .

STANZA 39

> The breathing of the air,
> The song of the tender nightingale,
> The grove without cares
> In the serene night, and the flame
> That consumes but gives no pain.

COMMENTARY

The breathing of the air,

This "breathing of the air" is a gift of the Holy Spirit, and the soul asks for it here in order to love God perfectly. It is called the "breathing of the air" because it is a most delicate touch and feeling of love ordinarily caused in the soul in this state through communication of the Holy Spirit. It is with this breathing of God, like an inspiration, that the Holy Spirit elevates the soul so she may breathe in God the same inspiration of love the Father breathes in the Son and the Son in the Father. Through the Holy Spirit, both breathe in the soul in the said transformation. For it would be no transformation if the soul did not join and were not transformed also into the Holy Spirit as she is in the other two persons of the Trinity, though in a lower form given the low condition of this life. This becomes for the soul such high glory and deep joy, that it cannot be spoken with mortal tongue, nor can human understanding explain it. For the soul, joined and transformed in God, breathes in God with the same divine breath that God, in her, breathes Himself to her.

The grove without cares

. . . "Grove" here means God and all His creatures as they rest in Him. For as plants and trees have their lives in groves, in the same way heavenly and earthly creatures have their roots and lives in God. . . .[40]

. . and the flame
That consumes but gives no pain.

. . . This flame is here understood as the love of God already perfectly established in the soul. The soul needs two properties to be perfect: first, that she be consumed and transformed into God, and second, that the burning and transformation of this flame does not cause pain to the soul. Thus this flame is now soft love, for as the soul becomes transformed into a flame there is satisfaction and conformity on both sides, and there is no pain in the soul of being dependent on greater or lesser amounts of love, as she was before she reached the fullness of this love. Having reached this state, the soul is as transformed and one in God, as the burning coal is with fire, neither letting out smoke nor sparks as it used to do before it burned fully, and without the darkness and roughness it had before it became penetrated by fire. These qualities of darkness and of letting out smoke or sparks are properties of the soul that experience a certain suffering and tiredness in the love of God, before she reaches that state of perfection of love when she is penetrated by its fire in fullness, softly and totally, without pains of smoke and passions and natural accidents. She is transformed into a soft flame that consumes all those things and changes her into God, where her movements and actions are now divine. . . .

LOVE'S LIVING FLAME:
The Soul as Living Flame

Commentary on the stanzas dealing with the most intimate and select union and transformation of the soul in God, written by the poet at the request of Doña Ana de Peñalosa.

NOTE: Doña Ana de Peñalosa was a benefactress of the Reformed Carmelites. She died in Madrid on March 27, 1608.

PROLOGUE

I feel, very noble and devout lady, a certain reluctance in trying to comment on these four stanzas as Your Grace has asked me. They deal with such interior and spiritual matters that no language is appropriate to them, for spiritual things exceed the senses, and it is difficult to say anything of their substance. One could speak badly concerning the depths of the spirit if one does not do it with spiritual depth. . . .

There is no reason to marvel at the fact that God grants such high and extraordinary gifts to the soul He has chosen to pamper. It does not seem unreasonable if we consider that it is God, and that He bestows those gifts as God with infinite love and goodness. He himself promised that if anyone loves him, the Father, the Son, and the Holy Spirit will make in that person a home (John 14:23), as the soul explains in these stanzas.

It is to be understood that the soul here speaking is already transformed and shares the inner quality of the fire of love, and that she is not only joined to Him in this fire, but this fire now makes a living flame in her. The soul feels this and in this manner she declares it in these stanzas, with a delicate and intimate sweetness of love burning in her flame, stressing in these verses some of its effects as they appear in her. . . .

THE COMMENTARY BEGINS

STANZA I

O Love's living flame,
Tenderly you wound
My soul's deepest center!
Since you no longer evade me,
Will you, please, at last conclude:
Rend the veil of this sweet encounter!

COMMENTARY

The soul now feels all inflamed in this divine union; her taste is all bathed in glory and love, and her most intimate substance is pouring no less than rivers of glory, abounding in delights. She feels running out of *her own stomach rivers of living water* (John 7:38), as the Son of God declared would happen in such souls. Since the soul feels transformed with such power into God and so highly possessed by Him, and in possession of such gifts and virtues, she feels very close to beatitude, with only a thin veil separating them. The soul becomes aware of the fact that the delicate flame of love burning in her glorifies her softly and powerfully each time it enters and penetrates her, feeling that in one of its thrusts she will reach eternal life, breaking the veil of mortal life, and that this is to happen within seconds, and that this waiting for the veil to be broken is the reason why the soul is not glorified. And so the soul speaks with great desire to the flame, the Holy Spirit, to break this mortal life at last in that sweet encounter during which He could communicate at last what He appears to be about to communicate; that is, the whole and perfect glory. Thus she says:

O love's living flame,

This flame of love is the Spirit of the soul's Bridegroom, the Holy Spirit. The soul feels Him within herself not only as the fire that has consumed and transformed her into sweet love, but as the fire that also burns within her and has become a flame, as I mentioned. This flame bathes the soul in glory and refreshes her with the strength of eternal life each time it is kindled. This is the work of the Holy Spirit on the soul transformed into love. The inner acts He produces are the kindling of that flame, inflamations of love, through which the united will of the soul loves in the highest form possible, made one love with that flame. Thus these acts of love of the soul are most valuable, and accrue more merit and are worth much more than all the soul had performed before she became transformed during her lifetime, regardless of how sublime those acts may have been. . . .

We may thus compare the habit of the soul normally within this state of transformation in love to the log engulfed in fire, and the acts of this soul to be the flame born of the fire of love. We see that this fire is more intense the greater is the union, and that this flame unites and carries up the acts of the absorbed and stolen will into the Holy Spirit, just as the angel rose to God in the flame of Manoah's sacrifice (Judg. 13:20). In this state the soul is not able to act on her own. It is the Holy Spirit Who performs all her actions and moves the soul. For this reason, the acts the soul performs in this state are divine, for the soul is moved and the acts are performed by God. The soul thinks, therefore, that each time the flame shoots up, forcing her to love with divine taste and temper, she is receiving eternal life, for she is raised to acts of God in God. . . .

. . . This flaring up of the Holy Spirit in the soul causes such high delight that the soul learns how eternal life really tastes. Thus this flame is called *living flame*, not because it is not always alive, but because it causes such effects on the soul as to force her to live in God spiritually and feel life in God, in the manner of David: *My heart and my flesh rejoiced in the living God* (Ps. 84:3).[41] The intention here is not to establish that God is always alive, but rather that his senses and spirit were alive with the taste of God, had become God, and this is equal to stating that they tasted the living God, that is, the life of God, eternal life. . . .

Tenderly you wound

This means that with your flame you tenderly touch me. For this flame is a flame of divine life and wounds the soul with the tenderness of the life of God. It wounds and softens it so much and so deeply that it makes it melt with love. . . .

How can we say, however, that the flame wounds the soul, since there is nothing in her left to wound, for the soul is all cauterized with the fire of love? This is a marvelous thing, for love is in continuous movement, just as the flame flares up here and there, and since love's job is to wound in order to cause love and joy, and since it is a living flame transformed in the soul, it keeps sending flares of fire causing tender wounds of delicate love, exercising the soul in the arts and play of love joyfully and festively. . . .

My soul's deepest center!

. . . By *my soul's deepest center* it is meant that when the soul's substance, virtue, and strength is reached, then the soul is wounded and taken over by the Holy Spirit. But the soul does not mean it to be understood that this vision is as the beatific vision of God in the other life, for this is unattainable while the soul is in this life, though at times God may grant something very similar. The soul speaks in this manner in order to declare the abundance and delight of the glory she feels in this manner of communication with the Holy Spirit. This delight is deeper and more tender the stronger and more substantial is the transformation and concentration of the soul into God. This is the utmost one can reach in this life, not as perfect as can be reached in the next, and for this reason it is called *my soul's deepest center.* It is possible, however, for the soul to possess the habit of love with the same perfection in this life as in the next, though not the acts or the fruits thereof, even though the fruits and acts of love grow in quality so much in this life that they are very similar to those of the next. With this in mind, the soul dares to speak as one would in the next life, and say: *my soul's deepest center.*

Considering, however, that strange things and those of which we have little experience appear extraordinary and less believable, it is understandable that what we have been saying of the soul in this state may seem to many, not knowing of it through science or experience, to be unbelievable or exaggerated. I answer to all these people . . . that this is what the Son of God promised: the Most Blessed Trinity will come and dwell within anyone who loves Him (John 14:23). This means that the intellect will be enlightened by the wisdom of the Son, that the will will find delight in the Holy Spirit, and that the soul will be strongly and vigorously absorbed within the deepest embrace of the Father's sweetness. . . .

. . . And this is how it happens (and even better than it can be said) when the flame of love rises in the soul. As soon as the soul is totally purged with regard to her substance, faculties, memory, intellect, and will, the divine substance, which as the Book of Wisdom says *touches everywhere by its cleanliness* (Wis. 7:24), absorbs the soul deeply and with subtlety within His divine flame. It is in this absorption of the soul within the wisdom of the Holy Spirit that He practices the glorious vibrations of his flame on the soul. . . .

STANZA 2

O cautery so tender!
O pampered wound!
O soft hand! O touch so delicately strange,
Tasting of eternal life
And canceling all debts!
Killing, death into life you change!

COMMENTARY

The soul explains in this stanza how the three persons of the Most Holy Trinity—the Father, the Son, and the Holy Spirit—work on the soul this act of union. Thus *hand, cautery, touch* are substantially the same. These names are given looking at the effect that corresponds to them. Thus, *cautery* is the Holy Spirit, *hand* is the Father, and *touch* the Son. The soul here praises the Father, the Son, and the Holy Spirit, stressing the three great gifts received from them, as they have changed death into life and the soul into Them. The first is *pampered wound,* and this belongs to the Holy Spirit; thus she calls it *cautery.* The second is the taste of eternal life, and this belongs to the Son, and is called *touch so delicately strange.* The third is the transformation of the soul, the *debt* with which the soul is well paid, and this belongs to the Father; thus it is called *soft hand.* Though the soul names the three gifts according to the properties of their effects, she only refers to one when she says: *death into life you change.* For the three gifts operate in one, and thus she attributes all of them to one, and one to all.

O cautery so tender!

This tender cautery is, as we have said, the Holy Spirit. Moses says in Deuteronomy, *Our Lord is a consuming fire* (Deut. 4:24), which means fire of love. Since this fire has infinite strength it may consume and transform to itself the soul it touches, though in an incomprehensible manner. This fire consumes each soul according to the readiness of the soul: some more, others less, and this according to its will, and how and when it wishes. Since God is an infinite fire of Love, when He wishes to touch a soul deeply the fire of the soul reaches such a degree of love that she feels herself burning above all the fires of this world. It is for this reason that she calls the Holy Spirit in this union *cautery*. For the heat of cautery is more intense and violent and produces greater effects than do other burnings, for in this union the fire of love is greater than anywhere else. And the soul is not only transformed by this divine fire, but she also feels the *cautery,* and the soul as a whole is made into a cautery of ravaging fire. . . .

It is thus that the happy soul through great fortune comes to this cautery where she knows all, tastes all, does all she wants, and grows in love. No one prevails against her, and she is touched by no one. The Apostle says of this soul: *The spiritual man judges all things and he is judged by no one* (1 Cor. 2:15); and again, *The spirit searches out all things, unto the deep things of God* (1 Cor. 2:10). This is the property of love: to search for all the possessions of the Beloved. . . .

O pampered wound!

The soul has addressed *cautery* first; now she addressed the *wound* made by the cautery. Since the cautery, as has been said, is soft, the wound must be proportionate to it; thus the wound from a *soft cautery* must be a *pampered wound.* For since the cautery is of love, the wound must be a wound of soft love, and thus it will be softly pampered.

Another way of cauterizing the soul is by means of intellectual

form, usually very high, and it is as follows. It may happen sometimes that the soul may be so inflamed with the love of God that she
will feel as if an angel, a seraph, were attacking her with an arrow or
dart all aflame with the fire of love, and that the dart is penetrating
into this soul already burning like a coal or a flame, and that the
angel cauterizes the wound instantly. It is then, in this penetration,
with the arrow and the cauterizing following it, that the flame of the
soul takes life and becomes vehemently inflamed, as when someone
uses a poker to stir the fire of a furnace or an oven. It is then, when
this burning dart wounds the soul, that the feeling becomes in-
tensely pleasing to the soul, for besides the fact that the soul is
moved about by the violent poking of the angel, when the soul is
burning and melting with love she also feels the delicate wound and
the herbs with which the angel tempered the arrow, forming a very
sharp thrust like the live tip of a dart, in the very substance of the
spirit, in the center itself of the pierced soul.

Who can adequately speak about this intimate tip of the
wound, which seems to reside at the center, the heart, of the spirit,
where it usually feels the most subtle aspects of things? For the soul
feels as if she held a very tiny mustard seed there, fully alive and
burning, sending into the surrounding circles of the soul a live and
burning fire of love; and this fire, born as it is from the very
substance and power of that live center where the seed is, radiates
itself in a subtle manner through all the spiritual veins of the soul
with all its power. The soul feels this heat of love becoming so
intense that she feels as if seas of loving fire are spreading in all four
directions, filling the earth and skies. The soul feels as if the whole
universe were a sea of love within which she moves, seeing no limits
to that love, feeling within herself the very tip and wound of this
love. . . .

Let us return, then, to the work the angel carries out, which is
truly to make the soul sore and wounded internally in the spirit.
Thus, if God sometimes allows for these internal wounds to appear
on the outside, they may appear on the body, as in the case of St.
Francis, wounded in the flesh in the manner he was wounded internally by love. God usually does not grant the body any gifts He has
not first granted the soul; and the greater is the delight and strength
of love that the wound causes in the soul, the greater is the external

manifestation in the body; as the one increases, so does the other.
This happens because these souls are so purified and abiding in God
that they experience pain and suffering in their carnal body while
their soul thrives with sweetness because of its strength and health.
Thus it is a marvelous thing to observe how pain grows out of
pleasure. This same marvelous thing did not escape Job, who when
observing his own wounds spoke to the Lord: Returning to me, you
torment me wondrously (Job 10:16). This is an indescribable
wonder and worthy of the generosity and sweetness God has hidden
for those that fear Him (Ps. 31:20)—to make them enjoy the taste of
pleasure when the pain and suffering is greatest. . . .

It must be noted that the more subtle and delicate this touch is,
the more joy and intimate pleasure it communicates where it
touches, infinitely smaller is the size of the touch. The divine touch
has no size or width, for the word producing it lacks any shape,
form, and figure, and this is what sets the limits to substance. Thus
this touch, of which we speak here, insofar as it comes from the
divine substance, is ineffable. O finally, delicate and ineffable touch
of the word, since nothing happens in the soul but through Your
most simple being and it is infinite, and it is infinitely delicate,
therefore it touches with such a subtle, loving, delicate, and lofty
touch that it leaves the soul—

Tasting of eternal life

Though this does not happen in a perfect manner, yet, its effect
leaves a certain taste of eternal life, as we have said earlier. . . .

Killing, death into life you change!

The soul calls here *death* the disappearance of the natural man,
the natural use of the faculties—memory, intelligence, and will—as
used to address the things of this world and the appetites of creatures. All this is the exercise of a decadent life, the death of an old
way of life which causes the death of the new life, that is, of the
spiritual life. The soul will not be able to live her spiritual life
perfectly if the old life does not die first, as the Apostle admonished:
Take off the old man and put on the new man who according to God

is created in justice and holiness (Eph. 4:22–24). In this new life, that is, when the soul has reached this perfect union with God, all the appetites and faculties of the soul and their habits . . . are transformed into divine operations.

Since, according to the philosophers, living beings live according to their operations, and since the soul lives now in God through the union she has with Him, she now lives God's life, thus her death has been changed into life, from animal life into spiritual life. . . .

In this state of perfect life the soul moves about, internally and externally, as if on holiday, the palate of her spirit tasting a deep joy of God, a song constantly renewed, wrapped up in joy and love at the knowledge of her happy state. . . .

STANZA 3

> O lamps of fiery lure,
> In whose shining transparence
> The deep cavern of the senses,
> Blind and obscure,
> Warmth and light, with strange flares,
> Gives with the lover's caresses!

COMMENTARY

. . . The soul, in this stanza, praises and thanks her Bridegroom for the many gifts their union has brought to her. She states how through such union she received many deep signs from Him; that these signs are all of love and that they light up and make the faculties and senses of the soul fall in love, faculties and senses which earlier had been blind and in the dark. And now the faculties and senses are clear and with the heat of love they can in turn give light and love to the One Who cleared them and made them feel in love. . . .

O lamps of fiery lure,

. . . To understand the kind of lamps the soul mentions, and how they light up and warm the soul, we should remember that God in His unique and simple Being is the whole range of all the virtues and powers of His attributes. He is almighty, wise, good, compassionate, just, strong, and loving. He is also many other attributes and marvels of which we do not know. Since He is all of this in His simple being, when the soul is joined to Him, and when God decides to flood the soul with His signs, then the soul sees all these virtues in Him in a different manner. . . .

Insofar as the soul receives the signs of these attributes in one single act of this union, God becomes for the soul many lamps at once, all shining and giving warmth separately. The soul receives signs from each separately and is inflamed in love by each. Thus, the soul loves with an inflamed love caused by each lamp and all the lamps at once, for all these attributes are one being, as we have said, and all these lamps are one lamp. . . .

One should realize that the delight the soul receives in this rapture of love produced by the fire of the light of these lamps is extraordinary and immense. It is abundant because it comes from all the lamps at once, and from each separately also, for each burns with love, while the heat of one increases the heat of the other, and the flame of one adds to the flame of the other, and the light of one to the light of the other, for each attribute is sufficient to know all the others. Thus all the lamps become one light and one fire, while the soul, totally absorbed within these delicate flames, and deeply wounded by love from each one, and at the same time even more deeply wounded and alive in the love of God from all of them at once . . . that the soul fully experiences here and understands the truth of the verse in the *Song of Songs,* that the lamps of love are lamps of fire and flames (Sg. 8:6). . . .

Who can say, then, O blessed soul, what you now feel, knowing yourself to be so loved, and by this love so raised? Your bosom, your will, is like a bride's, a mound of wheat covered and surrounded by lilies (Sg. 7:2). For while you are enjoying the grains of the bread of life, you are, at the same time, feeling the delight of those lilies of virtue circling you. These are the king's daughters mentioned by David, *they delighted you with myrrh, amber, and aromatic spices* (Ps. 44:9–10). Those signs the Beloved sends you are His daughters, His graces and virtues, and in them you bathe and are engulfed by them. You are also the well of living waters running impetuously from Mount Libanus (Sg. 4:15), that is, from God.

And in this you are gloriously filled with joy in the whole harmony of your body and soul, transformed into a paradise with divine irrigation. . . .[42]

. . . Thus, though it is fire it is also water; for this fire is the fire of the sacrifice lit by Jeremiah in the well: while it remained hidden it was water, and when they drew it out for the sacrifice it was fire (2 Mc. 1:20–23). Thus, the spirit of God hidden in the veins of the soul is like soft and fresh water quenching the thirst of the spirit, but as soon as it is exercised in the sacrifice of loving God it becomes living flames of love,[43] and these are the *lamps* in the act of love, and the *flames*. As we said above of the Bridegroom in the Canticle: *Your lamps are lamps of fire and flames* (Sg. 8:6). Thus the soul here calls them "flames, for she not only tastes them as waters, but exercises them in the love of God like flames." . . . The soul becomes the daughter of God through participation in Him and His attributes, and these are here called *lamps of fire*.

In whose shining transparence

Let us clarify what the soul calls *shining transparence* and how the soul shines in them. . . . The soul shines with the light of love, and this shining is not like the one produced by material lamps lighting the things around them. This shining is from within the flames, for the soul is within this shining transparence; thus, the soul says in whose shining transparence, meaning within. And this is not all, for as we have said the soul becomes transformed into that shining transparence, becoming one with it. Thus we may assert that it is as the air within the flame, for the flame is no more than air inflamed; and the movements and light given by that flame are neither air alone nor fire, but the combination of air and fire, and that it is the fire that causes the air to shine as it has inflamed it with fire.

We may thus understand that the soul and its faculties are made to shine within the light of God. The movements of these divine flames, which are the vibrations and flames we have described above, are not produced by the soul alone transformed into the flames of the Holy Spirit, nor does the Spirit produce them by Himself alone, but the Spirit and the soul together, He moving the soul, as the fire moves the inflamed air. Thus, these movements of

God and the soul together are not only shining transparencies, but also glorifications of the soul. These movements and flames are the game and joyful festival the Spirit causes in the soul, as we said in the commentary to the second stanza of this poem. It seems as if the Spirit were finally about to grant the soul eternal life and transport her to her perfect glory, bringing her finally into Himself. . . .

One may gather with greater clarity, from what we have said and are about to say, how exceedingly bright the light of these lamps is, as may be seen from the fact that they are also called *overshadowings*. This means something like casting a shadow, as much to protect, favor, and grant gifts, as to rest. For if a person's shadow covers us it means the person is close enough to grant us favors and protect us. Thus we find the Angel Gabriel describing the conception of the Son of God, that favor granted to the Virgin Mary, as an overshadowing of the Holy Spirit: The Holy Spirit will come upon you and the power of the Most High will overshadow you (Luke 1:35).

For a clear understanding of how God's casting of shadows, or overshadowings, or shining transparency (for they are all the same) comes about, let us consider how each thing casts its own shadow according to its height and property. If the object is opaque and dark, it will make a dark shadow, and if the object is clear and subtle, the shadow will be clear and subtle. Thus the shadow of the dark will be a darkness proportionate to it, and the shadow of a light a shadow proportionate to it.

God's attributes and virtues being, as they are, shining and resplendent lamps, and the soul being as near as she is to them, these lamps will not be able to avoid touching her with their shadows. But these shadows will also be resplendent and bright, in proportion to the lamps producing them; thus these shadows will turn out to be shining too. . . .

The deep cavern of the senses,

These caverns are the faculties of the soul: memory, understanding, and will. They are as deep as they are capable of receiving the greatest gifts. They fill only with the infinite. The emptiness they suffer without God will give us a measure of the joy they experience when they are filled with Him. . . . It must be pointed out that when these caverns of the faculties of the soul are not empty, purged, or clean of all affection toward creatures, they do not feel the emptiness of their deep capacities. Anything that attaches to them in this life is sufficient to keep them occupied and distracted, preventing them from feeling the harm caused, or missing greater good, or even knowing their great capabilities. It is also worth pointing out that it is enough for the soul, capable of the greatest good, to receive the least of them to be satisfied, and the soul cannot progress any further unless they are totally empty, as we shall soon see. But when the soul is clean and empty, the thirst and hunger for spiritual life is intolerable. The stomachs of the caverns are deep, and thus they suffer deeply, for the food they miss is also deep. . . . This great feeling for the spiritual life comes usually toward the end of the illumination and purification of the soul, just before reaching union, where the feeling is satisfied. Since the spiritual appetite is empty and purged from all creatures and affections towards them, and the natural disposition is lost, it is then that this spiritual appetite, forged in divine temper, with all its emptiness ready, finds itself frustrated with the lack of a total union with God. The soul, then, feels the suffering of this emptiness and thirst even more deeply than if it were death, the more so since through some sparks and cracks she is able to spy some divine rays, but not the complete vision. These souls suffer impatiently for love and cannot last very long without either receiving it or dying. . . .

What these caverns may hold is deep—it is God Himself, deep and infinite. Thus their capacity is, in some way, infinite, and so is their thirst, their hunger; their detachment and suffering are death. . . .

"Oh," you will say, "the soul understands no particulars and therefore she will not be able to make any progress." To this I answer that if the soul understood particulars, she would make no progress. The reason is that God, who is the object of the intellect, far exceeds the intellect, and thus He is incomprehensible and inaccessible to it. When the intellect begins to understand it is not moving closer to God, but away from Him. Thus the intellect must withdraw from itself and from its knowledge in order to reach God. Its path is faith, not knowledge. It is thus that the intellect reaches perfection, for it is through faith, and not through knowledge that it joins God. The soul travels to God not knowing rather than knowing. . . .

. . . In this state of perfection, even not to slide backwards is progress. The progress of the intellect is to turn itself to face faith, and thus it becomes darker, for faith is darkness to the intellect. . . .

"Oh," you will say, "if the intellect does not understand particulars the will remains idle and it does not love, and this must always be avoided in the spiritual path! The will is not capable of loving except what the intellect knows." This is true, particularly in the natural acts and operations of the soul, where the soul only loves what the intellect distinctively knows. But in this contemplation we are talking about, by which God infuses Himself in the soul, it is not necessary to receive knowledge of particulars, nor for the soul to perform acts of understanding, for God communicates to her in one single act light and love simultaneously. This is loving, supernatural knowledge, like a light giving warmth, for this light infuses love simultaneously. This light is dark and obscure to the intellect, for it leads to contemplation, and is like a ray of darkness for the intellect, as St. Dionysius teaches (Pseudo-Dionysius Areopagita, *De Mystica Theologia*, c.1:PG 3, 999). Thus, the intellect is to the understanding what love is to the will, for as this knowledge infused by God is general and obscure to the intellect, so the will loves in general without any distinction of particulars. . . .

. . . As for God: the soul, though not loving Him with any particular act, nor enjoying Him in a particular and distinct manner, loves Him, in that secret and obscure union, more than all particulars put together. It is then that the soul realizes that no particular gives her more joy than that solitary touch. . . .

Blind and obscure,

The soul was also blind insofar as it enjoyed some other thing. Appetite is the blindness of the rational and superior faculty. This appetite blocks and hangs over the eye of reason like a cataract or cloud, preventing it from seeing. Thus, while proposing something joyful to the senses it was blind to the divine riches and beauty hiding behind the cataract; one small object placed over the eye is enough to stop it from seeing greater things, regardless of how small the object covering the eye is or how large are those away from it. Any small or frivolous act performed by the soul is enough to block all those divine gifts waiting beyond the desires and appetites the soul reaches out to. . . .

. . . For as the cataract or cloud settles over the eye of judgment, it sees nothing but cataract or cloud—now of this color, now of another color, as the obstacles present them, and the soul takes this to be God. I have said that all we see is the cataract over the eye, and that God does not fit within the senses. It is in this manner that our appetites and sensual longings become an obstacle to knowledge of higher things. . . .

People who are not spiritual, not rid of animalistic tastes and desires, believe that those things the spirit considers low and base, which happen to be the things most filling their senses, are the highest; and those the spirit considers highest and most valuable, which are those most distant from the senses, these people will consider worthless and they will pay no attention to them—they might even consider them to be madness. In the words of St. Paul: *The animal man does not perceive the things of God; they are foolishness to him and he cannot understand them* (1 Cor. 2:14). *Animal man* here means whoever lives by natural appetites and affections, for even if some affections are borne from the spirit upon the senses, as soon as such a man tries to hold onto them with his natural appetites they then *become* natural appetites. It does not matter that the object or motive is supernatural, for if the appetite arises from our natural inclination where it has its power and root it remains natural, for it has the same nature as if it were a natural motive or object.

You may argue that when the soul desires God she desires Him supernaturally, and that therefore this desire has merit in the eyes of God. I answer by saying that when the soul desires God this desire is not always supernatural, but is so only when God infuses such a desire. God grants the strength of such a desire, and this is very different from a natural appetite, and it is then that this desire gains merit. Thus, when you wish to have the desire of God by yourself, this is only a natural appetite, and it will stay that way until God informs it supernaturally. And thus it follows that when you want to hold on to the taste of spiritual things and become attached to them, you do so out of your own natural appetite; you block your eyes with cataracts and remain an animal. You will not then be able to judge or understand spiritual matters, for they are above our senses and our natural appetites.

> *Warmth and light, with strange flares,*
> *Gives with the lover's caresses!*

When these caverns of the soul's faculties are so miraculously and wonderfully impregnated by the admirable splendors of those lamps, as we have said, that the faculties burn within them, they return their light of God to God, in addition to surrendering themselves to Him. They return the same shining transparency they have received in loving glory, leaning towards God in God, they themselves having become flaming lamps within the divine flames, returning to the Beloved the same light and heat of love they receive. For here the soul's faculties are returning what they receive to the one that gives and receives them, and with the same *strange flares* He gives. . . .

Strange flares means strange to our common way of thinking—above all praise, beyond every way and manner. The first strange flare is the way the intellect receives divine wisdom, as the intellect becomes one with God, and this is the same way the soul gives it back, for she cannot do it otherwise than the way it was given to her. The other strange flare is the way the will is joined to goodness, for it is this same goodness the soul returns to God in God, for this is the reason the soul received it in the first place—to give it back. And the same is true of the strange flare by which the soul is known in God's greatness, is united to it as the soul shines with the warmth of love. The same is true of all the other attributes of God communicated to the soul: fortitude, beauty, justice, and so on. These are the strange flares the soul is returning through her senses in joy to the Beloved, the same light and warmth she is receiving from her Beloved. The soul transformed in God becomes God in a certain manner, through participation, though as we have said, not in as perfect a manner as in the next life, but as the shadow of God. The soul operates in God and through God exactly as He operates in her by Himself, in the same way He does it, for the will of both is one, and so is the operation of both, one. . . .[44]

 . . . It is there that the soul realizes God is hers in truth, and that she possesses Him by heredity, by right, as God's adopted daughter, out of the gift God made of Himself, and that belonging to Him He may dispose of this gift as He will. Thus He gives it to His love, who is God Himself in His own gift, and here the soul pays back to God all she owes Him, for she pays Him out of her own will whatever she receives.

God gives the soul in this gift the Holy Spirit out of His own will, so that God may be loved in Him as He deserves. The soul receives inexpressible joy and delight in this exchange for she returns to God what belongs to her, and shares in God according to His infinite being. Though it is true that the soul is not able to add anything to God in this gift, for God is always the same in Himself, nonetheless the soul gives back a perfect gift, returning all she has received to gain love, and this is giving back as much as she received. God pays Himself with this gift of the soul (nothing less would do), and God receives it gratefully as a gift from the soul, and in this same gift God loves the soul anew, and in this surrender of the soul's gift the soul loves again as if for the first time. . . .

STANZA 4

How tame and loving
Your memory rises in my breast,
Where secretly only you live:
And in your fragrant breathing,
Full of goodness and grace,
How delicately in love you make me feel!

COMMENTARY

It is as though the soul said: "Your memory, O Divine Word, rises from the center and depth of my soul, and this is her pure and intimate substance, where in secret and silently, as her only Lord, You live, and not as if she were Your house, or even Your own bed, but within my own breasts, intimately and tightly joined to me, and it is here that I feel You tame and loving.". . .

Your memory rises in my breast,

. . . This memory is a movement that the Word creates in the substance of the soul, so deep, powerful, filled with joy, and of such intimate softness that the soul feels as if all the spices and fragrances from the flowers of the whole world are moving gently to perfume the soul. She feels as if all the kingdoms of the world and all the powers and virtues of the heavens are also moving, and that all the virtues, perfections, substances, and graces of all creatures and of all created things also shine and make the same movement, all at once within one. . . .

The above comparison is not accurate enough, for in this experience all these things not only appear to be moving but each one uncovers the beauty of its being, all their virtues, graces, loveliness, and the root of their duration and life. The soul soon realizes, in that experience, that all creatures from above and below receive their life and strength from Him. . . .

In this experience the soul sees how all these things are different from God insofar as their being is created, and she sees them in Him as His power, root, and strength; but she also realizes that it is God in His infinite immanence she knows inside, and in Him she knows all these things, and thus she knows these things better in herself than in themselves. And this is the great delight of this memory: to know creatures through God, and not God through creatures.[45] This is knowing the effects by their cause and not the cause by its effects.

It is a marvelous thing to realize how this movement takes place in the soul, for God is immovable. Though God does not really move, it appears to the soul that He is moving, for since the soul is the one that is changed and moved by God so that she may behold this supernatural vision, and this divine life and being, and the harmony of all the movement of creatures within God appears to her with such novelty, the soul thinks it is God Who moves, and gives to the cause the name of what belongs to the effects, for according to the effects we may say that God moves. . . .

This is the way God acts, as the soul saw, moving, leading, granting being, virtue, graces, and gifts to all His creatures while holding them virtually, in presence and substance, in Himself. The soul sees what God is in Himself and in His creatures at a glance, as if, through the open door of a palace, she saw the eminence of the person within and all he was doing. This is the way I understand how this comes about: the soul is substantially in God, as is every creature, and God removes from their eyes some of the many veils and curtains they carry over them so that they may see Him as He is. It is then that that face full of graces is partly and vaguely delineated, for not all the veils are removed. And since this vision comes together with the movement of all the creatures that are moving by His virtue, it appears as if God were moving with them in continuous movement. Thus the soul thinks it was God who moved and so she remembers it, while in fact the soul is the one that was moved.

The soul loses her fears as she shares these moments with the King of Heaven in an amicable exchange, as equals and as brothers. For God shows the soul the fortitude of His power with gentility, not fury, while the love of His goodness communicates strength and love from His bosom, coming to the soul from the center of the soul, like the Bridegroom leaving his bridal chamber (Ps. 18:6), where He was hiding, leaning over her, touching her with the scepter of His majesty, and embracing her like a sister. In this embrace we find the royal garments and their fragrance, God's admirable virtues; the shining of gold, charity; the shining of precious stones, the knowledge of all superior and inferior substances; and the face of the Word, full of graces that attack and dress the queen of the soul, so that when transformed into these virtues of the King of Heaven she becomes the queen. And so David's saying may apply to her: The queen sat by your right in garments of gold and surrounded with variety (Ps. 44:10). And since all this takes place in the innermost being of the soul, she adds:

Where secretly only you live:

The soul says He lives in her bosom, secretly, for as we have said, it is in the innermost being of the soul that this embrace takes place. God lives in all souls in secret and covered within their own substance, for if this were not the case, they could not last. . . .

And in your fragrant breathing,
Full of goodness and grace,
How delicately in love you make me feel!

This stanza, full of glory, goodness, and delicate love of God towards the soul, seals my lips, and there is no way I may speak about it, for I know clearly I will fail with words, and this is how they would come out if I tried. For here we have an inspiration from God to the soul, in which the remembrance of high knowledge of the Divinity is taken up by the Holy Spirit. . . .

NOTES

PART I: *THE LIFE*

CHAPTER ONE: THE PROPHETIC VOICE

1. Richard L. Rubenstein, "Religion and Cultural Synthesis," *The World & I* (April 1986).
2. Antonio T. de Nicolás, *Powers of Imagining: Ignatius de Loyola* (Albany, NY: SUNY Press, 1986).
3. Victoria Lincoln, *Teresa: A Woman,* ed. and intro. Elias Rivers and A. T. de Nicolás (Albany, NY: SUNY Press, 1985).
4. Emilie Zum Brunn, *St. Augustine,* trans. Ruth Namad (New York: Paragon House, 1988).
5. Herbert N. Schneidau, *Sacred Discontent: The Bible and Western Tradition* (Baton Rouge: Louisiana State University Press, 1976).

CHAPTER TWO: THE LIFE

1. The poet does not actually "write" poetry; that is, "writing" is not the originating act of poetry. The poet, while writing poetry, channels experience within the bounding shores of language. In this manner experience becomes public. The original act of poetry is the creation of experience. This experience could become lost or destructive, like the waters of a flood, but for the bed of language the poet builds. In this way experience reaches out with a controlled touch, in manageable proportions of sensation.

239

2. It is not known on which day Juan de la Cruz was born. The registry of baptisms at his parish of St. Cebrián has been missing since the early part of this century. The reason why this registry is missing is also unknown.

3. See José Jiménez Lozano, *Poesía: San Juan de la Cruz* (Madrid: Taurus Ediciones, 1982), 26.

4. Marcel Bataillon, *Erasmo y España* (Mexico–Buenos Aires: Fondo de Cultura Economica, 1966), 179–82, 542–43; Alvaro Huerga, *Historia de los Alumbrados: Los Alumbrados de Andalucía,* vol. II (Madrid: Fundación Universitaria Española, 1978), 595–96; Gerald Brenan, *St. John of the Cross* (New York: Cambridge University Press, 1983), 21, 77, 89, 96–98.

It might make it easier to understand the reaction of the Inquisition to the "*alumbrados,*" "*iluminados,*" and "*beatas*" if we consider that they had become a universal fashion, that "the whole country was covered by the doctrines of the *alumbrados* as if by a plague," and that eroticism and sexuality had taken over religious practice among people who behaved unethically under the pretense of "*alumbramiento,*" divine inspiration.

The *Song of Songs* was the center of controversy between the professors at the University of Salamanca, when John of the Cross was there as a student, and the Inquisition. Three professors of Jewish descent, Fray Luis de León, Grajal, and Martín Martínez, took the *Song* as a "*carmen amatorium,*" an erotic poem between its author King Solomon and his wife. The Church took it to be an allegory of the soul's love for God. It is also known that some of these professors were accused of reading the Arabic version of the *Song* to their students, and they were also accused, as Juan de la Cruz has been accused in his poetry, of "Arabic shades." See Luce López Baralt, "Huellas del Islam en San Juan de la Cruz. En torno a La Llama de Amor Viva y la espiritualidad musulmana israquí," *Vuelta* 45 (1980): 7–8.

CHAPTER THREE: SPIRITUAL PRACTICE

1. This statement is the epistemological epigram of mysticism in its many practiced varieties. It stresses the primacy of images in perception, their link to the will and affections, and their possible transformation by manipulation of images, or through the mediation of images.

This epistemological stance is contrary to theology, for theology deals with propositions, concepts, their relations, their link to the intellect, and the immutable truths of intellectual principles.

It is obvious that some theologies will accept mystical experience as the ground of religion, while others consider the "written word" the only ground of religion. These two attitudes towards religious experience were evident at the time of Juan de la Cruz in the opposing views of the Reformation and the Counter-Reformation theologians, and continue to cause disagreements in our own time between fundamentalist theologians and others who take experience as the foundation of religion, be they Catholic or members of any of the many extra–Biblical religions. A democratic society should give legitimacy to all these varieties of religious experience, not because they are religious but because they represent the whole range of human acts.

2. For a longer description of this project see my book *Powers of Imagining: Ignatius de Loyola* (Albany, NY: SUNY Press, 1986).

3. See Victoria Lincoln, *Teresa: A Woman* (Albany, NY: SUNY Press, 1984).

4. See Teresa Toulouse, *The Art of Prophesying: New England Sermons and the Shaping of Belief* (Athens: The University of Georgia Press, 1987).

5. See *Power of Imagining,* chap. 2, on imagining and the making of images in meditation.

6. See, for example, Masters, Roberts, and Jean Houston, *Mind Games: The Guide to Inner Space* (New York: Dell, 1973).

7. This act of dismemberment is as old as the Ṛg Veda and runs through the practices of the mystery religions and mystics in general. See Antonio T. de Nicolás, *Meditations Through the Ṛg Veda* (York, ME: Nicolas-Hays, 1976) also Joseph Fontenrose, *Python: A Study in Delphic Myth and Its Origins* (Berkeley: University of California Press, 1959).

8. Three mystic contemporaries, Ignatius de Loyola, Teresa de Avila, and Juan de la Cruz, may serve to provide an easy comparison of a practice common to all mystics. This chapter is the summary of such practice. I have already developed in more detail the practice of Ignatius de Loyola in *Powers of Imagining*. He is the best of the three in his description of the initiation to meditation. Teresa and Juan provide us more detailed information regarding the inner gifts souls receive in this practice, the description of inner signs and spiritual gifts. No one surpasses San Juan de la Cruz in his detailed description of the highest stages of meditation, although he advises that in the absence of spiritual gifts one should return to the cultivation of imagination and wait.

It might be instructive to summarize here Teresa de Avila's description of the same journey. As regards the use of imagination she writes: "God is not the product of the imagination: but it is through the imagination that God becomes present," (*Life*, 28:10). She also reminds us with Castilian irony that "The toad does not fly," (*Life*, 23:13).

On the difficulty of meditation, principally at the beginning, she writes: "And very often, for many years, I was more anxious for the hour I had determined to spend in prayer to be over than I was to remain there . . . and so unbearable was the misery I felt on entering the oratory, that I had to muster all my courage," (*Life*, 8:7).

On the transformation of the soul through meditation she writes: "The soul undergoes a change; it is always absorbed. . . . The intellectual vision is represented to the imagination so that in conformity to our weakness this presence may last in the memory and keep the thought well-occupied," (*Life*, 28:9).

On the use of the faculties in meditation she writes: "The faculties are like wild horses, they run in all directions; meditation proper begins with the technologies that gather them within," (*Life*, 14:2); "There the faculties are not lost, nor do they sleep," (Ibid.); "Only the will is occupied," (Ibid.); "Without knowing how, it becomes captive; it merely consents to God allowing Him to imprison it as one who well knows how to be captive of its lover," (Ibid.).

On the dark night of the soul she writes: "The water of grace rises up to the throat of this soul," (*Life*, 16:2); "This experience does not seem to be anything else than the almost total death to all earthly things," (Ibid.); "It seems to me that the soul is crucified since no consolations come to it from heaven, nor visits heaven; neither does it desire any from earth, nor is it on earth. . . . It is as though crucified between heaven and earth. . . . The intense pain takes away sensory consciousness . . . and this experience resembles the death agony with the difference that the suffering bears along with it great happiness. . . . It is arduous, delightful martyrdom," (*Life*, 20:11).

CHAPTER FOUR: THE POETIC VOICE

1. Crisógono de Jesus, *Vida de San Juan de la Cruz* (Madrid: Biblioteca de Autores Christianos, 1982), 404: "And his body, earlier on full of sores, begins to let out the smell of roses."
2. Mystic experience, unlike experiences derived from fantasy, are neither purely private nor subjective. Because of the embodied condition of the subject using these technologies of imagining, the experiences these technologies produce are as objective and capable of human articulation as the cognitive technologies derived from logic. Both require that

those reading the signs of such technologies be not only experts in the practice but also in the reading of the signs.

3. The writings of San Juan de la Cruz are gathered in *Obras Completas,* eleventh (critical) edition by Lucino Ruano de la Iglesia (Madrid: Biblioteca de Autores Cristianos, 1982). Juan de la Cruz's Life is told by Crisógono de Jesus in *Vida de San Juan de la Cruz,* Biblioteca de Autores Christianos, Madrid, 1982.

4. See *Obras Completas,* and the several introductions to those poems.

5. The poems called minor, like "Romance on the Gospel" give a clear idea of how the Saint instructed the young souls under his care to "gather memories" for meditation.

6. See *Powers of Imagining,* chap. 1; Francis A. Yates, *The Art of Memory* (London: Penguin, 1969); and Alexander Koyre, *Mystiques, spirituels, et alchemistes* (Paris, 1955).

7. Two famous bathrooms of the sixteenth century are Juan de la Cruz's and Martin Luther's.

8. Marcel Bataillon has shown the influence of St. Augustine on San Juan de la Cruz through the *Soliloquies,* a work attributed to Augustine during the sixteenth Century but later seen as not belonging to the Saint. "Sobre la génesis poética del Canto Espiritual de San Juan de la Cruz," in *Varia lección de clásicos españoles* (Madrid: Gredos, 1964), 167–82.

9. The most complete study on the influences of others on San Juan de la Cruz, particularly his poetry, is given by Domingo Yndurain in *San Juan de la Cruz: Poesía* (Madrid: Catedra, 1983). See page 32 on biblical influences. He also provides a bibliography on the subject.

PART II: *THE POETRY*

This is a partial list of the main expressions found in San Juan de la Cruz's poetry and in other earlier authors:

San Juan de la Cruz: *Adonde te escondiste,/Amado, y me dejaste con gemido?* (Where did you hide, my love, and left me thus to moan?) This expression appears in Garcilaso: *un agua clara con gemido;* in St. Augustine: *cum gemitu* (Confessions, VII, 7); in the *Aeneid,* last verse: *cum gemitu fugit.*

San Juan de la Cruz: Span-lang version precedes trans. version (like the stag you fled), *Como el ciervo huiste.* This appears in Virgil, *Aeneid* IV, 69, 78, and in Garcilaso. In San Juan de la Cruz it is the stag that causes the wound, and not the other way around, as in the others.

San Juan de la Cruz: 3. *Buscando mis amores/iré por esos montes y*

riberas;/ni cogeré las flores, ni temeré las fieras,/ y pasaré los fuertes y fronteras.
María Rosa Lida suggests these lines are found in Garcilaso's *Egloga I,*
vv. 401–5: *contigo mano a mano/busquemos otro llano busquemos otros montes
y otros ríos/otros valles floridos y sombríos/donde descanse y siempre pueda
verte.*

   San Juan de la Cruz in 4: *Oh bosques y espesuras etc.* María Rosa Lidia
suggests Garcilaso's *Egloga I,* vv. 216–24 as an influence: *Ves aqui un
prado lleno de verda,* etc.

   San Juan de la Cruz in 7: *un no se qué que quedan balbuciendo.* This is
found in: Boscán, *Historia de Leandro y Hero,* "El Cortesano," chap. VII
(Madrid: CSIC, 1942), 383.

   San Juan de la Cruz in 8: *no viviendo donde vives,* etc. This is found in
Teresa de Avila: *vivo sin vivir en mi;* in Diego Hurtado de Mendoza,
Epistola VIII, p. 154: *Y ansi, pues mi juicio no recibe,/percepción que el
sentido no refiera/diré lo que de tu dolor concibe.* The same or similar in
Ramirez Pagán (fol. 117, v.); Don Manuel de Portugal (C. Borges
Cancionero, p. 83–84); Garcilaso, *Canción* IV.

   The "wounds of love" are already in Leon Hebreo, *Diálogos de
Amor* (Madrid, 1947), 57.

   San Juan de la Cruz in 9: *Y pues me lo has robado;* A. Blecua points
out the *Song of Songs* and other sources in this "robo sin robar, (To Steal
Without Stealing)" *La literatura como signo* (Madrid: Playor, 1981),
110–44.

   San Juan de la Cruz in 11: *sino con la presencia y figura;* figura (figure)
as representation, traces on wax or on a mirror is found in Erasmus'
Enchiridion: "as within a mirror and as a figure," (Madrid, 1971), 246.
Also St. Paul, 2 Cor. 5:7; 1 Cor. 10:6; and Heb. 1:3; P. Laynez, *Obras,* ed
Entrambasaguas, II, p. 212 et al.; (Madrid: CSIC, 1951); Pedro Padilla:
"*Sin ti me offende cuanto veo/porque no representa tu figura*" *Thesoro, fol.* 203,
v.); Gregorio Silvestre: "*Siendo el esperar cosa tan dura/me pone en tal
estrecho su alegría,/Dios mío! qué será ver la figura?* (ed. Marin Ocete. p.
241); Ramirez Pagan: "*y que aunque goze el bien de tu figura . . .*" (Flo-
resta, fol. 135, v.; cfr. 138 v.)

   Juan de la Cruz in 12: "*O Christalina fuente,*" etc., is one of the
stanzas most dense in earlier references. See for example D. Alonso, *La
poesía de San Juan de la Cruz, Obras Completas vol. II* (Madrid: Gredos,
1973), 871–1075. From the Latin classics to the contemporaries of Juan
de la Cruz, everyone seems to follow the theme.

   Juan de la Cruz in 15: "*la noche sosegada/en par de los levantes del
aurora,*" etc. Garcilaso in *Egloga II,* 551–52: "*Denunciaba el aurora ya
vecina/la venida del sol resplandeciente.*"

This list of partial examples of the influences of others on the poetry of San Juan de la Cruz should be sufficient to give the reader a clear idea of the diverse methodologies which can be used in approaching his poetry. For more detailed information in this area I refer the reader to the above mentioned work by Domingo Yndurain.

PART III: *THE PROSE*

1. This prayer summarizes the many pages of prose San Juan de la Cruz will write to comment on his poems. The work of the soul does not cause the coming of God, yet God will not come without it; the desires of the soul will not bring God to it, for God Himself must put those desires in the soul. The negative way of the soul's journey is here sketched; the soul must remove all that impedes the arrival of the Beloved, yet the arrival, the presence, and the continuity of the stay of the Beloved is a gift, a grace of the Beloved of Himself with the soul to Himself.

2. The structure of Juan's prose commentaries is always the same: he uses one stanza from the poem to clarify the experience implied in view of the current theological doctrines. It is true that this method of explanation deprives the poem of its poetic value, but it is also true that San Juan de la Cruz uses the poem to make explanation dependent on experience, and thus his prose is more liberating than most of the doctrinal treatises of the period.

   This passage leads commentators to imply that San Juan de la Cruz was close to "illuminism." Wadding in *Annales Minorum* (1524) presents this influence as *"perniciosa pestis haeresos nuncupatae Illuminatorum seu Viae Illuminativae aut dimittentium se divinae dispositioni, nihil volentium facere nisi quod ultro per dinivas inspirationes seu revelationes sibi suggeri facile et erroneecredebant,"* in A. Hauck, *Realencyclopedie F. protestantische Theologie u. Kirche,* Leipzig, 1900, I, p. 388ff. This question of "illuminism" has lost contemporary interest, since a less intolerant Catholic theology has recognized that there is "spiritual value" in other forms of spirituality, including extra-biblical spirituality, as in Zen practice which resembles illuminism.

3. It is clear from this passage that San Juan de la Cruz has an audience in mind, and it does not include everyone. This audience is composed mainly of those with spiritual experience and who have abandoned the things of this world. Since the doctrine applies to all those souls with spiritual practice, it is obvious one does not have to belong to a

monastery to read these lines with profit. Nowadays the whole world is the monastery.

4. The starting point of the ascent is "desire," the desire of the appetites. The painful and anguished perception that desire is at the root of human decision making sets the soul looking for the way to the original desire of all life, and of the life of the soul. This is not the Thomistic starting point of the intellect searching for truth, but the starting point of a soul trying to extinguish the anguish of a bad choice. Chapters 1, 6, 7, 8, and 9 of *Ascent of Mount Carmel* are a reflection on this starting point, of the acts of the faculties that "tire, fatigue, torture, afflict, darken and dirty," the soul. Thus the light of the whole analysis falls on the "positive evil" of the *anguish dwelling on desire*. The ascent of the soul rests on this solid base of the state of anguish of the soul on its own.

5. San Juan de la Cruz accepts the appetites as an immediate, nonreflective act. See Hegel, *Jenaer Philosophie,* Ullstein Buch, 1974, 214ff. This immediate act with its nonreflective character, is distinct from "desire" and "will," which reflectively operate on "our inclinations" to generalize and modify them. Inclinations are not, therefore, denied, for they may be reoriented and transformed.

6. The "night of the senses" is not simple repression of their movement; the senses are mortified, or their fire extinguished, only to reorient them. Mystics do not suffuse desire, they reorient it. In the writings of Juan de la Cruz it is obvious that he does not consider ascetic practices very important or decisive. See Gershom S. Scholem, *Jewish Mysticism* (New York: Schocken, 1941), 49ff.

7. This "heat of the appetites" has been expressed in this manner since Plato. The soul, "psyche," is etymologically linked by him to fresh air, "anapsychon." Oxford Classical Texts, *Platonis Opera,* I, 329.

8. San Juan de la Cruz develops in detail his understanding of this "concentrated and gathered" virtue in the *Flame,* (Love's Living Flame). See also V. Jankelevitch, *Traite des vertus* II (Paris: Bordas, 1979), 301–11.

9. This is the part missing in the *Ascent*. The *Dark Night* provides the continuation of what was left incomplete. This has led to the conclusion that San Juan de la Cruz intended to write only one commentary. See Dicken, *The Crucible of Love* (London, 1963), 220.

10. This quick aside by San Juan de la Cruz reveals the instantaneous quality of the event when the soul charges from acting for herself to acting for God. It is quicker than the categories of active/passive indicate. Beginning and end meet in the same experience of God

pulling the soul out. See Baruzzi, *Saint J.de la Croix et le problem de l'experience mystique* (Paris: P.U.F., 1927), 393. The act of negating has a positive foundation, or origin.

11. When San Juan de la Cruz should have been sketching the "purgation of the appetites" he suddenly ends up "purging the will." He was not overly respectful of scholastic divisions.

12. The clarification of the passive and active appetites appears more clearly in certain descriptions in the commentary on *Love's Living Flame*. See particularly the commentary on Stanza 3, paragraphs 72–76: "I answer by saying that when the soul desires God this desire is not always supernatural, but only when God infuses such a desire."

13. Blasphemy, satanism, and lust are only signs of the ascent. It cannot be otherwise, for the consciousness of the mystic transforms the whole range of human desires, and therefore carries them along. Flaubert in *La tentation de Saint Antoine, Oeuvres Completes* (Paris: Club de l'honnete Homme, 1972), IV, 311, makes the same point: "La fouterie est une projection dans l'infini-Formes ignoble et cependant qui excitent. Donc, ce n'est pas la chair en soi qui excite, mais un certain esprit qui est en elle."

14. The spiritual form occurs in the ontological reality of "privation." Without this privation of the senses there is no real *"gesunde Leib,"* novelty of sensation, promised to the new man. However, things do not happen exactly as described. When movement occurs privation has also occurred, and only God knows exactly when this takes place. Could not a certain readiness in the soul be sufficient for God's action, rather than an internal judge measuring the degrees of privation until perfection in privation is reached?

15. This is the synthesis of the previous description: this destructive "fire" is properly contemplation, and in the experience of nothingness the gates of light open.

16. Love is painful in this state; there is emptiness and absence. Pseudo-Dionysius said: "God . . . on account of his preeminence not improperly is called Nothing," in *Dictionary of Philosophy and Psychology* (New York: Macmillan, 1902), II, 125.

17. "In the darkness with light" summarizes the night with its fears and realities, the return to chaos, and the birth of a new order. Buddha, Christ, the revelation of Koran—all took place in this night.

18. These passages proclaim that in this "second night" the soul joins the depths of faith. But faith here is not understood as an intellectual agreement with certain dogmatic propositions, but rather, willful union with an image and likeness that is absolute and incomprehensi-

ble. Vatican II defined the truth of faith as: "Christ's self and what He has done for men, not a series of theological or anthropological propositions."

19. A contemporary of San Juan de la Cruz wrote in his *Book of Job* (*Libro de Job* [Madrid: BAC], 312) a similar paragraph, stating that what does not belong to the senses is revealed through the abolition of the senses: "De arte que cuando fu revelado fu de noche y en los mas hondo y oscuro della, cuando las tinieblas espesas y la soledad que nace del silencio de todo causan horror en el ánimo . . . y cuando el humor melancólico que es calentado con el sueño y acrecentado con el alejamiento del sol, se mueve en el cuerpo . . . , y cría sueños pesados y horribles; que es decir a media noche . . . , y en lo mas hondo della; que es el tiempo, cuando según el vulgo, andan las sombras y estantiguas que espantan . . . Esta revelación fue de noche muy de noche."

20. San Juan de la Cruz rejects without second thoughts the whole charismatic tradition. He rejects the signs that appear in meditation, in the belief that signs are not the real thing, or at least, impede the real thing from appearing. They are messengers. There is, however, another tradition close to him which uses the signs in a different manner, in which spiritual life is based on the ability to read these signs and guide oneself by them. Teresa de Avila depended on signs all her life, and it would never have occurred to her not to call them real. In fact, the last time Teresa and Juan met in Granada, when Teresa had decided, on the basis of signs, to go to Burgos to open a convent, they spent the whole night arguing the merits of such a decision, and parted on unfriendly terms. See Victoria Lincoln, *Teresa: A Woman* (Albany: SUNY Press, 1984), 383–88. St. Ignatius de Loyola, founder of the Jesuits, also relied on the "signs" of meditation for decision-making. Was San Juan de la Cruz concerned with what the Inquisitioin might have to say if they examined his doctrine in this matter? His position had already been taken earlier by St. Paul and the Fathers of the Desert; perhaps he felt safe on this account rejecting the examination of such signs.

21. San Juan de la Cruz includes in this "second night" the theme of purging the "inner sense." This is consistent neither with the articulation of his experience, nor with the distinction he has established between contemplation and meditation. The natural contents of fantasy and imagining have already been purged in the "night of the senses," the first night; the "second night" takes place when the soul is taken by God "anxious, by love inflamed." Meditation at this stage does not help much; one may say it is unnecessary. See Baruzzi, *Saint J. de la C. et le probleme de l'experience mystique* (Paris: P.U.F., 1927), 393 et

al. Also, Dicken, *The Crucible of Love* (London, 1963). Also, *Oxford Dictionary,* op. cit., 898 on the relation between meditation and contemplation.

22. This is a clear description of the nebulous passage from meditation into contemplation. The journey from imagining and its signs to the life of faith and its operation on the soul is accomplished in inverse proportion to the will of the meditator. The more one tries the more one is operating, and the easier the movement of the soul, the deeper the operations of faith. The first leads to the second, and the second only occurs with the preparation of the first.

23. The moment contemplation begins, even before the purging of memory (*Ascent* III), the soul experiences forgetfulness of sensation as she knew it before, and experiences a general loving presence, in such a way that the soul does not really know what it is she loves.

24. It is in passages like this that San Juan de la Cruz offers his most subtle negativity. It is not enough to cancel the concrete signs that appear on the soul as the product of meditation, or even contemplation. One must also be careful with those forms of indirect light coming to the soul without passing through imagination. They lack form and profile: they are simply light. As when looking on a mirror, we must not only renounce the images in the mirror, but also the light with which the mirror gives images. This, in meditation, is an intelligible light and therefore must be rejected. We need to renounce not only signs and creatures, but also products of the spirit. This negativity is more in consonance with extra-biblical traditions, like Ibn Abbad of Ronda (died 1394) and Ibn Arabi. See: Asin Palacios, "Un precursor hispano-musulmán," *Etudes Carmelitaines* (April 1932); Ibn Arabi, *La parure des Abdals* (Paris: Editions Traditionnelles, 1951), 10.

25. The idea of acting, as if it were, through inspiration, occasioned one of the attacks against San Juan de la Cruz because of its similarity to doctrines held by the *iluminados*. See *Dictionnaire d'Histoire et de Geographie Ecclesiastiques* (Madrid: Letouzey et Ane, 1914), II, 850. Similar statements are found in Novalis and Nietzsche.

26. San Juan de la Cruz here gives a radical doctrine on virtue. Virtue is not to be practiced because of the satisfaction it gives. The ground of virtue is not ethical. The substance of virtue must be its loving origin. Thus "morality," and "human acting" are enclosed within the erotics of religious practice. They are inner moments of the manifestation of that love, not means leading to that love. In Luther's system this position would sound solid, for he also derived virtue from the ground of faith.

27. San Juan de la Cruz means "total union," nothing less.

28. "Search for Him as hidden" might better have been expressed "finding Him hidden." The erotic encounter requires for its fulfillment the renunciation of *theorein,* the theoretical component that sets distances and exteriority. The separation of the two elements of the encounter is real, however, because of the separate reality of both. The search, however, is within, at the center of the soul.

29. Love—spiritual love—starts as a wound that evolves to the point of causing death, a death that is by itself the space within which revelation and union take place. It is not only the point of departure for eternity, but also for freedom.

30. This terse paragraph covers the different dimension of the wound of love: flight of the soul to the Beloved and His touch, which intimates separation; the wound stands at the center of an erotic experience gathering to itself all the pains and impulses of love.

31. This wound of love has been left behind by the absence and presence of the Beloved: "Tali vulnere decet Deum percutere animas, talibus iaculis telisque configere, ac salutaribus eas vulneribus sauciare . . . Et quidem in hoc quasi amatorio dramate sponsa charitatis se dicit vulnera suscepisse," Origenes, *Patrologiae Cursus completus,* L. P. Migne, 1857, XIII, 162.

32. San Juan de la Cruz is here serving a master other than Christ, or being faithful to the description of his experience. Paragraphs 2 and 3 should be compared as two opposite descriptions of faith. The first is in consonance with San Juan de la Cruz's project in the commentaries, a *faith* originating in God. The second takes faith as a set of truths that are obviously obscure, but dogmatically determined. The superficiality of faith in this second version can hardly cover up the poverty of poetic expression with the metaphor of being silver-covered. This is an instance where Juan's commentary falls short of his poetic voice. It does reconfirm, however, the fact that experience is not generated *exclusively* by language, but rather that language is enlarged by experience and at times reduced by it, for experience must manifest itself through the particular language and powers of a period.

33. The wounded stag appears in Classical mythology long before Hölderlin picks it up: *Menons Klagen um Diotima,* I, 5–7. See footnote 9, Chapter 4.

34. This theme that desire breads desire desiring itself, or love breeds love loving itself, is the theme of *Love's living Flame.*

35. It is clear that San Juan de la Cruz separates in an irreconcilable difference the union of God with His creatures. In Him all things are

God, though creatures. It is union, identity in separation. This is the theme of *Love's Living Flame:* the whole of creation is in exercise of transformation from flesh into light and flame.

36. This is clearly a metaphor for the call of God to the soul, and also of the fascination it exerts over her.

37. It is clear the soul does not read the written word in her search for God. The soul listens, and in this sound coming from the inside, interiority and exteriority come together, soul and world, with the presence of God.

38. This audible penetration of the sound of God into the soul creates a bridge between two experiences commonly understood to be different—the mystic and aesthetic. The "whistle of the air," both sensible and spiritual, enters the body with the power of an uncommon experience; the mystic and the aesthetic join here in an ontological reality where beauty and truth coincide.

39. The Beloved infuses love in the lover, lights it up, sustains it, and in this love and infusion (passivity) virtues appear. It is obvious their origin has no practical consequence whatsoever; they are simple manifestations of the Being of Love being in love. Passivity leads to activity, but God is the ground of both.

40. San Juan de la Cruz takes literally the reality of the "incarnation." The incarnation of the Word equals the transformation of man into God, repeating Master Eckhart's intuition: *"Quidquid Deus Pater Filio suo Unigenito in natura humana dedit, hoc totum . . . mihi dedit. Nihil excipio, nec unionem nec sanstitatem,"* Denzinger: *Enchiridion Symbolorum et Definitionum,* 1888, 141. Thus spiritual activity does not destroy the sensible; the sensible is restored via contemplation.

41. This quotation is not as innocent as it appears. The living God is in the world and lives in the world—the senses are here divinized, and the spirit reenters the world. This is the general theme of *Love's Living Flame.*

42. The style of *Love's Living Flame* even in prose is radically different and of a more lyrical quality than the previous writings. The commentaries have much the same lyrical quality as the poetry, and the doctrine is freer from prevailing dogmatisms. It is obvious that both the writer and his experience have matured.

43. Water and fire have a unity in transformation, the turning of the soul from laboring for herself to a life under God's power. Once again, these transformations are more common in extra-biblical revelations than in Juan's own tradition.

44. This formulation may in theory sound like that of an *"iluminado."* But

in the context of the whole description it is obvious that within the union there is also a difference.

45. No other formulation of doctrine is as close to the intention of San Juan de la Cruz as this one: "To know creatures through God, and not God through creatures."

SELECTED BIBLIOGRAPHY

BIBLIOGRAPHICAL WORKS

Archivum Bibliographicum Carmelitanum. Rome: Edizioni del Teresianum, 1956.

Bibliographia Internationalis Spiritualis. Rome: Edizioni del Teresianum, 1966.

Bilbao Arístegui, P. *Indice de bibliografía sobre San Juan de la Cruz*. Bilbao: La Editorial Vizcaína, 1946.

Matías del Niño Jesús. "San Juan de la Cruz y su bibliografía, y Catálogo de la Exposición." *Homenaje a San Juan de la Cruz en el IV Centenario de su nacimiento*. Barcelona: Biblioteca Central, 1945.

Peers, E. Allison. *The Complete Works of St. John of the Cross*. London: Burns and Oates, 1964.

Ruano de la Iglesia, Liciano. *San Juan de la Cruz: Obras Completas*, 11th ed. Madrid: Biblioteca de Autores Christianos, 1982, 911–41.

EARLY EDITIONS

Obras espirituales que encaminan a una alma a la perfecta unión con Dios, Alcalá. Widow of Andres Sánchez Ezpeleta, 1618.

Obras espirituales que encaminan a una alma a la perfecta unión con Dios. Barcelona: Sebastián de Cormellas al Call, 1619.

Cantique d'amour divin entre Jésus-Christ et l'Ame Dévote, composé en espagnol par le B. Pere Jean de la Croix, traduit par M. René Gaultier. Paris, 1622.

Obras del venerable i místico dotor F. Joan de la Cruz. Madrid: Viuda de Madrigal, 1630.
Obras del venerable y místico dotor F. Joan de la Cruz. Barcelona: Sebastián de Cormellas, al Call, 1635.
Obras del venerable Padre Fray Juan de la Cruz. Madrid: Gregorio Rodriguez, 1649.
Obras del venerable Padre Fray Juan de la Cruz. Madrid: Bernardo de Villa Diego, 1672.
Obras espirituales que encaminan un alma a la mas perfecta unión con Dios, en transformación de Amor. Barcelona: Vicente Suriá, 1693.
Obras del Beato Padre Fray Juan de la Cruz. Madrid: Julián de Paredes, 1694.
Obras espirituales que encaminan a una alma a la mas perfecta unión con Dios, en transformación de Amor. Sevilla: Francisco de Leefdael, Ballestilla, 1703.
Obras espirituales que encaminan a una alma a la mas perfecta unión con Dios, en transformación de Amor. Pamplona: Pasqual Ibañez, 1774.

MODERN EDITIONS

Obras del Bto. Padre Juan de la Cruz, in *Escritores del Siglo XVI.* Madrid: B.A.E., 1853, vol. XXVII, prol. by Francisco Pi y Margall.
Obras del Místico Doctor San Juan de la Cruz. Edición crítica . . . , con introducciones y notas del Padre Gerardo de San Juan de la Cruz, 3 vol. Toledo: Vda. e Hijos de J. Pelaez, 1912–1914.
Obras de San Juan de la Cruz, Doctor de la Iglesia, 5 vol. Ed., annotated by Fr. Silverio de Santa Teresa, O.C.D. Burgos: El Monte Carmelo, 1929–1931.
Poesías completas de San Juan de la Cruz y comentarios en prosa a los poemas mayores, Poetry ed. Dámaso Alonso with intro.; prose ed. Eulalia Galvarrieto de Alonso. Madrid: Aguilar, 1st ed. 1963, 3rd 1968.
San Juan de la Cruz: Obras, intro. and notes Jose Luis L. Aranguren. Barcelona: Vergara, 1965.
San Juan de la Cruz: El Cántico Espiritual, ed. and prol. Matías Martínez Burgos. Madrid: Espasa-Calpe, 1924.
Vida y Obras completas de San Juan de la Cruz, Doctor de la Iglesia Universal. Biography by Crisógono de Jesus and Matías del Niño Jesús, Critical edition and notes by Lucinio Ruano de la Iglesia (Madrid: B.A.C., 1946). The latest edition of these works is the eleventh with great improvements, notably that the biography and the complete works are in two separate volumes.
San Juan de la Cruz: Cántico Espiritual Primera Redacción Y Texto Retocado, ed. with notes and intro. Eulogio Pacho. Madrid: Fundacion Universitaria Española, 1981.

ENGLISH TRANSLATIONS

The Complete Works of Saint John of the Cross, trans. and ed. E. Allison Peers, 3 vol. Westminster, MD: Newman Press, 1953; reprint, New York: Sheed & Ward, 1 vol., 1978.

The Collected Works of Saint John of the Cross, trans. Kieran Kavanaugh and Otilio Rodriguez, 2nd ed. Washington: ICS Pub., 1979.

John of the Cross: Selected Writings, ed. and intro. Kieran Kavanaugh. New York: Paulist Press, 1987.

The Poems of St. John of the Cross, trans. Roy Campbell. London: Harvill Press, 1951; Penguin Books, 1960.

The Poems of St. John of the Cross, trans. Willis Barnstone. New York: New Directions, 1972.

The Poems of St. John of the Cross, trans. John F. Nims, 3rd ed. Chicago: University of Chicago Press, 1979.

BIOGRAPHIES

Bruno de Jesus-Marie. *Saint John of the Cross,* ed. Benedict Zimmerman. New York: Sheed & Ward, 1932.

Crisógono de Jesus Sacramentado. *The Life of St. John of the Cross,* trans. Kathleen Pond. London: Longmans, Green, 1958.

Hardy, Richard. *Search for Nothing: The Life of John of the Cross.* New York: Crossroad, 1982.

José de Jesús María (Quiroga), O.C.D. *Historia de la vida y virtudes del Venerable P. Fr. Juan de la Cruz.* Brussels, 1628.

Jerónimo de San José, O.C.D. *Historia del Venerable Padre Fray Juan de la Cruz.* Madrid, 1641.

Brenan, Gerald. *St. John of the Cross: His life and Poetry.* Cambridge: Cambridge University Press, 1973.

————. *San Juan de la Cruz.* Barcelona: Laia, 1974.

Chaudebois, H. *La lección de Fray Juan de la Cruz.* Barcelona: Ariel, 1942.

————. *Portrait de Saint Jean de la Croix. La flute de roseau.* Paris: Grasset, 1947.

Gómez Menor, Jose. *El linaje familiar de Santa Teresa y de San Juan de la Cruz.* Toledo: Graf. Cervantes, 1970.

Peers, E. Allison. *Spirit of Flame: The story of St. John of the Cross.* London: 1943.

STUDIES: THE MAN AND HIS WORK

Ahern, Barnabas. "The Use of Scripture in the Spiritual Theology of St. John of the Cross." *Catholic Biblical Quarterly* 14 (January 1952): pp. 6–17.

Asín Palacios, Miguel. *Huellas del Islam*. Madrid: Espasa, 1941.

―――. *Saint John of the Cross and Islam*, trans. Elmer H. Douglas and Howard W. Yoder. New York: Vantage, 1981.

―――. "Un precurseur hispano-musulman de Saint Jean de la Croix." *Etudes Carmelitaines* 17, 1932.

Baruzi, Jean. *Saint Jean de la Croix et le probleme de l'experience mystique*. Paris: Felix Alcan [1924], 3rd ed. 1931.

Bendick, Johannes. "God and World in John of the Cross." *Philosophy Today* 16, Winter 1972, pp. 281–94.

A Benedictine of Stanbrook Abbey. *Medieval Mystical Tradition and Saint John of the Cross*. Westminster, MD: Newman Press, 1954.

Bord, Andre. *Memoire et esperance chez Jean de la Croix*. Paris: Beauchesne, 1971.

Brice, Fr. *Journey in the Night: A Practical Introduction to St. John of the Cross*. New York: Frederick Pustet, 1945.

Centner, David. "Christian Freedom and the Nights of St. John of the Cross." *Carmelite Studies* 2, 1982: pp. 3–80.

Crisógono de Jesus Sacramentado. *San Juan de la Cruz: su obra científica y su obra literaria*, 2 vols. Madrid: Mensajero de Santa Teresa y San Juan de la Cruz, 1929.

―――. *San Juan de la Cruz: El hombre, el doctor, el poeta*. Barcelona: Labor, 1935.

Cugno, Alain. *St. John of the Cross: Reflections on Mystical Experience*, trans. Barbara Wall. New York: Seabury, 1982.

Culligan, Kevin G. "Toward a Contemporary Model of Spiritual Direction: A Comparative Study of St. John of the Cross and Carl Rogers." *Ephemerides Carmeliticae* 31, 1980; reprinted in *Carmelite Studies* 2, 1982: pp. 95–166.

Dictionnaire de Spiritualite, Ascetique et Mystique, Doctrine et Histoire, s.v. "Jean de la Croix," by Lucien-Marie de Saint-Joseph. Paris: Beauchesne, 1937.

Edward, Denis. "Experience of God and Explicit Faith: A Comparison of John of the Cross and Karl Rahner." *Thomist* 46, 1982: 33–74.

Eulogio de la Virgen del Carmen. *San Juan de la Cruz y sus escritos*. Madrid: Cristiandad, 1969.

Frost, Bede. *Saint John of the Cross*. London: Hodder & Stoughton, 1937; New York: Harper, 1937.

Gabriel of St. Mary Magdalen. *St. John of the Cross: Doctor of Divine Love and Contemplation*. Cork: Mercier Press, 1947.

―――. *Visions and Revelations in the Spiritual Life*, trans. by a Benedictine of Stanbrook Abbey. Westminster, MD: Newman Press, 1950.

Galilea, Segundo. *The Future of Our Past: The Spanish Mystics speak to Contemporary Spirituality.* Notre Dame, IN: Ave Maria Press, 1985.

Garrigou-Lagrange, Reginald. *Christian Perfection and Contemplation According to St. Thomas Aquinas and St. John of the Cross,* trans. by M. Timothea Doyle. St. Louis: B. Herder, 1937.

Gaudreau, Marie M. *Mysticism and Image in St. John of the Cross.* Frankfurt am Main: Peter Lang, 1976.

Gicovate, B. *San Juan dela Cruz (St. John of the Cross).* New York: Twayne, 1971.

Lopez-Baralt, Luce. "Huellas del Islam en San Juan de la Cruz." *Vuelta* 45, 1980.

Maio, Eugene A. *St. John of the Cross: The Imagery of Eros.* Madrid: Playor, 1973.

Merton, Thomas. *The Ascent to Truth.* New York: Harcourt, Brace, 1951.

————. "Light in Darkness: The Ascetic Doctrine of St. John of the Cross." *Disputed Questions.* New York: Farrar, Straus & Giroux, 1960, pp. 208–17.

Nemeck, Francis Kelly. *Teilhard de Chardin et Jean de la Croix.* Montreal: Bellarmin, 1975.

Nieto, José C. *Mystic, Rebel, Saint: A Study of St. John of the Cross.* Geneva: Librarie Droz, 1979.

Orcibal, Jean., *Saint Jean de la Croix et les mystiques rhenoflamands.* Paris: Desclee de Brouwer, 1966.

Pacho, Eulogio. "El Cántico Espiritual retocado." *Ephemerides Carmeliticae* 27, 1976, pp. 382–452.

————. *El Cántico Espiritual: trayectoria histórica del texto.* Rome: Teresianum, 1967.

————. "La antropología Sanjuanística." *El Monte Carmelo* 69, 1961:47–70.

Ruiz Salvador, F. *Introducción a San Juan de la Cruz: El hombre, los escritos, el sistema.* Madrid: B.A.C., 1968.

Stein, Edith. *The Science of the Cross: A Study of St. John of the Cross,* trans. Hilda Graef. Chicago: Henry Regnery, 1960.

Thibon, Gustave. *Nietzsche und der heilige Johannes vom Kreuz: Eine characterologische Studie.* Paderborn: Verlag Ferdinand Schoningh, 1957.

Thompson, Colin P. *The Poet and the Mystic: A Study of the Cántico Espiritual of San Juan de la Cruz.* Oxford: Oxford University Press, 1977.

Vilnet, J. *La Biblia en la obra de San Juan de la Cruz.* Buenos Aires: Desclee de Brouwer, 1949.

Wojtyla, Karol. *Faith According to Saint John of the Cross,* trans. Jordan Aumann. San Francisco: Ignatius Press, 1981.

Zabalza, L.. *El desposorio espiritual según San Juan de la Cruz*. Burgos: El Monte Carmelo, 1963.

STUDIES: LITERARY

Alonso, D. *La poesía de San Juan de la Cruz (Desde esta ladera)*. Madrid: Aguilar, 1942.

————. "El misterio técnico en la poesía de San Juan de la Cruz." *Poesía española. Ensayo de métodos y límites estilísticos*. Madrid: Gredos, 1957, pp. 219–305.

Azorín. "Un sensitivo." *Los valores literarios* [1913]. Buenos Aires: Losada, 2nd ed. 1957.

————. "Juan de Yepes." *Los clásicos redivivos. Los clásicos futuros*. Madrid: Espasa-Calpe, 1973, 4th ed.

Ballesteros, M. *Juan de la Cruz: De la angustia al olvido*. Barcelona: Peninsula, 1977.

Bataillon, M. *Varia lección de clásicos españoles*. Madrid: Gredos, 1964.

————. *Erasmo y España*. Mexico: FCE, 1966, 2nd. ed.

Bousoño, C. *Teoría de la expresión poética*. Madrid: Gredos, 6th ed., 1976.

Camón-Aznar, J. *Arte y Pesamiento en San Juan de la Cruz*. Madrid: La Editorial Catolica, 1972.

Cernuda, L. *Poesía y Literatura*. Barcelona: Seix y Barral, 1960.

Cossío, José María de. *Letras españolas (siglos XVI y XVII)*. Madrid: Espasa-Calpe, 1970.

————. "Lírica, subjetivismo. San Juan de la Cruz." *Poesía española, Notas de asedio*. Buenos Aires: Espasa-Calpe, 1952.

Diego, Gerardo. "Música y ritmo en la poesía de San Juan de la Cruz." *Escorial IX*, 1942, pp. 163–86.

————. "San Juan de la Cruz, poeta lírico." *Escorial IX*, 1942, pp. 13–22.

Dominguez Berrueta, J. "Paralelo entre fray Luis de León y San Juan de la Cruz." *Revista española de estudios Bíblicos* 3, 1928, pp. 253–65.

D'Ors, Eugenio. "Estilo del pensamiento de San Juan de la Cruz." *Revista de espiritualidad I*, 1942, pp. 241–54.

Duvivier, R. *La genèse de "cantique spirituel", de saint Jean de la Croix*. Paris: Les Belles Lettres, 1971.

Florisoone, M. *Esthètique et Mystique d'après saint Therese d'Avila et saint Jean de la croix*. Paris: Ed. du Seuil, 1956.

García Blanco, M. "San Juan de la Cruz y el lenguaje del siglo XVI." *Castilla II*, 1941–1943, pp. 139–59.

García Lorca, F. *De Fray Luis a San Juan. La escondida senda*. Madrid: Castalia, 1972.

Guillén, J. "Poesía de San Juan de la Cruz." *Paragone* 130, 1960, pp. 3–52.

———. "Lenguaje insuficiente. San Juan de la Cruz o lo inefable místico." *Lengua y poesía*. Madrid: Alianza Editorial, 1969, pp. 73–109.

Hatzfeld, H. *Estudios literarios sobre mística española*. Madrid: Gredos, 1955.

———. "Los elementos constitutivos de la poesía mística. San Juan de la Cruz." N.R.F.H. XVII, 1963–1964, pp. 40–59.

Herrera, Robert A. "La metáfora sanjuanista." *Revista de Espiritualidad* 25, 1966, pp. 587–98.

Hornedo, R. María, "El Renacimiento y San Juan de la Cruz," *Razon y Fe* 129, 1943, pp. 513–29.

———. "El humanismo de San Juan de la Cruz." *Razón Y Fe* 129, 1944, pp. 133–50.

Lida de Malkiel, María Rosa, "Transmisión y recreación de temas grecolatinos en la poesía lírica española," *La tradición clásica en España*. Barcelona: Ariel, 1975.

Lozano, José Jiménez. *Poesía de San Juan de la Cruz*. Madrid: Taurus, 1982.

López Aranguren, Jose Luis. *San Juan de la Cruz*. Madrid: Jucar, 1973.

López Estrada, F. *Los libros de pastores en la literatura española, La órbita previa*. Madrid: Gredos, 1974.

Morales, José Luis. *El Cántico Espiritual de San Juan de la Cruz: Su relación con el "Cantar de los Cantares" y otras fuentes escriturísticas y literarias*. Madrid: Espiritualidad, 1971.

Nazario de Santa Teresa. *La música callada. Teologia del estilo*. Madrid: Espiritualidad, 1953.

Peers, Allison E. *Studies of the Spanish Mystics*. vol. I, London: The Sheldon Press, 1927.

———. "Alleged Debts of St. John of the Cross to Boscán and Garcilaso." *Hispanic Review* 21, 1953, pp. 1–233.

Spitzer, Leo, "St. John of the Cross," *Essays on English and American Literature*. Princeton, NJ: Princeton University Press, 1962, pp. 153–71.

Trend, John B. *The poetry of San Juan de la Cruz*. Oxford: Dolphin Books, 1953.

Valverde, Jose María. "San Juan de la Cruz y los extremos del lenguaje," *Estudios sobre la palabra poética*. Madrid: Rialp, 2nd ed., 1958.

Vossler, K. *La soledad en la poesía española, Madrid*. Ed., Revista de Occidente, 1941.

Yndurain, Domingo. *San Juan de la Cruz: Poesía*. Madrid: Ediciones Catedra, 1983.

WORKS OF RELATED INTEREST

de Nicolás, Antonio T. *Power of Imagining: Ignatius de Loyola*. Albany, NY: SUNY, 1986.

Jiménez, Juan Ramon. *God Desired and Desiring*. New York: Paragon House, 1987.

Lincoln, Victoria. *Theresa: A Woman*. Albany, NY: SUNY, 1985.

Kavanaugh, Kieran, and Otilio Rodriguez. *The Collected Works of St. Teresa of Avila*. Washington, D.C.: ICS Pub., 1976.